LOTUS ESPRIT

Other Titles in the Crowood AutoClassics Series

AC Cobra	Brain Laban
Aston Martin: DB4, DB5 and DB6	Jonathan Wood
Aston Martin and Lagonda V-Engined Cars	David G. Styles
Austin-Healey 100 and 3000 Series	Graham Robson
BMW M-Series	Alan Henry
Datsun Z Series	David G. Styles
Ferrari Dino	Anthony Curtis
Ford Capri	Mike Taylor
The Big Jaguars:3½-Litre to 420G	Graham Robson
Jaguar E-Type	Jonathan Wood
Jaguar XJ Series	Graham Robson
Jaguar XK Series	Jeremy Boyce
Jaguar Mk 1 and 2	James Taylor
Jaguar S-Type and 420	James Taylor
Lamborghini Countach	Peter Dron
Land Rover	John Tipler
Lotus and Caterham Seven	John Tipler
Lotus Elan	Mike Taylor
Mercedes SL Series	Brain Laban
MGA	David G. Styles
MGB	Brain Laban
Morgan: The Cars and the Factory	John Tipler
Porsche 911	David Vivian
Porsche 924/928/944/968	David Vivian
Range Rover	James Taylor and Nick Dimbleby
Sprites and Midgets	Anders Ditlev Clausager
Sunbeam Alpine and Tiger	Graham Robson
Triumph TRs	Graham Robson
Triumph 2000 and 2.5 PI	Graham Robson
TVR	John Tilper
VW Beetle	Robert Davies
VW Golf	James Ruppert

LOTUS ESPRIT

The Complete Story

Jeremy Walton

First published in 1991 by
The Crowood Press Ltd
Ramsbury, Marlborough
Wiltshire SN8 2HR

Paperback edition 1997

British Library Cataloguing in Publication Data

A catalogue record for this book is available from the British Library.

ISBN 1 86126 066 0

Picture Credits

The majority of the photographs in this book were kindly supplied by The Motoring Picture Library, Beaulieu.

The line drawings on pages 40, 43, and 62 were drawn by Bob Constant.

Printed in Hong Kong by Paramount Printing Co. Ltd.

Contents

Acknowledgements

Lotus, whether in the Chapman founder era or under 1990 General Motors ownership, has always proved an exciting and educational company to visit. Most of the information in this Crowood AutoClassic, *Lotus Esprit*, was gathered as a result of individually credited interviews. However, I do not forget the debt I owe to Michael Kimberley, chief executive and managing director, Group Lotus, for setting an accessible example to his team.

Similarly, the majority of pictures were specifically commissioned for this publication and the National Motor Museum at Beaulieu was responsible for seeing this side of the project through. The excellent technical drawings, and some of the even rarer Esprits, were supplied by Lotus. I am indebted to Ken Sears, Lotus chief engineer, Vehicle Concepts, for his explanation of the details involved in the Esprit's rear suspension and the necessary spread of incoming suspension loads, and of his accompanying drawings.

Thanks also to Gweneth Kell, Group Lotus, for her efficient help.

Now that Lotus is over forty years old, there is naturally a pool of former employees whom I thank for their additions to our knowledge of the Esprit in 1990. I would particularly like to acknowledge the past co-operation of former Lotus Press Officers Donovan McLauchlan and Ian Adcock who were responsible for my first-hand Esprit experience between 1976 and 1990. I must also add that I would not have driven one of the first pre-production Esprits, nor interviewed Colin Chapman, without the backing of *Motor Sport* magazine and Denis 'DSJ' Jenkinson.

Thanks also to Roger Putnam, formerly a Lotus PR who became sales manager before departing for a directorship of Jaguar. He illuminated company history considerably and is still held in great affection at Lotus: part of the standard road test route ('Putnam's Leap') is still named after this master of the quick quip and shrewd insight.

I would like to thank Aiden Shutter. His experience in running an earlier (S2) Esprit in the nineties was invaluable and he also provided his car for the appropriate photographic session.

My thanks also to those guardians of copyright who allowed us to reproduce their material, particularly in respect of original road tests. I am particularly indebted to *Autocar & Motor*'s editor Bob Murray for allowing the use of their world-recognized test findings.

I have always enjoyed Lotus cars and respected the strong individual talents that the company encouraged. I hope you discover that a similar admiration of a distinctive Lotus product is created by the contents of this book.

Jeremy Walton

The Lotus Esprit in Context

Pre-Production

1966 Lotus move from Cheshunt to present base at Hethel.
1966–1974 Lotus build 9,887 mid-engined Europa two-seaters, their most popular offering in the USA, prompting an enlarged successor.
1968 Lotus become a publicly-quoted company.

July 1970 Tony Rudd, then Lotus Director of engines engineering, obtains board approval for a number of longer term projects. Thcsc include the M70 (four-cylinder) and M71 (V8) mid-engine Europa replacements.

March 1971 Giorgio Giugiaro approaches Lotus founder Colin Chapman at Geneva Motor Show with the suggestion that they should co-operate. Chapma agrees and cites the M70/71 as the ideal subject.

October 1971 Giugiaro's first prototype, the non-running 'Silver Car', is readied for Lotus examination on expanded Europa chassis. Subsequent quarter-scale model used for aerodynamic trials.

October 1973 Arab–Israeli war triggers oil production restrictions and artificial fuel crisis. Another reason for Lotus to drop their 4-litre V8 (M71) and concentrate on their four-cylinder common production engine with the Elite.

November 1973 Second prototype (wearing show plates 'I DGG 01') is jointly created by Lotus and Giugiaro in Turin upon a pre-production M70 backbone chassis.

May 1974 Launch of front-engine/rear-drive Elite, using 2-litre Lotus 16V engine that will serve in the Esprit.

October 1974 Paris Show preview of the Esprit on 2 November.

December 1974 Tony Rudd team meet Christmas deadline, constructing a functional Esprit for Colin Chapman to assess.

Production Esprit

June 1976–May 1978 Series 1 2-litre 160bhp Esprit; 744 are made.

June 1978 British Government commits cash to the De Lorean DMC–12 sports car project, with Lotus Engineering development apparent in the March 1980 Geneva Show debut. (In July 1984 an official 330-page report shows the loss of £76.92 million and 2,600 jobs from the failed project.)

June 1978–January 1980 Series 2 2-litre 160bhp Esprit, 1,060 are made.

February 1980–March 1981 Series 2.2 2.2-litre 160bhp Esprit; 88 are made.

February 1980–April 1981 Essex-liveried Turbo 2.2-litre 210bhp Esprit; 100 are planned. Also debut month of Series 3 Esprit with shared Turbo chassis (2.2-litre 160bhp).

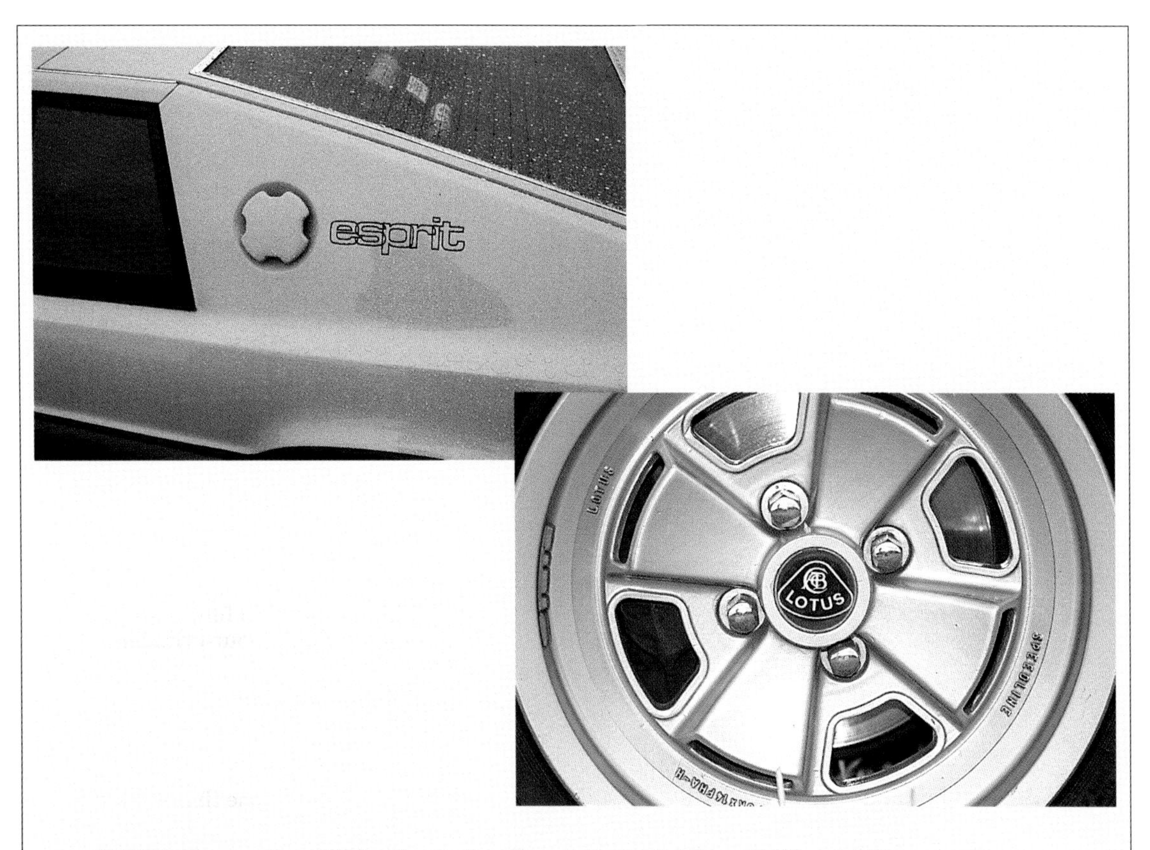

April 1981–September 1986 Production Esprit Turbo 2.2-litre 210bhp; 1,658 are made.

June 1981 Lotus announce future Toyota 'co-operation'.

December 1982 Anthony Colin Bruce Chapman, founder and chairman of Lotus Cars Ltd, dies on 16 December 1982. He is fifty-four years old.

June 1983 Company re-financed. As at close of 1985, the percentages settled as British Car Auctions (BCA) total 29 per cent; Toyota Motor Corporation 20 per cent; JCB 18 per cent; Schroeder Wagg 10 per cent.

January 1986 General Motors acquire a majority share-holding (later total) of Group Lotus PLC.

October 1986 Debut of 215bhp Esprit Turbo HC on 15 October. October also marks debut of an individually-numbered Limited Edition Esprit celebrating twenty years of Norfolk Lotus production.

October 1987 London debut of 'soft shape' Esprit Turbo and normally-aspirated Esprit.

May 1989 Esprit SE's chargecooled debut; 563 are made in 1989.

September 1990 Electronic anti-lock braking, deletion of normally-aspirated Esprit on 18 September. Range of 2.2 litres starts with the Esprit at 215bhp; the Esprit S at 228bhp and the retention of the Esprit SE at 264bhp.

esprit
EBO 307V

1 From Lone Genius to General Motors

'It is always the same. We totter from crisis to crisis.'

Colin Chapman

From its post-war foundations to the abrupt death in 1982 of its founder Colin Chapman, Lotus was a company that always seemed to be in a hurry to grow up. Did Lotus only reach maturity when the world's largest corporation, General Motors, bought the Norfolk company assets in 1986? Some observers tend to think so, but much of the 'crisis management' style reflected in the quote above was the direct result of Colin Chapman's increasing taste for technical sophistication and innovation, which in turn demanded ever-larger cash investments. In competition, Colin Chapman proved particularly adept at attracting new sponsors. Indeed, most trace back the current wave of logo-embossed single-seaters to the Gold Leaf Team Lotus sponsorship initiative of 1968.

Grand Prix racing success grew, culminating in the Indianapolis 500 victory in May 1965. Meanwhile, the E-prefix tradition of Lotus road car names reflected Lotus's desire to abandon their numeric competition and kit car origins. The first E-prefixed name was that of the Elite. The Elite was chosen as an attractive companion to the sports racing Eleven of the period, which had done so much at Le Mans and elsewhere to spread Lotus fame. Yet, numerals were retained for all but the Eleven racing cars and by 1990, the company had arrived at Grand Prix Lotus 102.

The dramatic impact of the early Esprit outline is certainly emphasized by this study. The car belongs to Aiden Shutter and the story of his ownership experiences is told in our last chapter.

The 1957–1961 Elite was a truly remarkable re-working of the 'tear drop' aerodynamic theme and widely regarded as one of the most beautiful road cars ever manufactured.

Commercially, the Elite (née Lotus 14) was not a success. Conceived as the company's first closed road car, production reached 990 in four sales years.

Sales success came with the first Elan (1962–1973) and the +2 Elan derivative (1970–1973) which sold 12,224 and 5,200 respectively. Both were powered by the first Lotus production engine, a double overhead camshaft (DOHC) design utilizing Ford cylinder blocks.

Both the Elite (1974–1982) and Elan (1990–) names were used a second time by Lotus and this second Elite generation provided a 2-litre DOHC 16-valve engine that was passed on to the Esprit. The model whose philosophy was closest to that of the Esprit was the 1966–1974 Europa mid-engined two-seater. Some 9,230 Europas were made: the earlier generations had Renault engines and gearboxes – initially sold in left-hand drive for export only – while a 1971–1974 stretched Europa descendant carried Lotus Ford DOHC power units aft.

Company histories can be very dull, but not so Lotus. The Lotus tale contains every twist and turn you would expect of a company that has created or refined original technical concepts, from telegraph poles to Grand Prix victors. And what better than the Esprit to capture that company spirit so perfectly?

LOCK-UP ORIGINS

The date 1 January 1952 marks the formal foundation of Lotus Engineering Company, but Colin Chapman was engaged in creating lightweight dual purpose competition and road cars from 1947 onward. A yellow and green company symbol (including the ACBC Chapman initials) was used from 1952 onward; a new corporate symbol without the Chapman initials was adopted during the eighties, but the initials were reinstated by the close of the decade.

The first Chapman creation was built in the lock-up garage behind the family house of Hazel Williams, who later became Mrs Chapman. That Lotus Mark 1 was based on a 1930 Austin Seven, but its two seater bodywork was considerably lighter in alloy and plywood.

The first Chapman special was ready for action in the spring of 1948, attacking the steep and muddy trails of Britain's sporting trials. The Mark 1, originally registered PK 3493 as an Austin Seven but subsequently OX 9292 as the first Lotus, reflected the Chapman addiction to low weight and admiration of aero industry practice. Not only was it capable of winning awards in its initial outings, but it also did nothing to hinder its creator's academic progress as Chapman graduated as a Bachelor of Science, also in 1948.

The second Lotus was also a special, but in this 1949 example, the Austin Seven chassis was equipped with a Ford 1,172cc four-cylinder engine and was the first Lotus to race. Constrained by demands from the RAF on the one hand and a full-time job on the other, Chapman's construction of the Mark 2 Lotus was slowed down and it wasn't until 1950 that he was able to tackle his first full competition season.

The founder died in December 1982, but Colin Chapman achieved so much in so many different spheres that it was no surprise when the world's largest car building organization, General Motors, purchased Lotus Cars.

Hazel Chapman, née Williams

Hazel Williams met Colin Chapman in 1945 and it was in the lock-up garage behind Hazel's family house that Chapman's first creation saw light. Hazel also provided the first £25 investment to turn Lotus into a Limited Company. They were married in 1954 and Hazel Chapman contributed to virtually every aspect of the embryo Lotus concern during the forties and fifties.

Following Colin Chapman's death in 1982, Hazel became a shareholder in Team Lotus, the independent Grand Prix company. In 1990, she retained a majority interest whilst son Clive was deployed as the marketing director.

Anthony Colin Bruce Chapman (1928–1982)

'Genius' is a much abused epithet, but it is the one most frequently used to describe the versatile talents of Colin Chapman. The man who gave Britain a marque to rival Porsche and Ferrari (and his initials to the Lotus monogram) was a restless visionary who wanted everything done, yesterday.

The amalgamation of such intelligence and impatience was ideally suited to Grand Prix racing and it is significant that Team Lotus have not won a World Championship since his totally unexpected fatal heart attack in December 1982.

Colin Chapman demonstrated considerable financial acumen when dealing to acquire components in that austere post-war period. It was soon also obvious that his ability to 'do a deal' was matched by a similarly exceptional driving talent and a good eye for publicity. Typifying his financial style was the acquisition of Gold Leaf and subsequent John Player Special (JPS) black-and-gold livery. These were both major steps in the fashioning of Grand Prix racing as a 'megabucks' sport sponsored by multinational corporations.

The darker side of Chapman's cashflow materialized in constant financial Stop-Go periods for the Lotus road car business (despite the company going public in 1968) and the De Lorean deals of the late seventies and early eighties.

Exotic air, marine, road and track transport occupied the majority of Colin Chapman's working life, but his energy and enthusiasm for digesting and utilizing information from other disciplines was also legendary. Witness the diverse letters after hs name: CBE ('Services to exports', December 1969); B.Sc. (Eng), FRSA (1968), plus a Royal College of Art Honorary Doctorate amongst others.

Colin Chapman's formal education was completed at the Stationer's Companies School, Hornsey and his B.Sc. was earned at the University of London. Typically, Chapman was by then constructing and later successfully campaigning his first special. Subsequently, neither the RAF (his life-long passion for flying had seen him log thirty-five solo hours by the time he had left university) nor employment at the British Aluminium Company (BAC) prevented him from pursuing this ability to live a number of lives simultaneously. He founded Lotus during that BAC period and finally started full-time employment at Lotus in 1955.

Affectionately known as 'The Old Man' and 'Chunky', Colin Chapman extracted the ultimate working performance from those around him. Such loyalty was generated by a crackling personality that flagged only under the most tragic circumstances. Once engaged by the Chapman character, most associates would then be drawn into further commitment by respect for his formidable abilities and a desire to work alongside such an original mind.

His most public engineering achievements were the execution and refinement of both the single-seater monocoque and ground-effect principles. Both allowed such considerable benefits in terms of handling that the opposition were initially outclassed and eventually had to imitate Lotus-Chapman initiatives.

RACING SEASONS

Wins and honourable placings were achieved from trials to circuit racing, and the Mark 2 carried on winning when it was sold. It also appeared in the 1957 British film classic comedy, *Brothers in Law*, pioneering a Lotus tradition for film and TV work that was continued by the Esprit in two major James Bond films.

The very first Lotus was also sold, but broken up into components rather than as a complete car, so that Chapman had adequate finance to tackle the 1951 season. His priority was to become much more involved with circuit racing. He was particularly interested in a then new 750 Formula (a descendant of which still thrives in Britain), in which the object was to design and construct a lightweight sports racing car.

The category attracted many innovative but impecunious designer-drivers over the years, perhaps the best known besides Chapman being Eric Broadley, founder of Lola Cars in Huntingdon.

Thus, the Mark 3 Lotus was created purely to race. The starting point, however, was still an Austin Seven chassis – albeit one radically altered, in line with Colin Chapman's own ideas on low-weight strength, engines engineering and suspension. In the latter case the rear springs were softer than standard. This was most unusual amongst competitors, who tend to stiffen suspension at every opportunity; even in 1990, Lotus were still implementing suspension layouts that used softer suspension settings than used on conventional performance cars.

However, it was the Mark 3 racing engine that attracted most attention at the time. Chapman's thoughts on carburation and inlet manifolding turned a Siamese-port Austin Seven unit into a split-port engine of considerably greater power. Approximate performance figures were 0–50mph (0–80kph) in 6.6 seconds; 88mph (140kph) maximum speed and over 50mpg (1,785km/100l) in leisure use. In its first race, all but the second-place man were lapped by the Mark 3, which was also used for weekend outings and holidays . . .

PRODUCTION PROGRESS

Although he was still employed full-time by the British Aluminium Company, Chapman was able to formalize his 1951 racing association with the Allen brothers by going into partnership with Michael Allen in 1952. That partnership sealed the formation of Lotus Engineering. From 1952–1959 the company – which became a Limited concern as from February 1953 – operated in a converted stable block at 7 Tottenham Lane, Hornsey, London N8.

Initially, Lotus produced more trials cars, namely the 3B and Mark 4, but demand was growing for a dual-purpose sports/club competition car that the customers could assemble themselves. Therefore, a plan to produce a 100mph (60kph) Mark 5 was abandoned in pursuit of the very first Lotus production car, the Mark 6.

Chapman, his two employees and partner Michael Allen could now abandon the Austin Seven chassis base and concentrate on a light, 90lb (41kg) tubular chassis/riveted and stressed aluminium panel body. The suspension featured an independent Chapman layout at the front and a coil-sprung Ford live axle.

In order to achieve his severe weight targets and functional efficiency, Chapman attracted the outside help of those outstanding alloy craftsman at Williams and Pritchard – quite an achievement for a company still in its formative years.

Major mechanical components, such as the 1.5-litre engine, the gearbox, the back axle and the braking system all came from Ford in customer assembly models. The flyweight Six proved so versatile on road and track that all sorts of engines were fitted, including a 2-litre BMW. Perhaps the most successful of the non-Fords was the variety of MG units, as campaigned by Peter Gammon in particular, but considerable power was also achieved by using Coventry Climax overhead camshaft motors.

ILLOGICAL PROGRESSION

The sleeker Lotus Seven naturally replaced the Six, both in its designated number and its engineering philosophy. In fact, there was a two-year gap between the two production models, and the Lotus Seven appeared in 1957. The company worked at the usual frantic Chapman pace during this period and 1957 proved something of a 'golden year' for Lotus. Two new road cars (Seven and

This is how the first production Lotus car appeared. In 1953 this 1,172cc Ford-powered Lotus 6 was the gleaming alternative for the sporting motorist, but barely accommodated the fashionable full race moustache.

The 1990 descendant of the 6 was this Caterham Super Seven racer. Unlike the array of Six and Seven models deployed in the background, this competition Seven was powered by Vauxhall.

Elite) were debuted at that year's London Motor Show; the sports cars carried on winning (including more class success at Le Mans) and the first Lotus single-seater, the Mark 12, was produced to meet new 1.5-litre Formula 2 regulations.

Lotus priorities had changed: they now seemed more preoccupied with increasingly specialized sports and single-seater racing cars. Yet the use of a site at Edmonton allowed Chapman and associates to work on the revolutionary Elite coupe.

LE MANS SPOILS

Before the marque became famous through Grand Prix successes, Lotus took part in an intense period of sports car racing, competing regularly at Le Mans in the late fifties.

Colin Chapman had long relied on the enthusiastic practical engineering expertise of Mike Costin, but in 1954, to gain the edge over the opposition in sports racing classes, Chapman involved Mike Costin's brother, Frank Costin, then an aerodynamics employee at the De Havilland aircraft concern in Chester.

The 1954 season also saw Colin Chapman found Team Lotus. This voluntary help organization was initially set up to make sure that racing did not get in the way of the Lotus Six's commercial manufacture. Later, however, this supremely professional outfit would net more Grand Prix wins than Ferrari between 1960 and 1982. It is a measure of the affection in which Colin Chapman held racing over road cars that it was the racing business that he retained when Lotus Cars went public in 1968.

The Lotus 8

The first sports racer to combine Chapman low-weight chassis engineering with the sleekest of shapes was the Lotus 8. The design brief called for a kerb weight of less than 1,120lb (10cwt); plus a maximum

Colin Chapman absorbed the message of clean aerodynamics for ultimate car performance in 1954. This Lotus Mark 8 could reach 125mph (200kph) on 85bhp. With Chapman at the wheel, the car is seen on its second outing at Goodwood in April 1954, still in the pristine alloy panels that followed an earlier road accident.

speed of 125mph (200kph) on just 85bhp from a hybrid MG-Morris 10 motor of 1.5 litres. Underneath the low-drag aluminium curves were a spaceframe chassis and a Chapman swing axle independent front suspension with a de Dion rear axle layout. That layout allied premium traction with excellent handling characteristics. The car's efficiency was shown when Colin Chapman scored its first class win in June 1954 (after three outings). It came fifteenth overall and was unlapped by the 4.9-litre Ferrari of Froilan Gonzales.

Later that season, Colin Chapman achieved one of his first motor racing ambitions, beating a quad camshaft works Porsche fair and square with the Mark 8. That car had become the fastest 1.5-litre racing combination in the UK – and a force to be reckoned with overseas, if more preparation time could be found . . .

In 1955, both Colin Chapman and Mike Costin decided to devote themselves exclusively to Lotus and the company moved up to the major leagues competing at Le Mans. Meanwhile, they were offering further Mark 9, 10 and (the most valued) 11 versions of the Mark 8 sports racing theme for sale.

Sarthe Success

Lotus first participated at the Le Mans circuit in 1955, but their 1.1-litre Coventry Climax engined Nine was disqualified when the boss reversed against traffic direction after a minor off. This was not a case of the French being bloody-minded as that year marked the biggest tragedy Motor racing has seen, in the Levegh Mercedes fatalities.

Continuing to be successful in shorter sports racing events all over the world, Lotus returned to Le Mans in 1956. This was the season in which Chapman decided to abandon the 'Mark' numerals before they became astronomical. Insted, he simply referred to the car as an Eleven, which amounted to one sports car racing design to accommodate a variety of engines. The tubular chassis beneath sleek and finned alloy panels was retained, but more of the panels were load-bearing and the kerb weight was down to a featherweight 840lb (7.5cwt) thanks to a pedigree Coventry Climax engine aboard. The starting price was £1,337 for a Le Mans model, but there were three Climaxes to choose from at extra cost. Alternatively, you could buy an Eleven for under £900 in simpler Sports specification.

At Le Mans in 1956, Lotus entered a trio of Elevens and came home with a win in the smallest (750–1,100cc) category, courtesy of Peter Jopp and Reg Bicknell. The 1.1-litre had reached nearly 120mph (190kph) on the legendary straight and 1.5-litre used its Climax power to top 128mph (205kph).

Naturally, Team Lotus returned in 1957. Together with privateers, there were five Elevens at *Les Vingt-Quatre Heures*. The 1957 season proved a good one for Britain with Jaguar winning – again – outright and Lotus scooping up two class victories (separate 750 and 1,100cc awards) and two other awards, including the coveted Index of Performance that Porsche and Panhard had striven to secure.

More Le Mans success accrued for Lotus in 1959. The 180bhp factory car was unable to start, but a quartet of private 1,216cc Climax-Elites performed with honour. They secured the 1.3-litre class, the Index of Thermal Efficiency and finished as high as fourteenth overall against far larger factory-prepared sports racers. By this (1959) period, Lotus were themselves involved in a vital factory move and the premier league of single-seater motor racing Grand Prix.

A NEW HOME FOR LOTUS AND THE SEVEN

Lotus moved to their new factory at Delamere Road, Cheshunt after a decade and more bursting at the seams of the Hornsey

February 1956 and Colin Chapman is on hand for the photo session that introduces the press to the Eleven.

Colin Chapman driving the Eleven (now with its headlamp cowlings screwed into place) at Silverstone in July 1956.

Elongated: the Lotus Mark 9 continued Lotus's exploitation of aerodynamic benefits and proved a popular purchase in the smaller-engined classes whilst the Mark 10 catered for 2-litre customers.

accommodation. The new facilities were officially opened in October 1959. There were two primary buildings; one devoted to manufacturing, and the second acting as the administrative headquarters, complete with a showroom large enough to house several of the latest products.

The suburban Hertfordshire site offered the space sorely needed to expand, and to meet a now bulging demand for road and race cars. This was served through Lotus Cars Ltd – most in demand was the Elite – and Lotus Components. The latter was then primarily concerned with the sale of a Seven successor to the Mark 6. Later on, as the customer arm of Lotus, Lotus Components sold racing cars and components before finally folding in the early seventies. In May 1973, sealed by a public ceremony in June, the Seven passed to Caterham Cars in Surrey, who still develop and manufacture the spartan two-seater to meet a burgeoning worldwide demand.

The Elite featured an eight-box section glassfibre monocoque, which was difficult to produce to an acceptable quality standard. The 1,216cc Coventry Climax power unit only added to the high prices that had to be charged to less than 1,000 customers prepared to pay the price of advanced technology. It

The Lotus Elite was intended to race, but continued the Lotus tradition for road and track versatility along with new construction techniques (glassfibre body) and amazing aerodynamic abilities.

made more sense as a competition car – the Elite was originally intended to compete at Le Mans of 1957, becoming a category winner with a top twenty result in 1959.

The contrast between the Elite and the Seven could not have been greater. The Elite's elegant lines differed from the Seven's uncompromising continuation of the stark Chapman lightweight principles that had brought Lotus much needed cash to support their more glamorous activities. Yet, neither brought Lotus the steady income and sheer production volume of the first Elan, which appeared for public consumption in 1962 at £1,095 in kit assembly trim with the original 1.5-litre (rather than 1,558cc) twin-cam power unit.

INSPIRED CONCEPTION

The conception of the backbone steel chassis to support an outer glassfibre shell was a master stroke. Lotus recognized that the day for an all-glassfibre construction had yet to dawn, but that a sensible compromise could be reached. Also, it was the 1961 development of the stressed steel structure that inspired Chapman and company to create the 1962 monocoque for the Grand Prix Lotus 25. As far as I know, there are few examples of a road car inspiring single-seater progress.

The double Y-shaped frame and central backbone chassis accommodated the twin-cam engine, four-speed gearbox and double-wishbone front suspension. The back half featured towers, on which to mount the classic Chapman strut layout of spring/telescopic damper and wide-based lower wishbones. Disc brakes were used all round, with rack-and-pinion steering sensitively guiding 145 or 155 section rubber at astonishingly high cornering speeds in excellent comfort.

The Elan was a truly versatile yet original interpretation of the two-seater convertible. It weighed little over 1,500lb (682kg) at introduction, and later spawned an attractive hard-top alternative and the elongated Elan +2. The latter was an 1,848lb (840kg) machine that could not match its tiny progenitor's accelerative prowess. It did, however, firmly set the tone of upmarket elegance that was first reflected in the Elite and which indicated Chapman's desire to enter Porsche and Ferrari territory, both on road and track.

The +2 was the first Lotus on the UK market to exceed £2,000 on its debut in 1970. As with all previous Lotuses, the Elan (especially in 26R competition trim) proved a popular sprint racer. It was a diminutive road performer: 144in (3.65m) long and less than 48in (1.22m) in track. This did not deter the buying public, among whom the +2 found a minority loyalty. Indeed, the original Elan inspired the 1990 rebirth of the Elan badge on an equally bravely-engineered descendant.

The most popular production Lotus to date has been the original Elan. This is the later S4 variant in hard-top guise.

MASS MANUFACTURERS

Largely forgotten in company records is the period in which Lotus first engineered a mass manufacturer's product to make it more suitable for competition. The first 'victim' was the Ford Cortina, and the original breed was radically equipped to accommodate:

1. Lightweight alloy panels.
2. Chapman A-bracket located rear axle on coil springs.
3. Uprated MacPherson strut front suspension.
4. Close ratio four-speed gearbox.
5. The ex-Elan Twin Cam engine, which had swift grown to 1,558cc and 105bhp.

The result was nearly 110mph (180kph) and 0–60mph (0–100kph) in some 10 seconds whilst recording 21–22mpg (750–785km/100l) overall.

The first Lotus Cortina was manufactured in far higher quantities than I, or any other author save Doug Nye, imagined. According to *The Story of Lotus, 1960–71* Lotus at Cheshunt made over 1,100 such Cortinas in 1965 and little less than 1,000 the following year. Ford took over manufacture of a much simpler version based on the second-generation Cortina in 1967.

Total Lotus production of the original must have been around 2,700 on this basis (I could find no figure for the launch year, 1963) and it set a precedent for rethinking mass-production saloons. This is one aspect which still profitably occupies Lotus Engineering: witness the 1990 Lotus Omega/Carlton twin turbo for Vauxhall-Opel, assembled at Hethel, and the 1980/81 World Rally Champion designated Lotus Sunbeam Talbot.

NEW HOME FOR FRESH MODELS

The Elan span was briefly interrupted by the move to a new factory. Lotus moved up to Norfolk at the close of 1966 (the foundation stone was laid by Chapman in July of that year) and has operated from these premises ever since. The Grand Prix Team Lotus, however, is separately housed (and owned) at Ketteringham Hall, about three miles away. For the buying public, the immediate effect of the move was that the company's first mid-engined road car, the Europa, was made gradually available. I say 'gradually' because from December 1966 onward, the Renault engine and transaxle machine existed in left-hand drive and was only released in right-hand drive in July 1969.

The Europa was designated type 46 in Lotus numerology. A racing cousin held the number 47 and utilized Twin Cam power from its winter 1966/67 debut in GT racing. The Europa was a marvellous supporting act to the Elan and could be regarded as the first affordable European mid-engined car.

A further-removed racing descendant, the 1969 Lotus 62, is also important to our Esprit story, because it utilized a Vauxhall slant four cylinder block at 2 litres with a

Direct ancestor to the Esprit was the Europa. It was originally offered with Renault engine and gearbox, but this is the later Lotus Twin Cam variant of 126bhp.

In amongst the heavy-metal Ford GT40s and Lolas, nineties Arrows/Footwork boss Jackie Oliver conducts the fleet 1968 Gold Leaf Team Lotus Europa Type 47.

Since its faltering start with Jensen Healey, the Lotus 16-valve DOHC engine has had a long and successful production life. It has grown from 140bhp and 2 litres to a 2.2-litre capable of yielding 280 production horsepower. This is the normally-aspirated 2.2-litre of 180bhp that was found in the front-engined Excel of 1990.

The later twin-cam five-speed Europas carried over the John Player Special black and gold colour theme, originally popularized (and seen below on the Lotus 72 of Ronnie Peterson) by Team Lotus in Grand Prix.

The Ford cylinder block/bottom half and Lotus DOHC cylinder head proved a production success, the company making over 30,000 such power units. This Big Valve example is installed in the mid-engined Europa.

Lotus 16-valve, DOHC, cylinder head to pump out 220bhp at 8,000rpm within an aerodynamically modified Europa body. Initially, Lotus had hoped that the Vauxhall blocks could be simply acquired and used as the basis for the new slant four that Lotus were to manufacture in the seventies – the power plant later transferred from the Jensen Healey to the Elite and Esprit. However, racing highlighted a weakness that made

Lotus design and manufacture their own blocks, leading to a more complete engine.

The Elan and the Europa made it commercially possible for Lotus to enter the seventies, the period in which the Lotus road cars made the Esprit possible.

ON THE GRAND PRIX TRAIL

The first Lotus single-seater racing car did not come to life until the company had reached the Mark 12, but its front-engine/rear-drive layout was a fine example of the Lotus trademark of lightweight body and agile handling. This was particularly true when the Mark 12 progressed from a de Dion rear suspension to the Chapman strut system. The latter was installed in many radically different cars including the original Esprit.

Those single-seater designs – 12, 16 and the first Lotus rear-engine racer, the 18 – paved the way for Lotus to naturally participate in Formula 1, and they debuted on 8 May 1958 at Monte Carlo. By 1960, Stirling Moss had won Lotus's first Grand Prix: both car and driver triumphed at Monte Carlo in the Rob Walker Lotus 18, just two years after Team Lotus had made their first appearance in the category . . .

A Winning Partnership

Colin Chapman and Frank Costin's association was not restricted to the Lotus sports racing designs of the fifties. Both were also consultants on the front-engined Vanwalls. It was with the Vanwalls that Tony Vandervell achieved his ambition of 'beating those bloody red cars' to the World Manufacturers' Championship in 1958. Chapman had begun the association when working on the 1956 chassis frame design, and he subsequently involved Frank Costin for the aerodynamics. Not unnaturally, the result was dubbed by many the 'mini-Vanwall'.

Later, Colin Chapman would admit that he felt the rear-engine 18 was 'our first true Formula 1 car'. In fact, it served many categories, but it is worth noting that the mid-engine and rear-drive layout, still retained for all 1990 Grand Prix contestants and an inherent principle for ultimate cornering prowess, was not a Chapman innovation. It was the Cooper Car Co that snatched the 1959 and 1960 World Championships for Jack Brabham, demonstrating that the front-engine/rear-drive Grand Prix era was over.

It was slightly ironic that the winning record for Team Lotus should be based on an outside design breakthrough and on the driving abilities of a privateer, even one of Moss's status. The golden years of Lotus's team success were, in fact, dependent upon factory cars and some of the greatest in-house drivers of motor racing history.

In their 1960–1982 heyday, Team Lotus recorded seventy-two wins, twenty more than Ferrari in the same period. This, however, remains shy of the Italian grand total, because Ferrari have been involved since the start of World Championship racing in 1950, and continue to win today, whereas Lotus success has been, at best, patchy since the death of Chapman in 1982.

INNOVATING TO VICTORY

Which Chapman innovations will be remembered as *the* most startling? The following can only be an unfair selection from the most inventive of current Grand Prix engineering teams but here it is anyway.

Sixties

The 1962 layout of the Lotus 25 was debut winner for Jim Clark, and it marked the first successful Grand Prix use of a monocoque chassis. This aircraft fuselage-style construction halved chassis weight and provided an

The Eleven was one of the best loved Lotuses. Just how much it is held in affection more than thirty years after its announcement can be seen from this 1988 Mille Miglia picture of a pristine 1956 example.

Hethel Aerodrome, Norfolk

The manufacturing and administrative home to Lotus road cars since Chapman laid the foundation stone on 17 July 1966, the Hethel site is a fitting legacy to Chapman. Some 40 acres ensured that there was plenty of space for growth. (The site now covers 55 acres.) Provision of both a 2.4-mile (4km) perimeter test track *and* a three-quarter-mile (1km) landing strip proved irresistible to the then thirty-eight-year-old Lotus boss.

In 1966, little over 100 cars were produced at the new site, but by 1969 a new record output of 4,506 Elans, Europas, Elan +2s and sundry Lotus Components cars emerged. Such an output was not matched until the nineties, particularly when Lotus cars went upmarket and became considerably more expensive without the kit-build option.

Production fell to less than 350 annually in the early eighties before climbing to the 1989 level of 1,060. Esprit variants accounted for all but 183 Excel (front engine) vehicles. This means that Esprit models formed 79 per cent of all production in 1989. The forward Lotus/GM plan called for manufacture of 4,500 Lotus cars annually 'by the early nineties'. It was expected that the Elan would account for 66 per cent (2,970) of that annual output.

For the nineties, Hethel has been the subject of a £35 million investment programme to make the new Elan. That is the biggest investment yet made in Lotus history. It also underlines the fact that the new Elan would not have made production, had GM not taken over Lotus.

Production area space has leapt from 85,737sq ft to 290,635sq ft and fascinating production aids such as the water jet cutting Fanuc robot (£250,000) explain how Lotus had spent £18 million on production hardware and buildings.

At first, the Lotus site looked a pretty daunting proposition for the labour force – only a hardcore of employees from Delamere Road, Cheshunt, likely to make the trip. Fortunately, many talented employees did stay on and the new workforce soon adapted to life at the car plant, where the most persistent smell is that of curing glassfibre.

In 1971, the first thoroughbred Lotus engine went into production (the 2-litre 907 for Jensen Healey). The computer tape control managerial system proved a nightmare to sort out when power cuts hit the plant but today, it is a thoroughly sorted facility that has made more than 26,000 of the 900-series 2.0-, 2.2- and 2.2-litre turbocharged Lotus 16-valve motors.

Employment figures at the site have naturally fluctuated along with the production figures: in 1966 there were 500 on the payroll, but as Lotus Engineering developed, so did a separate client list with its own factory facilities (1974: emission labs conform to Federal standards). Today, Lotus employ around 1,300 people. Approximately 50 per cent of them work on projects for twenty-six outside clients.

Lotus Cars at Hethel in the late eighties. Today the backdrop of the factory is far more cluttered, almost entirely filled with engineering Portakabins – where much of this book's key research was conducted.

almost ten-fold improvement in torsional strength. The figures were even better with a stress-bearing engine installed.

The year 1967 saw another debut winner, the Lotus 49, which christened the Cosworth Ford DFV V8 at Zandvoort. The 49 utilized those compact eight cylinders as an integral part of the structure. They were bolted to the back of the monocoque, behind Dutch Grand Prix victor Jim Clark.

Former Lotus employee Graham Hill initially led the race. Both Hill and Keith Duckworth – the creator of a V8 that went on to conquer 154 Grand Prix – were former Lotus employees in the Hornsey days. From the start, Chapman was an adept talent-picker.

Working alongside Colin Chapman prepared Michael J Kimberley for the rigours of steering Lotus through the eighties to berth with General Motors.

Seventies

For 1970, Chapman's talent was underlined by the co-design (with Maurice Philippe) of the Lotus 72 Grand Prix car. This wedge-shaped machine contrasted starkly with the cigar shapes then predominating in Grand Prix racing, but Lotus had already experienced some of its characteristics with their type 56 turbine cars and the 4 × 4 drive 1963/64 series. Running in conventional rear-drive trim with Ford Cosworth V8 power, the 72 popularized rearward and side-mounted radiators (there simply was not room in the needle nose for any other solution). Inboard disc brakes in the 72 were utilized all round, rather than simply at the rear.

The torsion-bar suspension allowed a notably smooth ride; it took time to sort the handling out so that the drivers felt confident in the machine, but when lead driver Jochen Rindt was motivated, a string of victories followed. The Austrian driver annexed the Dutch, French, British and German Grand Prix before his brutal death in practice at Monza, becoming the first posthumus World Champion in motor racing.

Such a record, both in terms of racing victories and innovation would have been enough for most men – another win followed at Indianapolis for the 1966 Lotus entries of Jim Clark – but Colin Chapman worked with aerodynamicist Peter Wright at Ketteringham Hall, Team Lotus's headquarters, to produce another handling revolution. This time, Lotus utilized shaped underbody panels to generate air displacement that literally sucked the car on to a race track. The result was a 1978 season-long domination of the championship tables by American driver Mario Andretti, loyally supported by Ronnie Peterson, until the untimely death of the popular Swede at Monza in that same year.

That was the last Lotus World Championship to date, but Chapman and company had one more potentially great chassis contribution to make to Grand Prix records. This was the double-chassis Lotus 88, designed to create downforce within regulations that had long since been framed to try and prevent any such manoeuvre. Despite Chapman's considerable persuasive powers, the Paris-based FISA ruling body prohibited the use of the Lotus 88 in Grand Prix, a rejection which, no doubt, embittered the Lotus founder.

The John Player Special colour scheme accompanied Team Lotus into the turbo era. Here Peter Warr (left) and Gérard Ducarouge examine the JPS 95T, which placed a Renault V6 behind Nigel Mansell rather than the normally-aspirated Renault V10 that the Briton deployed for Williams in 1991. By then, Team Lotus had consumed another sponsor (Camel) and had drifted toward the lower orders of Grand Prix racing.

Eighties

Of course, the death of Colin Chapman was damaging to Team Lotus, but managers like Peter Warr and Tony Rudd fought resolutely to re-establish the name throughout the eighties and nineties. However, it was French designer Gérard Ducarouge who raised team morale once more – as did a breed of drivers like Nigel Mansell and Ayrton Senna, who drove with a commitment to match that of a team only used to winning. Mansell went on to become a regular winner elsewhere, as did Senna, but the Brazilian proved that Lotus could win both with Renault and Honda power. Senna scored his first win for Lotus in 1985 in the soaking rain of Estoril and achieved two superb street circuit victories in 1987 in the Active Suspension Lotus Honda 99T.

Another Lotus racing development was a microprocessor-managed electro-hydraulic suspension control in 1983. It was premiered by Nigel Mansell at the Brazilian Grand Prix and also showed startling potential on Lotus, Chevrolet and Volvo development cars. At the time of writing, a major manufacturer has yet to announce full production plans, many opting for cheaper electronic damper control systems.

The only production companion for the Esprit during the late eighties was the Excel. Sales of the latter rarely exceeded those of the Esprit and the future for the Excel looked dubious in the nineties. This descendant of the second Elite shared the 16-valve engine, but it was mounted in the front and drove the rear wheels. This is a 1986 example, debuting the SE high compression variant of 180bhp.

PRODUCTION VOLUMES YEARLY (JAN TO DEC)

Year	Seven	Elan	Elan + 2	Europa	Elite	Eclat	Excel	Esprit	Turbo	HCPI	GMP4	Esprit SE	Elan	Total
1966	26	80												106
1967	164	1,117	261	443										1,985
1968	390	913	1,001	744										3,048
1969	581	1,148	1,158	1,619										4,506
1970	141	965	738	1,529										3,373
1971	241	748	378	1,315										2,682
1972	98	537	579	1,782										2,996
1973	130		916	1,776	6									2,828
1974			137	622	687									1,446
1975				57	459	20								536
1976					451	341		134						926
1977					210	280		580						1,070
1978					293	354		553						1,200
1979					276	281		474						1,031
1980					125	121		80	57					383
1981					13	31		185	116					345
1982					14	162		160	205					541
1983					1	214		84	343					642
1984						315		104	418					837
1985						232	130	127	262	62				813
1986							249	72	136	246				703
1987							337	78	186	198				799
1988							244	176	387	375	120			1,302
1989							183	90	103		121	563		1,060
1990*												759	1,193	1,947
	1,771	5,508	5,168	9,887	2,535	2,351	1,143	2,897	2,213	881	241	1,317	1,193	37,105

*Esprit SE and Elan volumes only

Lotus Production Road Cars, 1957–1990*

TYPE	LAYOUT	YEARS	TOTAL
Seven	F/engine, 2-seater, convertible	1957–1972	3,300
Elite	F/engine, 2-seater, coupe	1957–1962	990
Elan	F/engine, 2-seater, convertible and hard-top	1962–1973	12,224
Cortina	F/engine, 4-seater, saloon	1963–1966	2,671
Elan + 2	F/engine, 2 + 2 seater, coupe	1969–1973	5,200
Europa	Mid engine, 2-seater, coupe	1966–1974	9,230
Elite	F/engine, 4-seater, coupe	1974–1982	2,531
Excel	F/engine, 4-seater, coupe	1985–	1,143~
Esprit	Mid engine, 2-seater, coupe	1976–1990	7,549~
Elan	F/engine, F/drive, 2-seater, convertible and hard-top	1990	754^{+}

*Figures for pre-1982 from factory records of 1987
~Figures for Excel and Elite to close of 1989
$^{+}$Figures for new Elan, late 1990
?Figures for 1964–1966 only

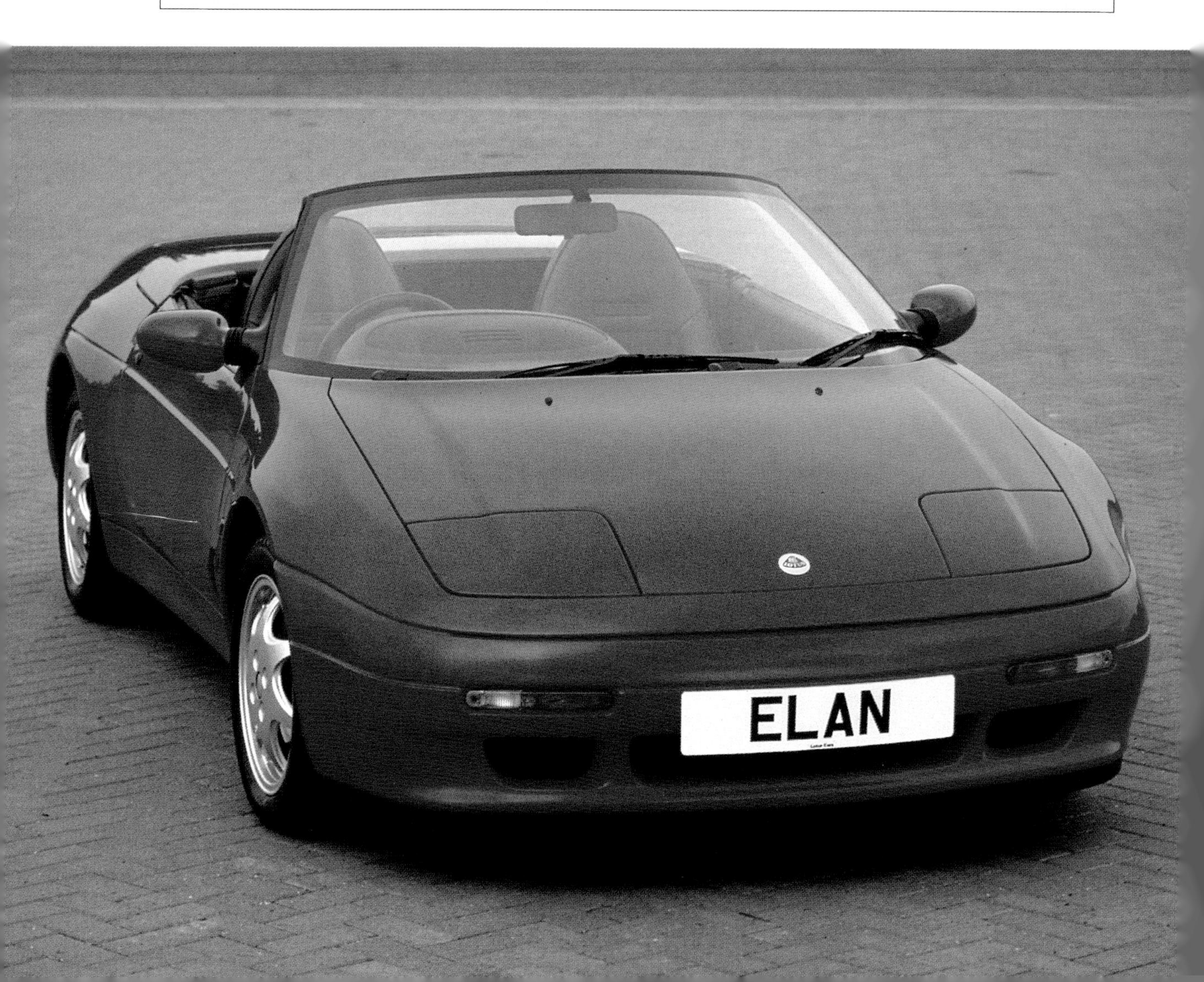

Since Senna departed in 1988 to pulverize pole position records and win a brace of World Championships for McLaren, Team Lotus has not been a winning force in Grand Prix. The 1988 season with Nelson Piquet and Honda V6 turbo power should have been magnificent, but proved to be disastrous, leaving both sides with stained reputations. Triple World Champion Nelson Piquet only regained his pride with Benetton-Ford in 1990.

To the Nineties . . .

For 1990, Team Lotus trusted two of the hardest workmen in the business – Derek Warwick and Martin Donnelly – with their jaunty yellow Camel 102Ts, but the shrill Lamborghini V12 machines had a job picking up stray points in the top six, never mind launching either driver on to the top three podium. As the 1990 season drew to a close, both Camel and Lamborghini announced that they were quitting and 1991 looked bleak for the Norfolk equipe.

By contrast, the road car future has never looked brighter, and it was the uncompromising mid-engine Esprit that somewhat surprisingly maintained company fortunes during the eighties. The Esprit outsold all its Lotus 16V-engined contemporaries to ensure that there was a Lotus to respect in the apparently interminable gulf between the original Elan and its front-drive successor of the nineties.

Now let us see how the Esprit was created in the inimitable Lotus fashion.

(Left) The second Elan was perhaps the bravest gamble Lotus ever undertook. The front-engine, front-drive two-seater entered production in 1990 and nearly 1,200 had been made by the end of the year.

2 Public Triumphs and Private Trials

'I reckon we solved 90 per cent of the problems.'
Tony Rudd, 1977

Although the Esprit made its official debut in the autumn of 1975, strong clues as to its main characteristics were revealed during the 1972 season. At the Geneva Show, in the opening week of March, the 2-litre Lotus 907 engine series, ('The only die cast 4 valve per cylinder engine to be produced in the country', said *Motoring News*) was unwrapped alongside the ill-fated Jensen Healey sports car.

Later in the year, November to be more precise, the Turin Show witnessed the Ital Design stand launch of the first Giorgio Giugiaro (silver) design study for what was to become the Esprit. Initial reactions were most enthusiastic. John Bolster reported in the *Autosport* of 9 November 1972:

There is a most attractive body on the stand of Ital Design, built on the mid-engine Lotus Europa. The work of the brilliant Giorgio Giugiaro, this body has flutes along the side of the bonnet in a style reminiscent of vintage Vauxhalls. Tartan seat covers are featured and the car is a real eye-catcher; Colin Chapman told me he is considering going into production with it in about 18 months' time. It is of great interest that the Lotus is fitted with the 2-litre 16-valve engine as used in the Jensen Healey.

GESTATION PERIOD

However, the first Esprit's obvious links with the Europa and the Jensen Healey hinted at the traumas suffered by Lotus in manufacturing their own engine and in mounting a genuine challenge to the most prestigious names in the performance car business. After all, Lotus were barely twenty years old!

Two main strands track back to the sixties: the need in 1965 for a new engine to supplant the Ford-based Twin Cam, and the success of the 1966 mid-engine Europa. Then, Lotus Engineering director, Tony Rudd recalled the gestation of the Lotus engine as stemming from, 'Chapman, who is really good at this crystal-ball gazing bit . . . '. Rudd continued:

[Chapman] was commissioning new engine designs and looking into sources of supply back in 1965. We made about 35,000 of those old Twin Cam engines, Ford kept on saying they would stop making the blocks, so the pressure was really on. Especially in the wake of the new Jensen agreement. The thing turned into a nightmare . . .

With hindsight, this was no surprise. Jensen Healey were suffering constant managerial re-shuffles and, consequently, the engine selection process was pushed aside until it came uncomfortably close to a public debut. Jensen Healey management had assessed wares from Vauxhall (that slant-four which Chapman was also to plunder for the first Lotus engine design and racing prototypes). GM could not get the 120bhp required, especially in emission-controlled specification. The Ford RS2600 Capri fuel-injection V6 was

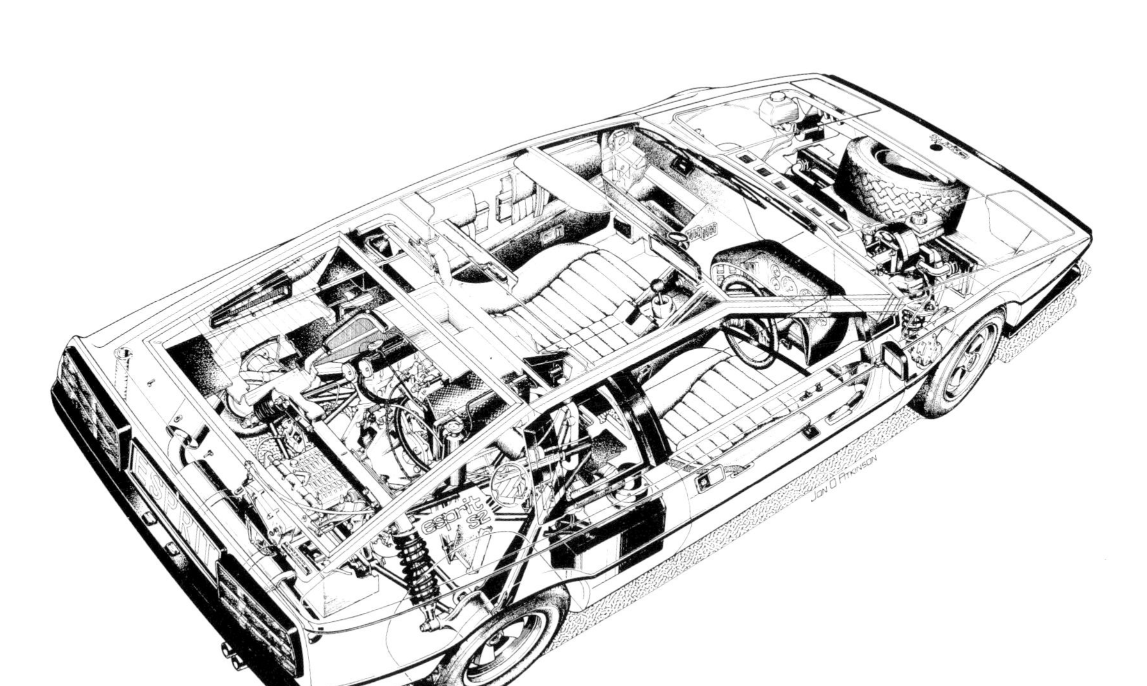

The first two Esprit models (S2 shown here) shared their running gear. Here, the distinctive rear suspension layout can be seen in its entirety, along with the Citröen rear transaxle and mid-mounted Lotus 16-valve engine of 2 litres and 160bhp. Also shown are the 'Z-section' aluminium door crash protection beams and front location of both water radiator and spare tyre.

also examined for the front-engine/rear-drive convertible (later a sporting GT estate, *à la* Reliant Scimitar GTE), and even the BMW slant-four came under close scrutiny before negotiations with Colin Chapman at Lotus were resumed. By then, the two sides were almost certain to run out of sync, and when Lotus installed some brand new electronically-managed production equipment, 'almost' became a dead certainty.

SHAMBLES

Jensen actually needed the motor before Lotus could supply it, let alone the 150–200 engines per week originally anticipated. Then, when Lotus had overcome the 'nightmare' of power cuts upon their delicate new engine tooling, Jensen started cutting back on order quantities. By an exclusive engine supply agreement, from the summer of 1972 Jensen Healey were selling their product way before any similarly-equipped Lotus could be readied. It was all a rather sad managerial shambles, and one, by 1976, that contributed to the untimely death of a brave new sports car project.

However, one result was that Lotus, at least, had an outside concern contribute to the development costs of their new 907 engine series. The 907 effectively replaced the Twin Cam, whose production (in enlarged 2.2-litre normally-aspirated and turbocharged guise) lasts to the present day.

Back in 1972, the Lotus engine powered

the 2,340lb (1,064kg) Jensen Healey two-seater convertible to 120mph (190kph), allowing 0–60mph (0–100kph) in 7.8 seconds on the best press demonstrators and averaging 21–23mpg (750–820km/100l). These were truly competitive figures for the time, and I can vouch for the fact that the later 5-speed Getrag gearbox and the 140bhp power level formed a very pleasant and untroubled alliance that deserved a far longer production life.

NAME GAMES

In 1971, Giorgio Giugiaro of Ital Design wanted to continue his line of long nose show cars. He also wanted to call the Turin débutante Esprit the Kiwi. Tony Rudd recalled Lotus's subtle reply to Giugiaro's suggestion: 'We pointed out to Giugiaro that Kiwi might be fine in Italy, but in Britain it meant a brand of boot polish!'

Lotus, you might recall, have used the letter E to start their brand names ever since the Eleven. That sports racing design was spelt out to avoid going any further up the numerical scale. It was therefore not surprising that senior Lotus personnel needed only 'a weekend with a dictionary' to cast their majority vote for Esprit.

The Concise Oxford Dictionary's definition of *'esprit'* is: 'sprightliness, wit. *Esprit de corps*, regard for honour and interests of body one belongs to.'

ENGINE LORE

The 907 engine, at 275lb (125kg) complete, did meet Lotus's constant call for low weight, but other aspects were not so satisfactory. Those iron liners suffered some distortion in Jensen's early experience and the oil consumption, never particularly frugal, was hard to raise to the target of 250 miles per pint. As Tony Rudd recalled in 1977:

The first 400 [engines] had terrible problems, especially with oil staying up amongst the camshafts when using over 6,000rpm, or with oil circulation during cold starts.

Mr Rudd explained how the rectification process continued during the birth of the company's first four-seater (more of a 2 + 2) design, the Elite:

When the Elite was finally put into production (during the winter of 1974 to 1975) we did a great deal of detail work on the engine,

Giorgio 'Giorgetto' Giugiaro (1939–)

Colin Chapman and Giorgio Giugiaro were both acclaimed as men of genius in their respective fields, so the pair who worked on the Lotus Esprit could be expected to create a truly remarkable vehicle.

Giugiaro was born in the Italian province of Cuneo. He was elegant in his personal dress – an elegance that was also visible in his designs. At twenty-six years of age, Giugiaro got his first job at the Central styling studio of Fiat.

It took less than four years for Bertone to recognize the talent of the embryonic international automotive designer, and the famous Italian coachbuilders took on Giugiaro in 1960. For five years, he participated in the birth of some classic Bertone shapes, the longest-lived belonging to the BMW CS coupes.

The combination of Giugiaro and the house of Ghia (now owned by Ford) was not the most likely, but it kept Giugiaro busy from 1965–1969. At this point, he emerged as a founder partner in Ital Design. His partners were Luciano Bosio and Gino Boaretti.

Since then, 'Ital' have conceived some outstanding work, in particular the original Volkswagen Golf and Scirocco and the Alfa Romeo Sud and GTV Coupe. These cars bear that most elusive of international automotive design hallmarks: elegant originality.

covering about thirty different aspects in all. Primarily, we tightened up valve gear tolerances for quieter top-end running, and enhanced the torque characteristics out of all recognition by profiling the camshafts along the lines we had explored for the Jensen Healey, to make the car easier to drive.

That development period would have beaten a less experienced and resilient engineer, particularly one responsible to the mercurial Chapman for a specific project. This was indeed the case for Rudd with the 2-litre 907 motor from 1969 onwards – and he must have made a fine job of it, for later he also assumed leadership of the small team that made the Esprit a pre-production runner.

EUROPA BASE

In July 1970, Tony Rudd was assigned to look at longer-term Lotus model prospects, and two versions of what was to become the Esprit were approved by the Lotus board. The first one, coded M70, housed the four-cylinder 907 engine. The second one, coded M71, housed the projected Lotus 4-litre V8 – this much delayed engine would have been made from two 907s. Both versions were logical 'grown-up' replacements for the Europa.

Meanwhile, the first mid-engine Lotus was now reaching its ultimate production trim. The Europa became home to the Twin Cam engine (115bhp) from December 1971, but it was still allied to a wide ratio Renault 4-speed gearbox. Lotus then mated the more powerful Big Valve Twin Cam (126bhp) to a Renault-based 5-speed transaxle for the Europa Special in 1972. That machine echoed the John Player black-and-gold livery and so linked Lotus's road and race activities.

Tony Rudd (1930–)

A key figure at Lotus since his arrival in 1969, Tony Rudd's 66th year on earth was characteristically vigorous. Instead of the dark suit and vaguely rumpled air of the world-class engineer that we encountered through the earlier days of the Esprit project, the Tony Rudd of 1990 sported a yellow track uniform and answered to the titles of: executive chairman, Team Lotus; technical director, Group Lotus and deputy chairman, Lotus Engineering. All these are fitting rewards for one who has achieved so much in so many differing areas of advanced engineering.

Mr Rudd began his career at Rolls Royce as a teenage apprentice. From 1939–1951, he did far more than learn a craft, but his considerable knowledge of aero engines is carried comfortably in the chuckling and self-deprecating style that has made him such an accessible source of information for this book. In 1951, Tony Rudd took on his first racing car technical post, rising from development engineer to racing team manager at British Racing Motors (BRM), now defunct, in Lincolnshire. This was not an enviable task, as BRM were autocratically governed and subject to many of the emotional and patriotic forces that have caused chaos at Ferrari in the past.

Despite the inevitable politicking, Rudd was at the managerial helm when it mattered, Graham Hill securing the world title for drivers, and ensuring that BRM won the parallel world series for manufacturers.

Tony Rudd established original concepts such as the H16 BRM engine (which won a World Championship round in the back of the Lotus driven by Jim Clark in 1966), established a very advanced computer-controlled engines manufacturing facility at Lotus and led the Esprit project team. He also worked closely on the revolutionary ground-effect Grand Prix Lotus cars, remaining a key figure at Team Lotus into the troubled nineties, until his retirement in 1991.

1972 Lotus 907 Engine
(As supplied to Jensen Healey)

Block Gravity cast LM 25 WP alloy, cast-iron liners, block slanted 45deg from vertical. Four in-line cylinders, wet sump lubrication.
Cylinder head LM 25WP die-cast alloy, twin overhead camshafts driven by 1in wide Powergrip belt and activating sixteen valves at an included angle of 38deg. Unleaded fuel compatibility for the USA. H&G Lotus design solid skirt pistons operated on a compression ratio of 8.4:1.
Induction Europe: twin, double choke, side-draught Dell'Orto 40 DHLA carburettors; USA: twin side-draught, single choke, Zenith 175 CD.
Cubic capacity Bore × stroke of 95.28mm × 69.24mm gave 1,973cc.
Power ratings 140bhp at 6,500rpm; 130lb ft at 5,000rpm.

Stretch

More significant than the Europa's increased power was a stretch in wheelbase. Cabin space also grew to meet the demands of the 6ft 5in tall Mike Kimberley and of the US market: 80 per cent of Europa production was now heading for the States. Quite possibly, the idea of stretching the Europa was retained for that car's successor.

The first Ital Design study of 1971 (debut in Turin, November 1972) was based on what Tony Rudd described as:

A diabolical cut-and-shut Europa chassis. It was wider and longer than a Europa, to the planned M70 dimensions, with the wheels and tyres that we wanted to use, plus the 2-litre (907) engine and a sort of filigree arrangement to show what the gearbox would look like. We had not got one of those, because we had yet to get thinking about that.

Giorgio Giugiaro caused the first Europa-based show car to be created in a remarkably short time. He only put the proposition to Colin Chapman in March 1971, yet his first attempt at the car was exactly right, even down to the tartan interior, which theme was echoed in the first production Esprits.

Another original detail retained on the first Esprits was the use of Wolfrace alloy wheels. I was told, however, that the massive 265-section rear Goodyears were simply specials made up to complement the show car's rakish appearance. One of the later pre-production tasks was to adapt the Esprit to the 205-section Dunlop tyres that were more realistically supplied to suit the car on the road.

The show car went down well with the press at Turin, and Lotus were impressed enough to also commission an aerodynamic study on quarter-scale. The results of those Motor Industry Research Association (MIRA) investigations and a euphoric sport show examination of production practicalities meant that a second 'red' prototype had to be created.

PRODUCTION REALITIES

The realities that had to be addressed in the second Ital Design study were:

1. To body the car in the top- and bottom-half sections that could be withdrawn from the unique Lotus Vari moulds.
2. To marginally decrease front-screen rake (it went from 22 to 27.5 degrees).
3. To meet American safety requirements.

Another safety-orientated move was to relocate the petrol-filling arrangements;

accessibility via the off side quarter light glass was changed to a pair of exterior fillers, high on the rear-quarter panels. The radiator air flow was also modified: the venting on the bonnet was deleted after the aerodynamic studies had shown far too much front-end lift with the 1972 show car.

Another change to the original metal show car (Giugiaro had never worked with glassfibre prior to the Lotus co-operation) was to remove the racing-car style opening back section in favour of a more conventional deck lid to surround the rear window. The Esprit can be called a hatchback, but one where the engine invades a heated luggage bay. One aspect which always left a lot to be desired with Lotus cars, particularly in comparison with the 1990 Honda NSX, was the engine cover. This glassfibre lid was also introduced to the second Esprit show car in the move towards production practicality.

Ital Design Giorgio Giugiaro Number 01

This second prototype, which wore the artificial registration IDGG 01 (Ital Design Giorgio Giugiaro number 01), required the attention of Colin Chapman, Michael Kimberley, and Lotus design chief, Oliver Winterbottom. Oliver Winterbottom camped out at the Turin studio, down beside the River Po, while Chapman and Kimberley remained in Britain. Instead, they worked up a creative sweat, overcoming the terrors of frequent trips to Turin in a vulnerable small aircraft. Michael Kimberley recalled the period vividly as he commented:

Development of the second car seemed to go on forever. Once, twice, sometimes – albeit rarely – three times a week we would fly down, myself and Chairman Chapman. We had some really epic flights to and fro, including one occasion where the plane did not have enough oxygen and had to fly between the Alps to keep the occupants conscious! It made for a pretty long day, especially after that trip without oxygen. Then we landed, feeling a bit sleepy, and still had a full day of design development to do.

My best memory of that period was of working late at the styling studio and seeing both Colin and Giugiaro spark off each other to get the windscreen right. It was raked about 22 degrees on the original, and we felt it had to be more upright for impending legislation on visibility. The problem was how to keep the rakish look and be legal. Giugiaro was literally in there with bits of plaster, modifying things as we went along, but it just didn't look right. Finally Colin came up with the idea that we leave the centre of the screen where it was legally permissible, and move the outer, bottom screen edges forward – giving us a 'fast' A-pillar screen line. It was the sheer inspiration of two really original minds feeding off each other that produced the answers on that car.

Reviewing the crisp pre-production lines that emerged from those Turin sessions with the benefit of hindsight, Mike Kimberley felt that:

It was a memorable design; we often call it the folded-paper look in recognition of its sharp edges. The Giugiaro look served us well through much of the eighties, but when we re-examined the style of the Esprit again, from December 1985 onwards, it was felt that the square rigged appearance was really out of date . . . By then the Giugiaro style was *too* sharp-edged; held too much appeal for the gold medallion man!

FROM SHOW TO GO

Late in 1973, the second Giugiaro machine was ready for Lotus management to make

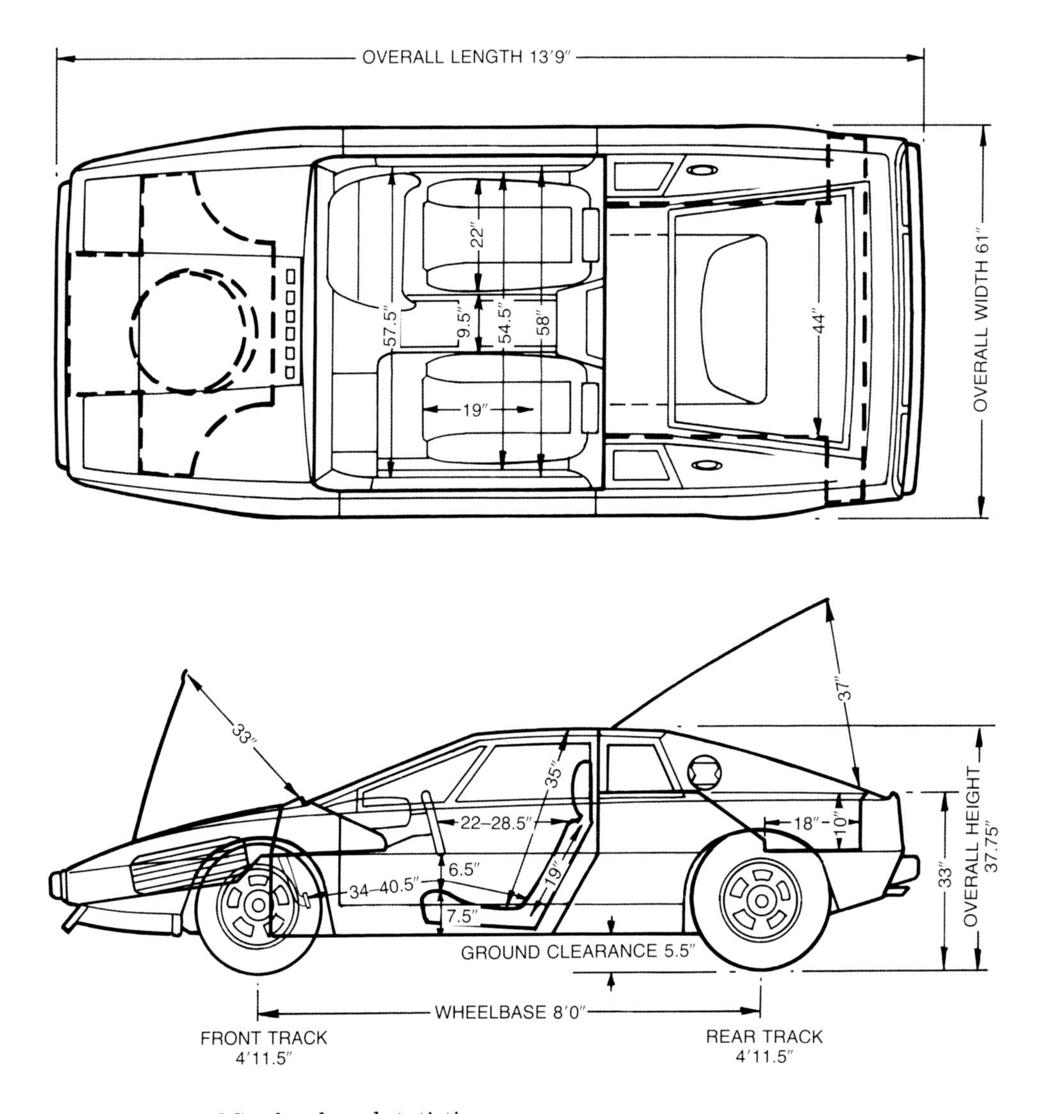

Dimensionally, the S2 and S1 also shared statistics.

an overall assessment. Tony Rudd commented:

The project was moving along well, but was rather overshadowed by the engine side of the business, and the priority of getting the new Elite out . . . at our third attempt!

Officially the Elan and Seven disappeared from Lotus production listings at this point. The Seven departed to Caterham Cars for a life that looks lustier than ever in the nineties, while the Elan (the largest production volume vehicle made by Lotus) was simply and sincerely missed. Lotus directors would later freely admit that the little two-seater with the pop-up headlamps was too readily dismissed but, at the time, they thought that the Elite and its 907 engine would be on the production line a lot earlier than its 1974 debut.

'That engine business' referred to the

durability programme for the 907 engine, a process not helped by the power cuts of the winter of 1973–1974. Lotus would ready the engine for Elite (and, subsequently, Esprit) production with an additional 20bhp. In turn, this demanded new camshaft profiles and a compression ratio increase from 8.4:1 to 9.5:1 besides the need for a bespoke exhaust system to suit the north/south disposition with clutch and unique bellhousing to mate that elusive gearbox.

Mike Kimberley (1938–)

Michael John Kimberley climbed the Lotus managerial tree in convincing fashion, becoming a director less than six years after his arrival (in 1969) as a project engineer.

'MJK' guided the GM-owned company into the nineties as chief executive officer and managing director, Group Lotus. At 6ft 5in he cuts a dapper figure in one of the inevitable dark suits that are as much his trademark as his welcoming grin and penchant for instant action that earned him the Lotus Cars nickname, 'Kimbo'.

Educated at Lanchester Polytechnic and the Coventry College of Advanced Technology, it was a natural progression for Mike Kimberley to join Jaguar as an apprentice. His time served, Kimberley progressed through design, development and project engineer status. His expertise in suspension and road noise insulation (mostly earned on the acclaimed XJ6 saloon) was valuable at Lotus.

Michael worked with Tony Rudd on the re-vamped Europa – he had a personal interest in accommodating his lengthy frame within the, later, stretched cabin. Thus, the two-seater Esprit always offered as much room as possible within that confined mid-engine layout.

The Citröen Solution

Messrs Rudd and Kimberley found what they were looking for: 5-speed manual transaxle unit at an affordable price. Unfortunately, they found it in the hands of Citröen, who would succumb to ownership by Peugeot after poor post-fuel-crisis sales. This led to the abandonment of the exotic Citröen Maserati SM and, indirectly, to the bankruptcy of Maserati who supplied the V6 engine that mated with said 5-speed transmission. Lotus were allowed to select their own ratios, which were then machined on Citröen tooling. The only significant Esprit changes in ratios between 1975 and 1987 were prompted by differing wheel and tyre combinations, particularly the increase of 1in (25mm) in wheel diameters for the original Turbo.

Because his brother, Brian Spooner, was also actively involved in power-train matters, particularly as Rudd did have other duties to attend to during this Esprit production engineering development crisis, Colin Spooner remembered one apt story about the Lotus-Citröen gearbox liaison:

We got right up close to our production dates, working along the assumption that we would have to machine our own Crown Wheel and Pinion (CWP) assembly. We thought our CWP would be needed because the gearbox would be installed the opposite way round to its original application. In fact, if we had installed our Lotus CWP, the only effect would have been to give the Esprit five *reverse* gears and one forward ratio! It was not until that *very* late stage that we discovered that the Citröen Maserati engine ran *backwards*, so there was absolutely no need to change the CWP gears . . .

Working to Beat the Clock

Easter 1974 saw an important managerial re-shuffle at Lotus. Mike Kimberley became chief engineer while Tony Rudd was given ultimate power to oversee and progress new projects, which specifically meant the Elite and Esprit. Now that the Elite was erratically surging into production – Lotus made

Colin Spooner (1950–)

Joining Lotus in 1967 from a 'non-automotive, Ministry of Defence' background, Colin Spooner HNC and his brother Brian both made significant contributions to the development of the original Esprit. Colin was a major driving force behind the 'soft look' re-styled Esprit of October 1987, and has continued to be associated with the car's progress into the nineties.

In the nineties, Spooner is to be found operating from one of the upmarket Portakabin offices that house many of the Lotus on-site engineers. Outside, Elans, Chevrolet Corvettes and Lotus-developed Omegas and Carltons bear witness to the variety of engineering challenges the company now meets. Within, most of Spooner's preoccupations were with progressing the 1991 Elan hard-top and meeting questions with disarming candour.

As an engineer and designer, Colin Spooner survived the Chapman and GM eras, keeping uncompromising standards and a strongly individual anti-bureaucratic streak. Colin left Lotus twice during the seventies, finally rejoining in 1978. His creed is in the informal, original, high speed development engineering (and engineers) that characterize Lotus.

six in 1973 and a record 687 in 1974 – Mr Rudd could concentrate his energies on the Esprit. The Esprit was badly needed in the USA, as the Europa was approaching its final 'sell by' date, so far as safety and emission regulations were concerned.

Tony Rudd now had a clear assignment from the Lotus board and a personal commitment to Colin Chapman to 'get the Esprit running by Christmas 1974'. To achieve this objective, a small team of key Lotus personnel was withdrawn from the main company headquarters at Hethel and relocated in the stables at Ketteringham Hall.

In the summer of 1990, Colin Spooner remembered that period vividly: 'I started off back at Lotus with a small office in the corner of the pattern shop, trying to panic-progress the Esprit into production. During 1973 we built a quarter-scale steel tube rendition of the backbone frame . . . ' The conversation breaks for barely a minute as Spooner sprints away and retrieves that stress analysis original ' . . . but it was obvious that something extra was needed if we were going to get the Esprit into production on the time scale that Chapman wanted.'

That 'something' was half a dozen staff, led by Rudd and including both Colin Spooner and his brother Brian, who adapted the Citröen 5-speed SM transaxle and bought it to life at the other end of a motor car, as well as executing suspension and hub designs. Chris Wynder acted as secretary to the 'emergency squad', whilst pattern-maker Charlie Prior (to be seen working back at Team Lotus in the 1989 season), and fitters Ted Fleet and Dennis Jewell put theory into practice with racing haste. Colin Spooner recalled:

One practical guy did so much to make it possible that you should tell his story to show the basics we had to master before meeting that Christmas deadline. Bob Hutchins was the man who took the chassis, and sundry other parts of the Europa, and made the red show car possible, even driving it back out to Turin in a rented 3-ton truck. More than that though, he made Ketteringham Hall stables work for us, he even swept the tiled floor, and rewired the telephones.

Almost There . . .

The Ketteringham Hall squad did not quite make the Christmas 1974 target of a completed runner. Items such as the green and white instrumentation supplied by Veglia went astray on the railway system, which delayed the whole process. However, Lotus did have such an Esprit, (complete with 250 weekend test miles (some 400km) recorded

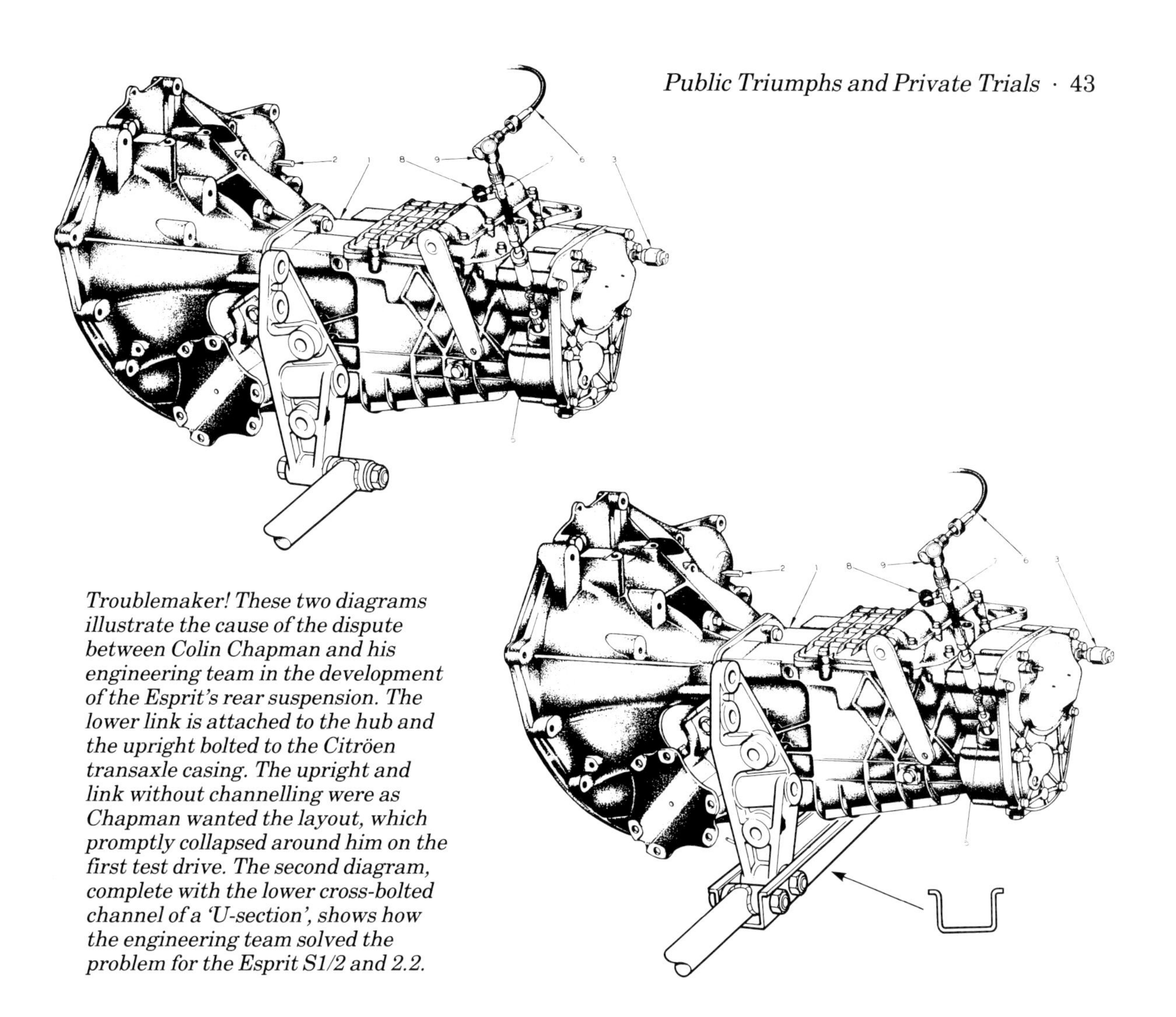

Troublemaker! These two diagrams illustrate the cause of the dispute between Colin Chapman and his engineering team in the development of the Esprit's rear suspension. The lower link is attached to the hub and the upright bolted to the Citröen transaxle casing. The upright and link without channelling were as Chapman wanted the layout, which promptly collapsed around him on the first test drive. The second diagram, complete with the lower cross-bolted channel of a 'U-section', shows how the engineering team solved the problem for the Esprit S1/2 and 2.2.

by Rudd and Colin Spooner) just after Christmas. The first operational Esprit met Colin Chapman at Heathrow on his return from the 12 January 1975 Buenos Aires Grand Prix. (In that Argentinian season starter, Team Lotus had struggled to make the now aged Lotus 72 competitive. Ronnie Peterson had retired and Jackie Ickx had attained a lowly, by Lotus standards, eighth place.)

Nevertheless, Colin Chapman was obviously delighted to see his new mid-engined product ready for its master's occupation. Colin Spooner reported:

Three of us, Dennis Jewell, myself and Tony Rudd, met an unshaven Chapman at one of those Heathrow hotels. He really was pleased to see the Esprit and he just jumped in with Rudd and roared off. In the Elite we struggled to keep up with the 'Old Man' but not for long . . . the rear north/south wheel casting collapsed! Chunky somehow managed to keep it under control in a shower of sparks and left Dennis and I to sweep up the bits whilst he resumed his journey in the back-up Elite.

Fifteen years later, Colin Spooner recalled the equally amusing story behind that premature failure, but this time from the engineering perspective:

When we were developing the running gear for the Esprit – a spell of almost a year, which I remember as composed of seven-day weeks and fifteen-hour days – the relationship between ourselves and Colin Chapman was particularly good. He really did keep a close eye on the project, especially on costs of the inboard disc-brake callipers beside the Citröen transaxle and the way in which we bracketed the single lower wishbone mountings, either side of the transaxle. The development squad had decided to additionally secure the lower link attachment loads by attaching a U-section metal link, colloquially known as a 'Top Hat' brace.

Colin Chapman was curious enough to climb underneath and asked, 'What's that?'

We told him that we had done a stress calculation and . . . But Colin interrupted and said: 'No, no. That'll be OK without.' The second time he saw our 'Top Hat' in place, running from inner lower link mounting to transaxle and bracket and thence beneath the transaxle to its counterpart on the other side, Colin was a bit more insistent. The third time, he gave us a real bollocking, I can tell you, effing and blinding about 'that piece of angle iron'. So we took it off, and had that Heathrow failure. To give Chapman his due, he did have the grace to

Colin Chapman was personally involved with the Esprit's development. Here, the photographer has caught him with the original 'Silver' Giugiaro design study in Turin. (Note that the shiny Wolfrace wheels and outline are substantially correct, but that the screen angle had to be raised and fuel filler necks and caps moved from within the car to the three-quarter rear panel.)

Giugiaro had never designed a glassfibre car before he tackled what became the Esprit, but got very close to the production shape in this first attempt. Deviations include twin wipers and chrome inlay bumper.

The Giugiaro original design for the Esprit had a detailed interior and was based on a stretched Europa chassis. Note the bonnet vents and lovingly chromed door handles, neither of which made it to the production Esprit.

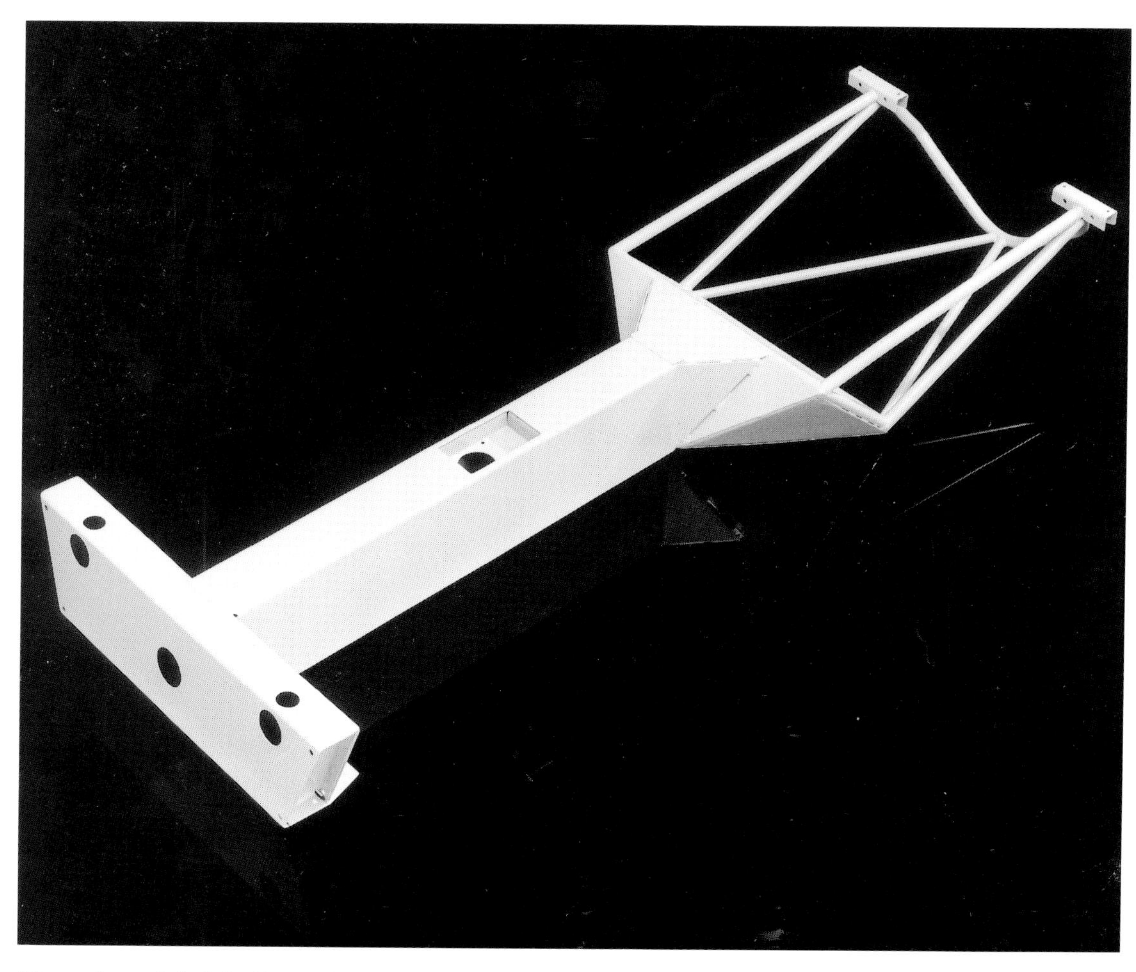

The scale model of the Esprit frame, photographed before torsional study, was located by Colin Spooner. The scale model is still to be seen in the engineering areas at Lotus. The workshop manual diagram (opposite page) shows how close that scale study was to the production reality and also identified (arrowed 6 and 10) the location of the rear suspension upright and cross-channelling that caused so much heated discussion between Colin Chapman and the original Esprit development team.

say to us afterwards, 'That'll teach me to keep my mouth shut', walking away with a boyish grin to step into his alternative transport.

RUNNING DEVELOPMENT

In the later stages of those seven-day development weeks, the Ketteringham Hall trouble-shooters had the services of up to half a dozen pattern-makers and produced three Esprits for three specific purposes: one show car apiece for Paris in the first week of October, another car for Earls Court, and that first running prototype for the Chapman demonstration and subsequent evaluation. Colin Spooner recalled: 'The press were virtually camped outside our gates, so we had

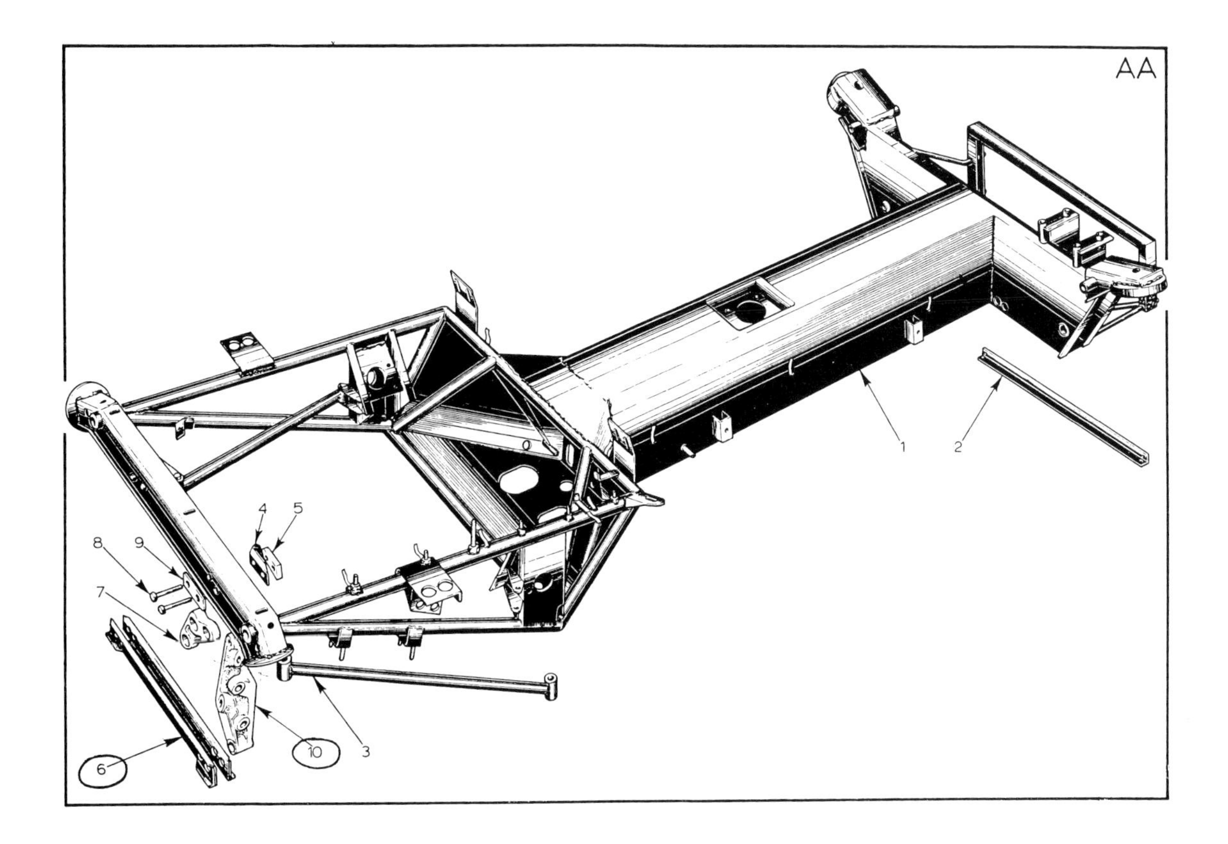

to do most of our running over weekends at Hethel, when they tended to take a break.'

Although Tony Rudd had thought that the Esprit might be a good point at which to depart from the tradition of Lotus backbone chassis, beneath 'belt and braces' glued and bracketed top and bottom body halves, his suggestion was over-ruled. A new chassis of primarily boxed-section steels was constructed, after the experience of the quarter-scale model and the variously expanded Europa prototypes.

The suspension story was initially simplest at the front, where Colin Spooner recalled: 'We virtually used a corner from the then current Opel Ascona.' That meant adapting a double wishbone arrangement with a coaxial coil spring and damper unit to a very different role. At the stage where Chapman drove the car, both Rudd and Spooner recalled that the car had 'dreadful problems with the steering, it was very heavy and suffered an over-centre effect.'

More Work

According to Colin Spooner, the main rectification work to the steering revolved around basic geometry, which was especially applied to the camber settings and the mounting angles at various joints. It is also worth noting that the earlier Esprits used the Ascona layout in association with Triumph TR6 uprights and trunnions, rather than the ball-joint set-up first found on the Esprit Turbo/S3.

There was also detail work to be done on the disc brakes. The front discs came from the Ascona and the rears from Ate supplies for Alfa Romeo, but calliper supply looked like being a problem throughout the prototype's gestation, until Girling decided that

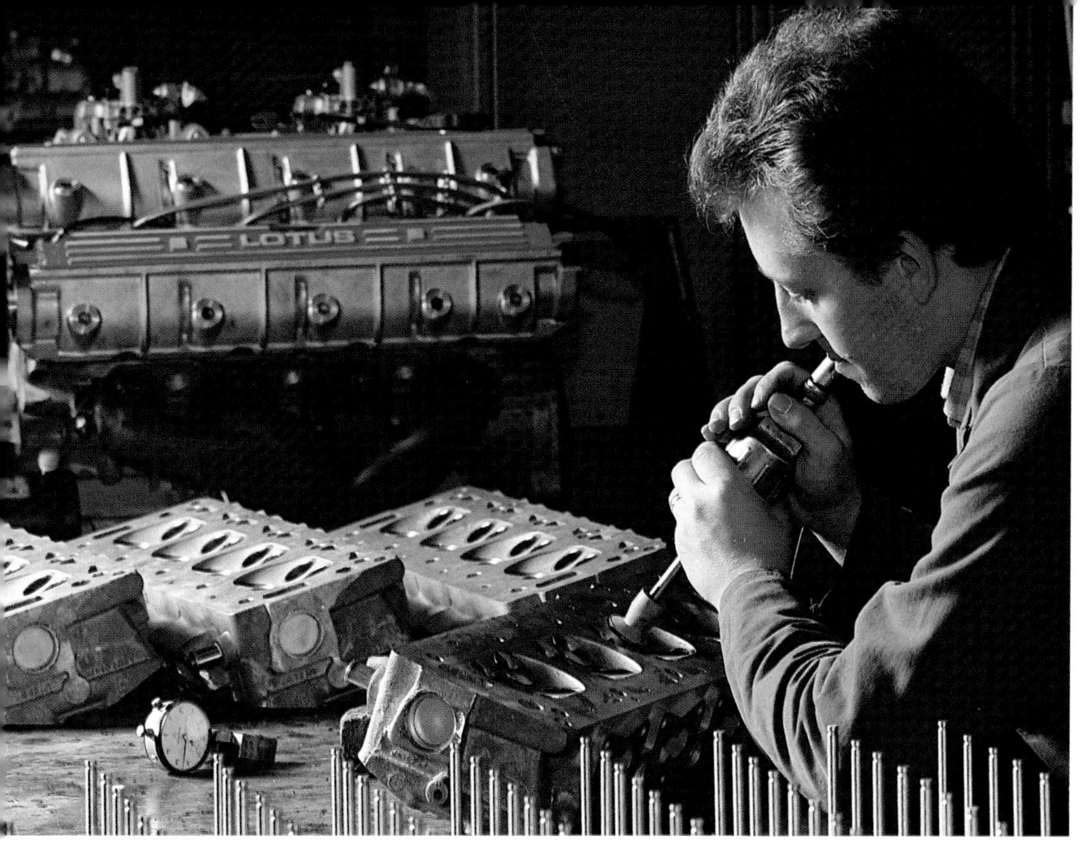

The Lotus twin overhead camshaft, 16-valve, alloy cylinder head has been at the efficient heart of every Esprit manufactured.

Lotus have always been at the forefront of emission requirements and their resources have long included the kind of test laboratory seen here. Today, the Esprit SE meets standards all over the world, thanks to the work of departments such as this one, which is recognized by the American Federal authorities.

What might have been? I know of no Lotus plan to produce an Esprit convertible, but this smart private example shows how well the two-seater adapts to open life at a Club Lotus Day in June 1990.

The end-result: pre-production Esprit S1 in glorious red at Hethel.

they would supply such a low-production requirement. No power assistance was specified but, like the size of the discs that was changed during the S2 Esprit series, vacuum servo assistance has always been part of the Turbo specification, along with enlarged brakes. These features were complemented in 1990 by the adoption of anti-lock (ABS) braking throughout the turbocharged Esprit range.

The trials and tribulations associated with the development of the back suspension have been noted, but it is worth adding that the rear suspension was characterized by the box-section trailing link and a transverse lower arm acting as a wide based triangulated bottom arm. The spring/damper unit fed its loads directly into the steel chassis towers. This layout survived until the 1980/81 birth of the S3/Turbo series, which did take on a top suspension arm and freed the drive shaft from its previous dual role as an upper-link and transmission component. This meant that the engine could be mounted with more compliance, and Noise Vibration and Harshness (NVH) levels became a lot more civilized in the cabin. Unfortunately, the car did have to be put into production before cockpit ventilation could be optimized. That item was a little lower down the priority list than legal requirements, which included toning the individual tubular branch exhaust system down to a respectable crackle.

RUDD'S REVENGE

Tony Rudd had the final quip to summarize the fraught business of developing the Esprit into a car fit for public sale. In November 1976, he stated:

I reckon we solved 90 per cent of the problems before manufacture, but there were others in the company who reckoned I solved 10 per cent – and they sorted 90 per cent trying to put it into production!

3 The First Edition

'The no compromise Lotus for its driver and one selected companion.'
Lotus S1 brochure, 1975

Paris, 2 October 1975. On that autumn Thursday, the Ital Design stand at the annual Parisian display of automotive *haute couture* was dominated by a single silver two-seater. Correctly gambling that the French show would be too good an opportunity to miss in terms of publicity, Lotus had changed their plans at the last minute, by bringing forward the official debut of their mid-engined successor to the Europa. Two weeks prior to the London Earls Court arena, the Esprit shared the limelight in Paris with the new Eclat (also on its debut). Both cars were powered by the 2-litre 16-valve motor that Lotus had uprated from the now bankrupt Jensen Motors application.

It was not just Jensen that had found times hard in the post 1973–1974 fuel crisis period. Lotus hit this troubled period in the history of car sales with a corporate plan to switch from the Elan/Europa generation into the new era of Elite, Esprit and Eclat (all powered by the 2-litre DOHC 16-valve unit that had served Jensen). Commercially, this proved a disaster. The new cars did not come into production fast enough to bridge the gap, and they also met economic conditions that were the toughest in their young history.

REDUNDANCIES

In the years 1973–1975, Lotus had slashed back their workforce from 830 to 450 employees 'and then,' said one Lotus executive of the period wrily, 'we concentrated on survival.' The factory was running well below capacity – in fact, the Elite was the only car Lotus produced after the Europa's production demise was extended to March 1975 – so that the Esprit was desperately required to increase production volume.

The front-engine/rear-drive Eclat was a cheaper descendant of the second Elite – which cost nearly £8,000 in its dearest variant – and went on to father the Excel. The Excel, now with 180bhp was still limping along in current (November 1990) production when this was written. An excellent front-engine/rear-drive machine, with a practical 2 + 2 layout, it was always outshone by the glamour of the Esprit, which really kept Lotus alive between the high volume Elan/Europa era and the new Elan of the nineties.

In his 1976 appraisal of a very early Esprit (MCL 100P) John Bolster shrewdly underlined the production potential of the Esprit:

As was to be expected, the announcement of the car caused something of a furore. The demand is already such that its production may well outstrip that of the Elite/Eclat range.

That was a brave prophecy to make in the opening months of 1976, and one that was proved entirely correct before John Bolster's untimely demise in the late eighties.

It is possible that this is the pre-production Esprit driven by the author for Motor Sport, *but the point is to show how Lotus depicted the Esprit S1 in an early brochure.*

MONEY TALK

After the two show cars, the debut of a production Esprit was greeted warmly. Under the heading 'Lotus announce the futuristic mid-engine Esprit at the Paris Show', *Motoring News* declared in their introduction that it was, 'a superb looking two-seater.' That comment summed up the overall reaction to a claimed 138mph (220kph) machine that looked like costing under £5,000.

In fact, Lotus personnel in Paris were overcome by show fever. They anticipated a price-tag of 'just over £4,500 including all tax', reported a contemporary issue of *Motoring News*. It would be June 1976 before the first Esprits of the Series 1 (S1) breed were available to the public, and the first list price (issued by the close of October 1975) proved to be £5,844.13p.

To put that in contemporary terms, a Jaguar XJ-S V12 coupe (which also made its debut in October) was listed at £8,900 whilst a Capri 3-litre was literally half the actual price of an Esprit S1, and an Aston Martin V8 more than double. There was a niche to be filled.

Just over a year later, the first road test examples were 'doing the rounds'. The yellow S1 Esprit (RCL 377R) borrowed by *Motoring News* had a recommended price of almost twice the original estimate: £8,548.03.

Lotus would vary their production tallies for S1 Esprit output between June 1976 and May 1978. The most consistent company quote, however, was for manufacture of 994 such Esprits, and the most outrageous claim (upon the birth of its S2 successor) was that '1,300 Esprits have been built'. What was the final production specification?

Lotus took the trouble to ensure that everyone knew a great deal about the machine that justified the *Motor Sport* headline 'Hethel secures its future with a spectacular new mid-engined sports car.' So let us just elaborate on what that development

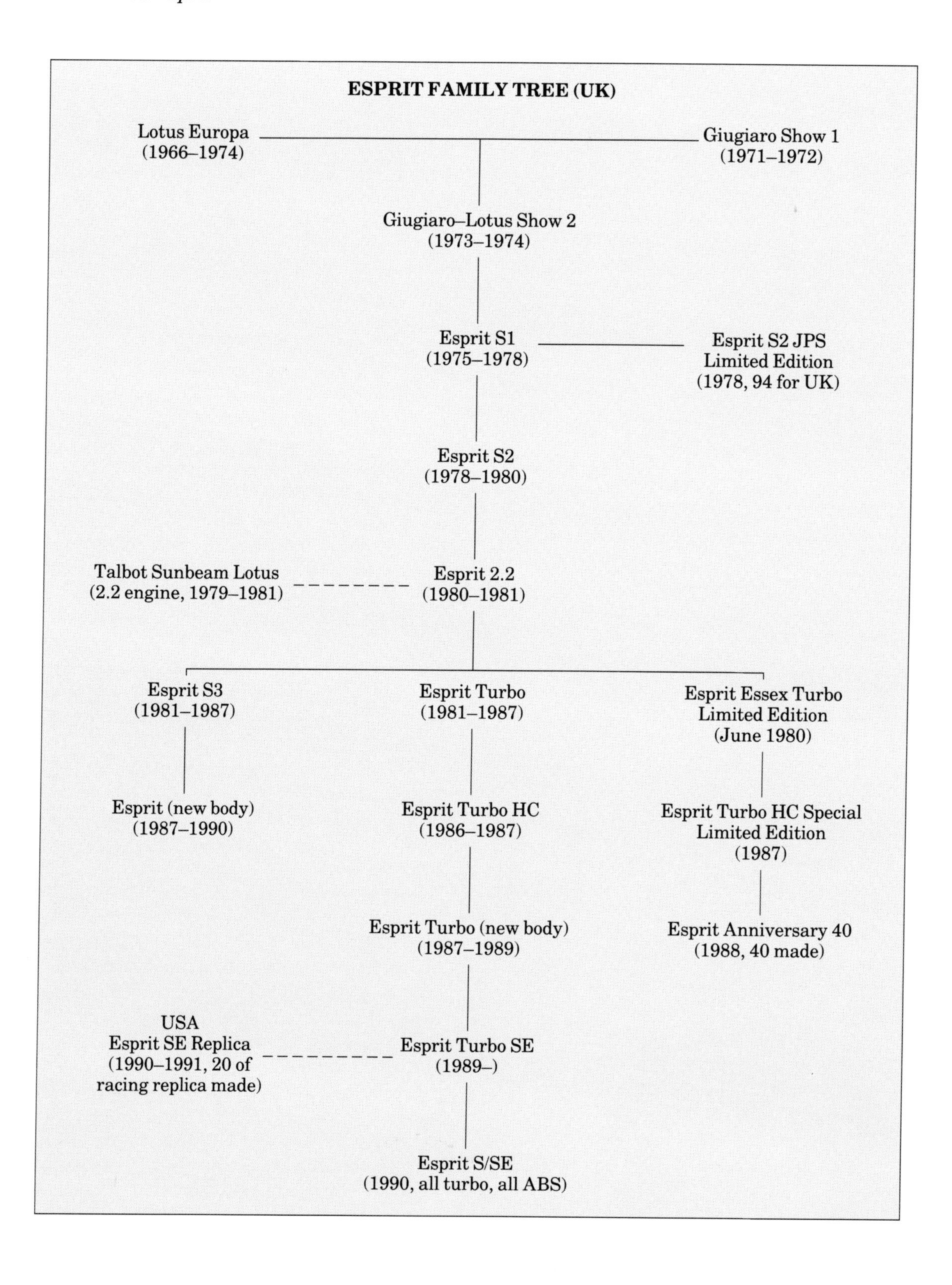
ESPRIT FAMILY TREE (UK)
Lotus Europa
(1966–1974)
Giugiaro Show 1
(1971–1972)
Giugiaro–Lotus Show 2
(1973–1974)
Esprit S1
(1975–1978)
Esprit S2 JPS
Limited Edition
(1978, 94 for UK)
Esprit S2
(1978–1980)
Talbot Sunbeam Lotus
(2.2 engine, 1979–1981)
Esprit 2.2
(1980–1981)
Esprit S3
(1981–1987)
Esprit Turbo
(1981–1987)
Esprit Essex Turbo
Limited Edition
(June 1980)
Esprit (new body)
(1987–1990)
Esprit Turbo HC
(1986–1987)
Esprit Turbo HC Special
Limited Edition
(1987)
Esprit Turbo (new body)
(1987–1989)
Esprit Anniversary 40
(1988, 40 made)
USA
Esprit SE Replica
(1990–1991, 20 of
racing replica made)
Esprit Turbo SE
(1989–)
Esprit S/SE
(1990, all turbo, all ABS)

team from Ketteringham Hall submitted for the 1976–1978 production span.

BODY TECHNIQUE

The strictly two-seater Lotus emerged from its international design and development period ready for manufacture in Glass Fibre Reinforced Plastic (GFRP). Such coachwork was formed in two primary moulds (upper and lower half, within a distinct crease marking the central joining point) and bonded and bolted upon the now equally traditional Lotus steel backbone chassis.

The injection mouldings initially saw a new paint, picked up from the Concorde programme, incorporated. It was abandoned after 1977, when Lotus used a unique ICI-Lotus self-colouring process to provide 'painted' exterior panels from the mould. When I watched early Esprits being made in the summer of 1977, the self-colour paint process required only light polishing to meet showroom standards, ex-mould.

Clad in red and green 'tartan' cloth trims conceived by Giugiaro, this was the first of many interiors worn by the Esprit over the sales seasons. Note the ugly two-spoke wheel that was standard equipment on original Esprits.

Lotus Press Release, 26 September 1975

(Embargo: 001 hours, 2 October 1975)

ENGINE
Lotus 907 2-litre 16-valve twin OHC power unit developing 160bhp.

GEARBOX
5-speed manual unit. Synchromesh on all forward gears; fifth gear is overdrive.

BRAKES
9.7in disc – front
10.6in inboard discs – rear
Dual braking system, split front/rear circuits.

BODY/CHASSIS
Glassfibre-reinforced plastic body with steel backbone chassis. Passenger compartment encapsulated in a 'safety-cell structure'.

SUSPENSION
Front *Independent unequal length wishbones and coil springs. Telescopic shock absorbers. Anti-roll bar. Camber 0 to 0.5 degrees, 3 to 5mm toe in.*

Rear *Independent diagonal trailing arms and lateral link with fixed-length driveshaft, coil springs, telescopic shock absorbers. Camber 0 to 0.5 degrees, 8 to 10mm toe in.*

STEERING
Rack-and-pinion
Castor: 3 to 3.5 degrees.
Kingpin: 9 degrees.

WHEELS
Front *6J × 14*
Rear *7J × 14*
Tyres *Goodyear Grand Prix*
Front *195/70 HR 14*
Rear *205/70 HR 14*

BASIC DIMENSIONS
Wheelbase: 96in
Overall Length: 165in
Overall width: 73.5in
Overall height: 43.75
Front track: 59.5in
Rear track: 59.5in
Mid-laden ground clearance: 5.5in
Weight (kerb): 1,980lb

PERFORMANCE
Maximum speed: 138mph
Acceleration: 0–60mph – 6.8sec
0–100mph – 20.7sec

FUEL CONSUMPTION
Average fuel consumption: 28mpg
Tank capacity: 15 gallons
Range: 450 miles
Oil: 550miles/pint

INTERIOR
Front headroom: 36in [914mm]
Steering-wheel to seat: 17.5 – 23.5in
Seat cushion front to pedals: 14–20in
Boot capacity: 7cu ft

GENERAL SPECIFICATION

Engine	*4 in-line Lotus 907*
Capacity	*1,973cc (120.4cu in)*
Bore/Stroke	*95.2/62.9mm (3.75/2.772in)*
Cooling	*Water*
Block	*Aluminium*
Head	*Aluminium*
Valves	*DOHC 4 per cylinder*

Valve Timing

Inlet opens	*30 degrees BTDC*
Inlet closes	*50 ABDC*
Exhaust opens	*50 BBDC*
Exhaust closes	*30 ATDC*
Compression	*9.5:1*
Carburettors	*2 Dellorto DHLA 45E*
Bearings	*5 main*
Fuel pump	*SU electrical*
Maximum power	*160bhp at 6,200rpm*
Maximum torque	*140lb ft at 4,900rpm*

ELECTRICAL
Negative earth, Lucas 18ACR (45 Ampere); 4 fuses.
Battery beneath rear side window.

TRANSMISSION
Type: 5-speed manual
Clutch: 8.5in diaphragm spring, hydraulically operated.

Internal ratios and mph/1,000rpm

Fifth	*0.76:1*	*21.85mph*
Fourth	*0.97:1*	*17.15mph*
Third	*1.32:1*	*12.58mph*
Second	*1.94:1*	*8.56mph*
First	*2.92:1*	*5.69mph*
Final drive	*4.375:1*	

PERFORMANCE
Speed in gears at 7,300rpm

First	*41.5mph*
Second	*62.5mph*
Third	*91.8mph*
Fourth	*125.2mph*
O/D Fifth	*138mph at 6,300rpm*

Acceleration from rest	***Seconds***
0–30mph	*2.4*
0–40mph	*3.3*
0–50mph	*4.9*
0–60mph	*6.8*
0–70mph	*9.1*
0–80mph	*12.0*
0–90mph	*16.1*
0–100mph	*20.7*
Standing ¼-mile	*15sec*

At the time, I commented in *Motoring News* (25 August 1977):

It's a good hard finish, but the self-colouring system is at present only applied for white, yellow, red, orange and blue, although experiments were taking place with black when I called.

The time spent trying to get such a finish in place at a good production pace must have been uneconomic, for the Elite did not use the system and the Esprit reverted to conventional paint-spraying techniques as well by the close of the year. Lotus loyalist (he joined the company in 1957) and current associate director, Composites, Albert Adams confirmed in 1990:

We are to re-address the problem of putting final colours into the moulding process. Then we could get a fair surface finish, from the mould, but the lasting snag was to get a colour match between items like the doors and the main panels. If we can get that matching and rectification process to the standards of the nineties, then we will re-introduce the paint and mould process.

EFFICIENT LINES

Despite the corpulent body width, Lotus brought the first Esprit on the market with a fine aerodynamic drag coefficient. At just 0.34Cd, this was an excellent figure for the mid-seventies, especially with such broad wheels and tyres to shroud and a mid-engine bay to ventilate.

The dramatically low lines and steeply raked flat screen (swept by a single pantograph wiper) helped to offset the 73.5in (1.87m) width and the angular styling theme, but the most obvious contribution was the jutting 'chin' spoiler. No other aerodynamic appendages were featured in the first Esprit series, so if the model you are examining lacks 'ears' around the rear-side glass and other engine bay air-feeds, then the chances are that you are looking at an S1 Esprit.

Ancillary components in and around the GRFP primary sections were in vacuum-formed mouldings of light plastics. These comprised items such as the headlamp covers, number-plate surround, tail-light accommodation and heater cowling. Such tooling was expensive for Lotus to acquire, but the speed and economy of its subsequent output justified the initial expense. It also contributed to explain why such a high percentage of car content could be claimed as 'Lotus-made' (Lotus quoted 63 per cent in July 1977).

Other features manufactured by Lotus in the 1977 period of the S1 were: air conditioning units; seats, interior trim panels and upholstery; heaters and, for the entire range, those 2-litre 16-valve motors. The steel backbone chassis and suspension links were also made within the Lotus of the late seventies, but we will detail those subsequently.

ROAD TEST
Lotus Esprit

Reproduced from *Autocar*
15 January 1977

Long awaited new sports car from Lotus. Excellent handling, road holding, and brakes with taut ride. Disappointing level of interior, engine and wind noise. Eye catching good looks not very practical, with difficult access and poor driver visibility. Poor value absolutely, but with few rivals in its class.

The Esprit is the latest of the new generation of cars designed to move Lotus away from the 'kit car' image and into the prestige sports car market. The Elite and Eclat before it have done much to make this movement a reality, but it is on the Esprit that

MANUFACTURER: *Lotus Cars Limited Norwich Norfolk NR14 8EZ*	
PRICES:	
Basic	£6,820.00
Special Car Tax	£568.34
VAT	£591.07
Total (in GB)	£7,979.41
Seat Belts	standard
Licence	£40.00
Delivery charge (London approx)	£20.00
Number plates (Approx)	£12.00
Total on the Road (ex insurance)	**£8,051.41**
Insurance	Group 7
EXTRAS (inc VAT)	
*Radio	£73.71
*Fitted to test car	
TOTAL AS TESTED ON THE ROAD	**£8,125.12**

Lotus' highest hopes are pinned. Compared with its mid-engined predecessor, the Europa, the Esprit is a giant stride towards the Porsche/Ferrari/Maserati market and it oh-so-nearly makes it as a worthy competitor to such marques. That it does not do so is really a question of development, since it is the high level of engine noise and body resonance that prevent the Esprit from being considered in the class. The Elite improved greatly in its first year of production and we must hope that this will be repeated with the Esprit which could become a very desirable cut-price rival in this very special market.

Following the lead set by the Elite, the Esprit is another two-part body design, the upper and lower halves of the car being moulded as just two sections with a join at the conspicuous waistline. Such a design is essential to give a competitive power-to-weight ratio for Lotus' 2-litre engine gives only 160bhp – much less than the larger engines found in many of the Esprit's class rivals. To show further movement towards the performance potential of rivals, the Lotus makes the best use of current thinking on aerodynamic design and the shape is very smooth and efficient.

Unlike the Elite and Eclat, the Esprit continues the mid-engined theme pioneered by Lotus (for road cars) with the Europa. Thus, the four-cylinder sits longitudinally in a simple space-frame attached to the broad of the backbone chassis. It lies on its side at 45deg to the horizontal with the induction face uppermost and drive from it is taken via a single dry plate clutch to the Maserati 5-speed gearbox. This is the box developed for the now obsolete Citröen SM and supplies of it have been guaranteed for five years. The gearchange uses a rod to select the gears and a cable to work the across-the-gate movement.

Suspension is by a mixture of off-the-shelf Opel Ascona components at the front and Lotus' own clever independent system at the rear. The latter is similar to that used in the Elite except that the bottom link pivots at the outboard end in the centre of a new hub carrier where on the Elite, the link attaches to the back of the bottom of the carrier. At the front of the car, the suspension is by unequal length wishbones and the anti-roll bar forms the forward legs of the bottom links. Steering is by rack and pinion, again 'borrowed' from the Elite but with a higher ratio through use of shorter steering arms.

Braking is by discs all round, those at the rear being inboard on the same mounting that supports the gearbox. There is a direct acting servo for the split circuit system which, at present, has solid discs at the front.

The design of the Esprit's body is very much a two-seater with no space in the cockpit behind the seats. The latter are bucket-shaped with no provision for rake, only fore and aft adjustment. The line of the roof is carried through to the tail by a very big engine cover which is nearly all glass. The whole of this cover can be lifted to gain access to the rear compartment that doubles as an engine-bay and luggage area. The engine itself is covered by a removable box which sits on insulating rubber around the engine and gives quite reasonable access to the engine when removed – better than other mid-engined designs in fact.

At the front, another cover lifts to give access to the spare wheel, brake reservoir, washer bottle and the headlamp lift motors. There is space in here for a little luggage, but only of the squashy variety as the space is really quite small. The body design smacks more of a styling exercise than a production design. It started as one of course, the Ital Design Europa-based special shown at the Turin show in 1972. The production car is less 'extreme' in its styling but since the Lotus pre-production car, which made its debut at the 1975 Paris Show, the windscreen has been made less steep by 2 deg to improve vision. Regrettably, nothing was done to slim down the front pillars, which are very thick and a long way forward, requiring a glance through the side windows when making anything more than a gentle turn. To give some rear vision, quarter windows are let into the body sides immediately behind the door pillars but there is still a lot of body in the direction of three quarter rear which means that junctions are best approached at right angles.

Performance

Though maximum torque is produced at relatively high revs (4,900rpm), the light weight and good aerodynamic shape do not give the impression that the Esprit is a 'top end' car. The acceleration figures reveal that it will pull from as low as 10mph in 3rd gear and that it will even pull the high 5th gear down to 30mph. 1st and 2nd gears are quite close with 1st gear pleasantly high, allowing 40mph at the indicated maximum 7,000rpm. 3rd gear is noticeably 'tall' and allows nearly 90mph to be reached before 4th is needed to take the speed over 100mph. Since the engine of the test car had only done some 2,000 miles, it is perhaps not surprising that we were unable to match the Lotus claim of acceleration to 60mph from rest in 6.8sec. On a wretchedly wet day, we returned 8.4sec which is due in part to the slow time to 30mph (2.9sec as opposed to the claimed best of 2.4sec by the factory). Of greater significance in demonstrating the unsuitability of the test conditions and the unrepresentative performance of the test car is comparison of the Esprit with the performance of the heavier and bigger (but similar-engined) Elite. The latter car accelerated from 40 to 80mph in 3rd gear in 10.9sec while the Esprit (with similar gearing) took 11.1sec; we would have expected the lighter car to have been significantly quicker here.

Lotus claim a maximum speed of 138mph at 6,300rpm in 5th gear, but our particular car could not be made to pull more than 5,675rpm.

Economy

During the 800 miles of the test period, the Esprit gave an overall consumption of 23.3mpg which is markedly improved over the Elite which gave 20.9mpg. The shape must help here as does the lighter weight and as the Steady Speed returns demonstrate, the consumption at high speeds is good. In the region 50–80mph, consumption is consistently around the high twenties, while no better consumption at lower speeds reveals the over-choked nature of the engine.

With 15 gallons of petrol available in the linked twin tanks, the fuel range comfortably exceeds 300 miles and with care, 400 miles might be approached. Filling the fuel tanks is an arduous business as there is severe blow-back and the fuel delivery of most pumps cannot be used. As the balance pipe between the two tanks is not quite big enough, it is necessary to fill up both sides through the two fillers provided. Though the test car's was a young engine, it did not use oil at a great rate; consumption was estimated at 1,000 miles per pint.

Roadholding, Handling and Ride

It is in this area that the Esprit is already very well developed. The usual Lotus formula of soft, long travel springs allied to taut damping means that at all speeds the ride is comfortable and relaxing. Only high frequency undulations such as patched road repairs can upset the suspension and under most conditions, the suspension copes well. The very wide tyres are guilty of serious bump-thumping over cats eyes and potholes but this is a reasonable enough price to pay for the response and grip that they give.

Just as you would expect of a Lotus, the Esprit handles very well indeed with just a slow build-up in understeer to show how the cornering forces are increasing. The build-up in steering effort is pro rata with the understeer and thus there is the best of messages to relay to the driver's hands. In extremis, *the understeer builds up until full lock is reached at which point there is a disconcerting but safe 'pitching' on the outside front wheel as the inside front wheel bounces. At no time during the test was there any indication that the rear wheel adhesion could be seriously upset. Even the most brutal of treatment such as turning quickly into a corner, lifting the accelerator and then quickly putting full power back on failed to produce an oversteering 'drift'. Thus one concludes that the handling is very safe with the proviso that the lightly laden front wheels can be made to run very wide on a slippery surface by application of too much power.*

If further proof is needed of the balanced nature of the handling, even heavy braking when turning into a corner will not allow the tail of the car to step out of line even though the braking is biased to the rear wheels.

On wet and dry roads alike, the Dunlop Sport Formula 70 Super tyres give quite outstanding roadholding and there are few cars that could stay with an Esprit in a hurry. It takes some time to find confidence in the roadholding and handling since the car feels so light on the ground. Once used to the fact that this is only caused by the wide tyres, confidence builds and the Esprit can be flicked around like a racing car.

Though three turns from lock-to-lock suggest high geared steering, the turning circle is not generous at a mean 35 feet between kerbs. In fact, the gearing is about right with enough leverage to turn the wide wheels easily at walking pace while not needing excessive amounts of lock at speed.

Plenty of experience of aerodynamic design ensures that the body of the Esprit does not allow a feeling of lightness at high speed. There is a tendency to wander slightly all the time, but again, this is due mainly to the tyre width and the great response that this gives. Provided that the steering wheel is not held too tightly, the Esprit runs true enough, though it does not have the arrow-straight reassurance of the better high performance front-engined cars. During the period of the test there was little discernible sidewind, but the buffeting effect of heavy lorries was shrugged off satisfactorily and there should be no misgivings in this area.

Brakes

Generous discs front and rear, the squat shape of the design and a pleasant servo action all contribute to ensuring that the Esprit's brakes are well up to the performance potential. The fade test served only to work the brakes up to their best operating temperature and they felt really good at the end of the tenth sucessive stop. Response checks revealed that the braking performance is progressive, building up in effectiveness with increased pedal pressure. Even on a wet road, the optimum performance proved to be as high as 0.9g and there is no reason to doubt that braking in the order of 1.0g would be possible on a dry surface. It is the rear wheels that lock first but they do this only just before the fronts – the right compromise. The handbrake proved to be particularly effective, giving a retardation on its own of no less than 0.35g – good enough to stop the car from 30mph in under 30 yards.

Noise

It is in this area that the development of the Esprit must go on. There are serious resonances at several points in the rev band, the first occurring at only 2,000rpm. This is not only wearing on the ears, it can be felt through the feet and seat too. The worst period is an exhaust-induced resonance on the overrun around 5,000rpm which is bad enough to cause discomfort.

The engine only approaches silence when the car is cruising on a light throttle at speed, when what noise there is streams out behind. Hard acceleration produces a high level of engine noise that is not particularly pleasant in its nature – certainly not as nice as the old Lotus Twin Cam of the Europa.

The test car was guilty of wind noise too from the leading and trailing edges of both doors and from the wing mirror.

By contrast, transmission noise is never obtrusive, despite all the ratios being indirect.

Fittings and Furniture

Getting into the Esprit for the first time is like walking into an Italian furniture shop. The materials used for the interior trim are conventional, contemporary 'good taste' with much use of suede-like material for the fascia and door trims and contrasting panels in brushed nylon. The roof lining is colour-keyed to the door trim relief panels and made in a moquette-like material. The whole effect is crisp and modern, very much in keeping with the body design. The brushed nylon seats have pronounced side support with a roll beneath the knees and a built-in head restraint.

All the instruments are contained in a banana-shaped console that sits on the angled fascia and surrounds the steering wheel. The shape allows a deep lid over the instruments that very nearly prevents any reflection in the deep windscreen. Set in the ends of the instrument pack are rocker switches in the left hand one for minor controls and the two slide levers for the heating system in the right-hand one.

Control of the lights, indicators and horn is given by a Leyland-type fingertip stalk on the right of the steering column while a matching lever on the left operates the single pantograph windscreen wiper and the powerful windscreen washers.

The gearlever falls readily to hand in its position atop the high, wide backbone section of the chassis. Ahead of it is the radio mounting position while behind are the controls for the electric window lifts and a neat lift-up lever for the choke. Though early versions had a central ashtray, there are now two, one on each side, set in the sill tops.

At the rear end of the backbone section that runs through cockpit is a vertical pocket set against the engine bulkhead and this is usefully shaped to take objects as big as a map and wide enough for a hand to be got in to reach things on the floor of the pocket. This compartment and the glove locker set in the steeply raked fascia top on the passenger's side, constitute the only places where on-journey paraphernalia may be put.

The release for the rear lid is set in the driver's door jamb while that for the front compartment is an over-centre bar that is positioned beneath the offside fascia.

Living with the Lotus Esprit

The Esprit proved to be a reluctant starter during the period that it was with us, needing several attempts before it would 'catch' and run cleanly. When hot, it starts better though when left to cool for half an hour or so, it needed quite a bit of churning to get going. The front-mounted radiator takes a while to warm up and this explains why no heat is available from the heater for the first three miles or so when starting from cold.

Before discussing starting, we should really consider getting into and out of the Esprit, a job for the fit and lithe. The low build of the car and the proximity of the steering wheel to the front edge of the seat mean that the only satisfactory way to get in is to put one leg in first, flop down on the seat and drag the other in afterwards. Once in, the driving position is immediately noticeable as 'Italian Ape' with the pedals close and the steering wheel seemingly a long way away. Thus a pronounced knees up attitude is needed and some taller drivers will find that the steering wheel rim fouls their knees. It might be better all round if the steering wheel rake was less vertical.

Though space around the pedals is limited, there is just room for feet of average size and even room alongside the clutch for the left foot (though, annoyingly, there is no foot rest); the pedals are arranged to allow for heel-and-toe operation.

All the controls, including the pedals, are light to use though the angle of the clutch pivot and its nearness to the floor mean that the action is a pushaway rather than just an ankle flex. The gearchange is conventional four-speed layout with 5th gear out to the right and forward with reverse below it. The action of the gearchange is light and unobstructive with the right degree of spring-loading into the 3rd/4th gear plane. Despite the length of the linkage the change feels pleasantly direct though naturally, the amount of inertia to be overcome does not allow it to be as light as a direct-acting lever.

The view out from the cockpit is panoramic and one has to lift oneself up to see the bonnet's far edges. To the rear, visibility is only limited badly in the direction of nearside three-quarter rear and a matching wing mirror to that tucked away on the driver's door frame should be standard. The wiper clears the screen well considering its size but does leave an unwiped portion adjacent to the offside pillar, worsening the visibility problem produced by the thick pillar itself. At night, the Lucas sealed beam headlamp system gives a bright, if uncontrolled beam pattern. On cars as low as the Esprit, a flat-top Continental beam would be better as one is sitting low enough to look down the beams and the back glare caused by upward light scatter can be very disturbing, especially in fog. Electric motors elevate the headlamps quickly enough for them to be used for flashing in daylight but in the up position, the headlamps flutter annoyingly over any bumps. The fuse controlling their elevation, in common with the heated rear window and interior light, failed repeatedly during our test.

Heating and ventilation are looked after by an air-blending system that lacks volume but is very controllable. There are fresh air vents for both driver and passenger and the air flow through both may be boosted by the heater fan, the latter being noisy only on the fastest of its two speeds. The extraction of stale air from the cockpit is rather lazy and it is necessary to have the fan operating on its slowest speed to keep the windscreen clear of condensation at low road speeds when humidity is high.

Because some water makes its way into the rear trunk area, the heated rear window must be used all the time to keep the rear window clear though little dirt or dampness stays on the outside surface of this window. The rear window is isolated from the cockpit by the vertical window immediately behind the seats, which in common with similar arrangements on other mid-engined cars can set up multiple reflections in the mirror at night.

With the rear window open and the engine cover removed, access to most components is good though the hidden distributor is a noteable exception. The battery is positioned below the offside quarter window and must be removed to check the electrolyte level.

SPECIFICATION

ENGINE

	Mid engine, rear drive
Cylinders	4, in-line
Main bearings	5
Cooling	Water
Fan	Electric
Bore, mm (in)	95.3 (3.75)
Stroke, mm (in)	69.2 (2.73)
Capacity, cc (in)	1,973 (120.5)
Valve gear	dohc
Camshaft drive	Toothed belt
Compression ratio	9.5-to-1
Octane rating	97 RM
Carburettor	Two-Dellorto 2-choke
Max power	160bhp (DIN) at 6,200rpm
Max torque	140lb ft at 4,900rpm

TRANSMISSION

Type	Citröen 5-speed all synchromesh
Clutch	Borg and Beck, sdp 8½in dia (hydraulic)

Gear	Ratio	mph/1,000rpm
Top	0.76	21.85
4th	0.97	17.15
3rd	1.32	12.58
2nd	1.94	8.56
1st	2.93	5.69

Final drive gear	Hypoid bevel (in unit with gearbox)
Ratio	4.375-to-1

SUSPENSION

Front – location	Independent, double wishbones)
– springs	Coil
– dampers	Telescopic
– anti-roll bar	Yes (forming part of bottom wishbone)
Rear – location	Independent semi-trailing beam cross link, fixed length shaft
– springs	Coil
– dampers	Telescopic
– anti-roll bar	No

STEERING

Type	Rack and pinion
Power assistance	No
Wheel diameter	14¾in

BRAKES

Front	9.7in dia disc
Rear	10.6in dia disc
Servo	Yes, direct-acting

WHEELS

Type	Cast aluminium alloy
Rim width	7J × 14 (rear) 6J × 14 (front)
Tyres – make	Dunlop
– type	Radial ply tubeless
– size	205/70 HR 14 (rear) 205/60 HR 14

EQUIPMENT

Battery	12-volt 50Ah
Alternator	45amp
Headlamps	Quadruple 150/120w
Reversing lamp	Standard
Hazard warning	Standard
Electric fuses	8
Screen wipers	2-speed plus single wipe facility
Screen washer	Electric
Interior heater	Air blending
Interior trim	Nylon seats, moquette head-lining
Floor covering	Carpet
Jack	Screw parallelo-gram
Jacking points	Front, beneath wishbone; rear beneath cross-beam
Windscreen	Laminated

MAINTENANCE

Fuel Tank	15 Imp gal (68 litres)
Cooling system	13½ pints (inc. heater)
Engine sump	10½ pints SAE 10W/50
Gearbox and final drive	4 pints SAE 90
Grease	Driveshafts front hubs
Valve clearance	Inlet 0.005/0.007in (cold), Exhaust 0.010/0.012in (cold)
Contact breaker	0.014/0.016in gap
Ignition timing	12deg BTDC (strobo) 8deg BTDC (static at 1,000rpm)
Spark plug	
– type	Champion N7Y
– gap	0.023in
Tyre pressures	F 18; R 28 psi
Max payload	380lb (170kg)

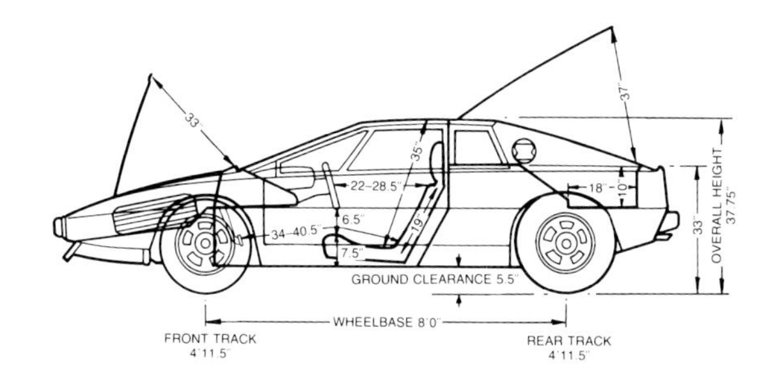

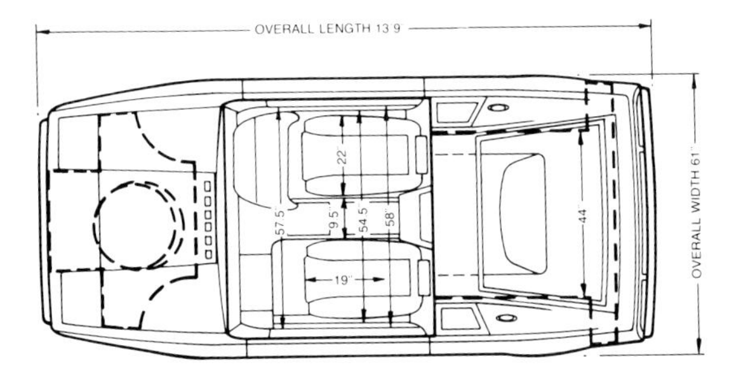

MAXIMUM SPEEDS

Gear	mph	kph	rpm
Top (mean)	124*	200	5,675
(best)	124*	200	5,675
4th	120	193	7,000
3rd	88	142	7,000
2nd	60	96	7,000
1st	40	64	7,000

**See* text

ACCELERATION

True mph	Time (sec)	Speedo mph
30	2.9	32
40	4.3	43
50	6.3	53
60	8.4	65
70	11.6	77
80	15.3	88
90	20.2	100
100	27.4	111
110	39.4	122
120	–	133

Standing
¼-mile:
16.3 sec, 82mph
kilometres:
30.2 sec. 102mph

mph	Top	4th	3rd
10–30	–	–	7.4
20–40	–	9.9	5.9
30–50	13.9	8.2	5.1
40–60	12.4	7.9	4.8
50–70	12.9	7.8	5.3
60–80	12.5	8.1	6.3
70–90	13.4	9.0	8.2
80–100	17.0	11.1	–
90–110	23.6	16.6	–

CONSUMPTION

Fuel
Overall mpg: 23.3
(12.1 litres/100km)
Calculated (DIN) mpg: 25.2
(11.2 litres/100km)

Constant speed:

mph	mpg
30	28.3
40	29.3
50	29.6
60	28.9
70	27.7
80	26.2
90	24.0
100	20.6

Autocar formula:
Hard driving, difficult conditions 21mpg
Average driving, average conditions 26mpg
Gentle driving, easy conditions 30mpg

Grade of fuel: Premium, 4-star (97 RM)
Mileage recorder: 3 per cent over reading

Oil
Consumption (SAE 10W/50) 1,000 miles/pint

BRAKES

Fade *(from 70mph in neutral)*
Pedal load for 0.5g stops in lb

	start/end		start/end
1	20–15	6	25–25
2	23–20	7	25–25
3	23–20	8	25–30
4	25–25	9	25–30
5	25–25	10	25–30

Response *(from 30mph in neutral)*

Load	g	Distance
20lb	0.30	100ft
40lb	0.60	50ft
60lb	0.77	39ft
80lb	0.90	33.4ft
Handbrake	0.35	86ft

Max gradient 1 in 4.

CLUTCH

Pedal 32lb and 5½in

TEST CONDITIONS

Wind: 0–5mph
Temperature: 3deg C (36deg F)
Barometer: 29.8in Hg
Humidity: 90 per cent
Surface: wet asphalt and concrete
Test distance: 800 miles

Figures taken at 2,000 miles by our own staff at the Motor Industry Research Association proving ground at Nuneaton.

REGULAR SERVICE

Change	Interval 5,000	10,000
Engine Oil	Yes	Yes
Oil filter	Yes	Yes
Gearbox oil	Check	Yes
Spark plugs	Check	Yes
Air cleaner	No	Yes
C/breaker	Check	Yes
Total cost	**£41.61***	**£54.55***

(Assuming labour at £5,50/hour)
**Approximate times taken as same as Elite. 10,000 mile service time plus 3½ hours if valve clearances need adjustment.*

PARTS COST

(including VAT)

Brake pads (2 wheels) – front	£10.58
– rear	£8.64
Silencers	£49.40
Tyre – each (typical advertised)	£57.75
Windscreen	£70.24
Headlamp unit (approx)	£14.00
Front wing (approx)	£100.00
Rear bumper	£41.00

Warranty Period
12 months/12,000 miles

WEIGHT

Kerb, 20.3cwt/2,275lb/1,033kg
(Distribution F-R 43.7/56.3)
As tested, 23.3cwt/2,601lb/1,185kg

Boot capacity: 7.0cu ft.

Turning circles:
Between kerbs
L, 34ft 5in; R, 36ft 2in
Between walls
L, 36ft 7in; R, 38ft 5in
Turns, lock to lock; 3

TEST SCORECARD

(Average of scoring by *Autocar* Road Test team)
Ratings: *6 Excellent*
5 Good
4 Better than average
3 Worse than average
2 Poor
1 Bad

PERFORMANCE	3.50
STEERING AND HANDLING	5.00
BRAKES	5.80
COMFORT IN FRONT	3.58
DRIVERS AIDS *(instruments, lights, wipers, visibility, etc.)*	3.50
CONTROLS	3.38
NOISE	3.00
STOWAGE	3.00
ROUTINE SERVICE *(under-bonnet access; dipstick, etc.)*	2.70
EASE OF DRIVING	4.18
OVERALL RATING	3.74

COMPARISONS

	Price (£)	max mph	0–60 (sec)	overall mpg	capacity (cc)	power (bhp)	wheelbase (in)	length (in)	width (in)	kerb weight (cwt)	fuel (gal)	tyre size
Lotus Esprit	**7,979**	**124**	**8.4**	**23.3**	**1,973**	**160**	**96**	**165**	**73**	**20.3**	**13.0**	**205/60 205/70 × 14**
Porsche 911	9,999	130	7.8	23.2	2,687	165	89½	169	65	21.2	17½	185/70VR15
Lancia Monte Carlo	N/A	119	9.8	25.2	1,995	120	91	150	67	20.4	13	185/70HR13
TVR 3000M	4,399	121	7.7	21.4	2,994	142	90	158	64	20.0	12	185/70HR13
Maserati Merak	10,793	135	8.2	17.4	2,965	190	102¼	171	70	28.5	18½	185–205/70HR15

For routine level checks, only the rearmost section of the engine cover need be hinged backwards, revealing the cooling system header tank and allowing the dipstick to be reached – a guide tube would help in returning the dipstick to its hole.

In Conclusion

Though the Esprit does most dynamic things well, there are some poor features in the design that will grate with some owners and potential owners. The front lid cannot be opened while the headlamps are up and it is a perpetual fiddle to get into the engine bay because so much has to be done before the engine can be reached. It is also very annoying that the best way to lift oneself out of the car is by pushing up on the sill as this gets very wet and dirty in rainy weather.

Perhaps one can argue that such things are the price one pays for such an exotic motor car – we are not so sure.

If like the Elite, the first year of Esprit production is used to sort out the shortcomings, then in time, the Esprit will join other Lotus models that have eventually come good.

As to whether the Esprit is value-for-money, who can say? It has no obvious rivals except the Lancia Beta Monte Carlo. The Lancia is certainly more practical, arguably less good looking, and likely to be significantly cheaper in Britain. But it isn't as 'exotic' and it is on this aspect that many Esprits will be sold.

A 120-MPH RETRACTION

It is worth noting that the original headlamp, with single-lift operating motor, was changed during S1 production for a twin-motor system. Lotus reported that the reason for changing to twin motors was that the 'long tie bar between left and right lamp pods allowed too much flexing and subsequent fluttering of the lights on rough terrain.' A straight corporate face was also maintained when the secondary reason for the change was given as 'the single motor struggled to retract lamps over 120mph (!)' . . .

Another unique feature within the Esprit body, and one which remains at the time of writing, was the provision of a safety cell around the cabin. The bulkhead behind the occupants was made in a light and particularly strong marine plywood. An almost vertical glass panel was let into that middle bulkhead, affording a view over the engine cover and through the ultimate in 'fastback' rear glass. The 'glass-back' was released by a pull handle in the door jamb.

Original S1 Esprits had their engines covered by a one-piece moulding, but this was changed during the production run to an engine cover that offered a hinged access hatch to check oil and water levels.

Luggage could be carried in two primary areas. A claimed 7cu ft (20cm^3) was provided in an upholstered bin that tended to heat your belongings (courtesy of hot engine and transaxle) on any journey over 15 miles. Alternatively, there was room to squash in some extra supplies around the spare wheel, which resided under the front bonnet.

INSIDE STORY

The side doors carried extruded aluminium beams of a Z-section that saved 5lb (2kg) per side compared to steel, yet offered comparable side-protection strength. Across the front scuttle and, at strategic points, in association with a wooden bulkhead, steel reinforcement sections were utilized.

The cabin earned the plaudit: 'Interior appointments are splendidly attractive, ultra-modern and practical' (*Motor Sport*, November 1975). Such warm comment seemed prompted primarily by the generous, and washable, expanses of green cloth applied to the fascia and the 'luxuriously body-hugging, high-back, bucket seats' (*Motor Sport*).

The seating had no adjustment of back-rest rake, but was extremely comfortable, once you had become accustomed to lying back. Both seat and upper-door panels were distinguished by an inlaid red 'tartan' plaid, whilst red was also reserved for the carpets.

The green theme was extended to the Veglia instruments, which was fine for colour-conscious 'dedicated followers of fashion', but the snag was that the dials were quite hard to read. However, there was at least a comprehensive display. This was headed by larger 160mph (260kph) speedometer and 7,000rpm red-lined tachometer, flanked by smaller green and white visages to proclaim: water temperature, oil pressure, volts, and the 15-gallon (68-litre) fuel tank contents.

The steering-wheel was rather plain – a two-spoke padded affair that looked as though it belonged with the flap-type marina door handles and other British Leyland stalks and switchgear. The binnacle around the instruments swept over the dials in dramatic fashion, but it also looked a bit cheap in contrast with the cloth trims, carrying more imported mass-production switch-gear at its extremities.

The massive central division between driver and passenger carried a king-sized ashtray fit for the heaviest smokers, switches for the standard electric windows (much needed in the absence of air-conditioning, which did not become available until the S2) and a simple choke lever for the twin carburettors. The handbrake was not quite so silly as previous Lotus 'umbrellas' beneath the dash had been, but it was (and is) parked on the door sill, to the right on a right-hand drive car, slightly forward of the driver. The fly-off action lever is superbly arranged to hook into stray trouser legs and generally impede ingress and exit.

THE ROLE OF STEEL

The steel chassis was not the galvanized unit of today; anti-rust treatment did not appear until the 2.2 of June 1980. However, there was unspecified undersealing from the start, along with an assortment of steel fabrication techniques. The major area, the central 'spine' if you prefer, was in box-section construction, but the rear engine frame and some lightly stressed front-end sections were tubular and accompanied by smaller rectangular transverse frame to pick up the Covrad front radiator.

That central steel spine was large enough to also serve as a passage-way for the front-to-rear water pipes, and also accommodated the rod gear linkage for the rear transaxle, passing the north/south engine installation to perform that task.

Glassfibre was used for the twin fuel-filler caps. These fed separate 7.5-gallon (34-litre) tanks that were placed low down in front of the rear wheels and interconnected to form a 15-gallon (68-litre) reservoir.

The springs and dampers fed their loads directly into top mountings upon the backbone chassis, front and rear. At the back, there was a large, diagonal trailing arm that went back to the cast-alloy hub and the much discussed tie bar offering transverse location, aft of the fixed-length drive-shafts.

As discussed, the front-end suspension featured a wider number of pressed-steel components, courtesy of GM Opel Ascona double wishbones and combined coil spring/damper layout. The brakes they carried were not servo-assisted or ventilated, but a complete Girling disc system was used. The rears were placed inboard and were larger than the front units, a remark which applies to the current Turbo SE models, although inboard location was abandoned.

The S1 featured the deeply-dished and highly-polished finish of the Wolfrace 14in aluminium wheel that Giorgio Giugiaro had preferred from the outset, and those unequal width (6in front, 7in rear) wheels remained an S1 trademark.

Original S1 Esprits used only Goodyear G800 Super steel covers of the 205 and 195 unequal sizings indicated on the Lotus press release, but my 1977 road test car carried Dunlop Sport radials 205 sections fore and aft. The Goodyears were initially specified as 70 series radials rather than the 60 series that were actually fitted at the front of many production S1 types, including the press demonstrators.

The rears remained 205/70, which was plumpish at the time but nothing like the giant sections of the show Esprits. Recommended pressures reflected the uneven weight distribution at 18psi front and 28psi rear. The spare wheel was usually a smaller 185/70 HR 13 acting as an early 'get you home' mini-spare.

ENGINE AND TRANSMISSION INSTALLATION

The slant-four was uprated for Lotus use in the Elite (up 20bhp on the trim in which it went to Jensen Healey), but the planned V8 never reached the buying public. This 4-litre unit apparently proved disappointing in action; undoubtedly, Lotus engineers could have overcome any shortcomings, but not without the development cash that was notably absent throughout the sixties and seventies.

The alloy 907 motor brought 160bhp at 6,200rpm and 140lb ft of torque at 4,900 revs, significant figures that reflected a four-cylinder of racing ancestry. To get the best out of the engine, high rpm were needed, and that led to some unacceptable cabin noise in the initial batch of cars. It was not simply that the alloy mid-mounted engine was noisy – all concerned had expected that – but rather that any attempt to soften the harshness and rumpus emitted by the power train, could affect the handling.

The First Production Lotus: Mark 6 Statistics

Body Two-seater; multiple tubular steel chassis, aluminium panels including sheet floor, bonnet, wings and nose cone.
Engine Most common was the Ford side-valve. It had four in-line cylinders of 1,172cc (63.5 × 92.5mm) and offered from 30–55bhp according to modifications incorporated.
Transmission Both 4- and 3-speed gearboxes were fitted, the bevel gear final drive almost always from Ford.
Vehicle Weight 952lb (432kg) with Ford side-valve engine.
Dimensions Wheelbase, 87.5in (2.2m); Overall length, 121in (3.0m); front track, 49.5in (1.2m); rear track, 45in (1.1m); overall height (no screen), 30.5in (0.77m).
Steering Burman worm gear.
Suspension Divided ('swing') front axle, independent with external coil spring/telescopic shock absorbers. Live Ford rear axle, coil sprung with telescopic Woodhead Monroe shock absorbers and Panhard Rod location.
Brakes Cable-operated Girling (ex-Ford) 10 × 1.25in (254mm × 31.75mm) drums.
Production Approximately 100 units, 1953–1955.

That handling quirk existed because the four engine and transaxle mountings had to be reasonably firm (transmitting higher noise levels than desired) to cope with the driveshaft loads. These arrived as a result of effectively using the shafts as top suspension links.

This balancing act, between soft mountings for lower noise transmission, and harder bushes to accompany legendary Lotus handling (a key sales point) dogged the Esprit until the 1980 Turbo brought a revised steel chassis. The latter allowed a top suspension link to take over those duties, thus freeing the mounts and allowing an immediate drop in cabin noise levels as well as improving handling.

Handling

The later Esprits did also go through a number of front-suspension changes from the original Opel specification, including new front-ends from Triumph and Toyota. (*See* Chapter 4.)

Lotus chose the five forward ratios in the indirect-layout Citröen gearbox (also used on the Maserati Merak) and quoted maximum gear speeds as corresponding to a maximum 7,300rpm, rather than the red-line advice of 7,000rpm.

The useful maxima, including more than 60mph (100kph) in second, could be read in Lotus press material, but what mattered more – especially to those who had suffered the earlier Europa gearchange – was the shift quality. Colin Spooner felt that it was: 'A super gear change on those early cars; in fact, I think they were the best. Since then, we have compromized a little, but immediately after the Europa our priority was to get the change right.' Before my first drive in the Esprit, Tony Rudd bluntly expounded that the gearchange was worth the selling price on its own 'and the rest is free!'

PERFORMANCE: DISAPPOINTING

The basic sales problem with the Esprit in its initial normally-aspirated trim was that the straight-line performance did not match up to either the Lotus claims, or to customer expectations – which were based on the price and appearance. In other words, the earlier Esprits looked a lot faster than they actually were . . .

Based on Lotus figures, some 181bhp per ton should have snapped the Esprit from rest to 60mph (100kph) in 7 seconds or less. In fact, it was hard to crack 8.3 seconds for this much quoted statistic. I managed 8.28 versus the *Autocar*'s two-way average of 8.4 seconds, both of which were way off factory expectations. Similarly, the standing quarter-mile was estimated at 15 seconds dead, but my own test-track efforts for *Motoring News* showed fractionally over 16 seconds, using the same demonstrator that *Autocar* had borrowed.

Top-speed reality was even further from Lotus expectations: they quoted 138mph (220kph), but the best independently conducted *Autocar* test was 124mph (199kph). Since Lotus quoted fractionally over 125mph (200kph) in *fourth* gear, it was not surprising that they did not like such test results, but the simple truth was that the first Esprits simply were not as fast as we had all expected. In my experience, only the advent of the 2.2-litre engine (for the rare 2.2 or far more accessible S3) made a significant difference to the 'real world' performance abilities of the good-looking, high-grip Lotus in non-turbo terms.

These disappointing Esprit performance figures were nothing compared to the results attained in the States. Instead of 160bhp, American testers had a Stromberg-carburated model that harvested just 130bhp from the sophisticated 16-valve unit in emission control trim . . .

HECTIC HETHEL

by Jeremy Walton

Reproduced from *Motor Sport*
January 1977

In which we take the chance to drive the mid-engined Esprit, are inspired through a vigorous Colin Chapman discussion, and meet most of the senior executives who play a major part in bringing the current three Es – Esprit, Eclat, Elite – to defend the Lotus name. The cars have been a long time in pre-production gestation, but now the signs are that Lotus will settle manufacturing and selling the existing cars before ultimately adding V8 derivatives to the range.

A day of mixed fortunes. I am fortunate in having D. S. J.'s companionship on the long slog to Hethel and back in a day out from Henley, but I am unfortunate in being adjudged as rotten a driver as (most of) the rest of you: sitting beside Moss does give a man standards, you know. I am fortunate in meeting so many people worth talking to, apart from the inimitable boat-building, car-constructing, Grand Prix contesting boss, but I am unfortunate in that there's only enough time to glimpse the problems they have (largely) overcome. I am fortunate in having the chance to drive the noisy but persuasively packaged charms of the Esprit, but unfortunate that the fuel pump packs up in a car destined for Mr. Chapman's use! One thing has to be lucky though, and in this case it's the interview which quite literally left me dazzled by a virtuoso performance. Colin Chapman is a man who actually seems to fulfil the kind of dreams that remain just that for most people. I have been privileged to meet and write about some of the most powerful people in both the motor industry and the sport, but I cannot recall anyone with the sheer personality and breadth of creative talent that Chapman can command. Obviously his companies, his own relationships with others and his products are far from perfect, but it is still a salutary lesson that Britain is very far from a dead duck when men like this are undimmed by the prospect of more Government controls and plummeting pounds. He simply says 'I'll tell you why I carry on . . . ' a grin from ear to ear as he leans back in the chair in self-mocking reply, 'because I enjoy it. It's in the blood now. The boats make a nice relaxation, but building cars and racing that is the real thing for me . . . '

Currently Lotus cars span the range from £7,544 for the Eclat 2 + 2, through £7,979 for the mid-engine Esprit up to £10,100 for the most expensive version of the four-seater Elite. All models share the 16-valve, four-cylinder Lotus engine, now developing 160bhp after a painful birth ahead of the Lotus schedule for Jensen.

We, and I mean that literally in this article for D.S.J. ranks with Royalty at Lotus, so the interviews seemed to come naturally as Jenks spotted a new face, began by talking to Tony Rudd. Tony can now regard his BRM engineering experience with equanimity, having been with Lotus since 1969. He has been an important factor in making aspects as different as engines, complete cars, labour relations and glassfibre bodywork. Which often meant setting the factory and its equipment up as well.

Rudd's Reflections

When you consider the trail of crisis that Lotus have followed in this Rudd period, which covers the slow death of Elan, Europa, Seven, Elan 2 + 2 and the racing car manufacturing business, then the introduction of a completely new model range, made by new processes and powered by new engines (though it must be said that Jensen suffered badly as the first operators of that 16-valve engine and paid a bitter price in reputation before the unit emerged in its present clean breath, high power form), it's amazing that through it all Rudd has retained his humour and persistence. Chapman tests any employee fully, but you have to enjoy outstanding technical knowledge ('I wouldn't argue with the old man about glassfibre, but anything else is fair game', Rudd chuckles) and adaptability to stay the pace when the boss wants it all to happen now. What's more Chapman is used to things happening now in racing so the difficulties are further increased.

Our main intention was to hear how the present family of cars were born, and what the biggest headaches had been from a Lotus viewpoint. Tony replied, 'Ah yes, well I can see you have a comfortable seat to listen for a month while I tell you!

'In Autumn 1970 our planning called for a four-seater quality car, a 2 + 2 derivative of *that car (both front-engined) and a wedge-shaped successor to the Europa, which would have the mid-engine. It was thought that 2-litres, the biggest size we could practically envisage for our four-cylinder engine, was too small an engine for such cars. Logic dictated that the four-cylinder be designed so that we could add a second bank to the basic slant of the four and turn it into a 4-litre V8.'* Tony stopped at this point, but it seems worth pointing out that the official Lotus line is that the V8 only exists in drawn form; however there are V8 prototypes at Hethel today.

Rudd continued, 'America got going with all this emission and safety thing and we started to alter our thinking. Sir (Colin Chapman) did not want us to get too dependent on the States as a car market – at that time it was the largest market for us – as we all felt that it would result in us building cars suitable only for American use. He wanted to keep building cars that would appeal in Europe.

'We were able to adapt and engineer the Europa and Elan models past most of the new regulations, but it was only stop-gap manoeuvring and there is no doubt that those cars died earlier than expected because of legislation. We also dropped them earlier than we should have done, because we thought we would have the new Elite in full stream.

'We made about 35,000 of those old Twin Cam engines. Ford kept on saying that they would stop making the blocks and so on – in fact Chapman, who is really good at this crystal ball gazing bit, was commissioning new engine designs and looking into sources of supply back in 1965. So the pressure was on for a new engine, especially in view of the Jensen agreement. The thing turned into a nightmare. The wonder machines we bought to make the engines – in the Twin Cam's case we had really been assembling other people's work, now we machine castings and make more of the cars than ever – were set up in our new engine shop after dramas that included finding an underground lake on the site which we had selected. When we did get the delayed programme under way, the power cuts of that winter were just really beginning to bite. There was the obvious problem of stopping and starting production, but worse was to come. Somewhat later we discovered that the machine tools we were using were voltage sensitive, so they were not operating correctly half the time they were working on reduced current – but much more important to the quality of the engines was the fact that these tools work beautifully when fully warmed up, holding tolerances precisely and so on, but while they are warming up all sorts of cock-ups on dimensions and machining occur!'

Not surprisingly with two separate companies working on a project one side would get ahead of the other. This plagued that engine too, for Jensen needed the engine before Lotus could supply. Then when Lotus could supply 150 engines a week Jensen were reeling from the effects of the introduction and didn't want as many as had been anticipated. The whole badly co-ordinated effort was a shambles that contributed to Jensen's untimely demise and is doubly sad when you think of the benefit both companies could have realised from a basically good idea.

Talking of the engine itself Rudd said frankly, 'The first 400 had terrible problems, especially with oil staying up with the camshafts when using over 6,000rpm, and cold starting. When the Elite was finally put into production (during the '74–'75 winter) we did a great deal of detail work on the engine, covering about 30 different aspects in all. Primarily we tightened up valve-gear tolerances for quieter top end running, and enhanced the torque characteristics out of recognition by profiling camshafts along the lines we had explored for the Jensen-Healey (power was increased by roughly 20bhp over the Jensen unit none the less) to make the car easier to drive.

'Initially with the Elite we were disappointed with the car's acceleration, and this was down to both the engine and bodies that were much thicker and heavier than we were able to produce in later models. Of course the glassfibre process was new too – the panels actually emerge with a hard gloss paintwork, where required, and consistency is now to the level where I reckon our body repair costs under warranty are at least as good, if not better than, metal-bodied cars.'

Paying credit to the man who succeeded him as head of engineering, and is now the day to day manager of the car company operations, ex-Jaguar man Mike Kimberley, Rudd says of another Elite problem. 'We had complaints of noise based along those big fat Dunlops too. That we got rid of them was just because Mike has so much experience with using rubber bushes in suspension systems without leaving them mushy and upsetting the car's handling.'

Talking to Kimberley later in the day revealed that his last major project at Jaguar had concerned the XJ13 aborted racing project. He showed us quickly and informatively around the company's products, covering subjects as diverse as the moquette trim for the Elite to the 4.1 final drive and 300lb weight-saving appeal of the Eclat in four-speed, steel wheel form, when it reminds him of Lotuses of yore. 'It really accelerates like anything, and on those narrow (6in) rims you can do anything.' A positive wealth of hard driving memories overcame this amiable young man's potted tour.

The Eclat seemed to rouse few dramas compared with the Elite and Esprit, but as Rudd said, 'The Elite was its parent. The bottom half of the two-part body is Elite, it's just the top reshuffled to give a fast back, better boot and more upright seating. Mind you, it didn't completely stop the dramas. The body was lighter and when I was travelling at a very illegal speed the rear window blew out! You do not put weight onto a car in this company, so I had to trace to the heart of the problem, rather than just try and strengthen the rear window surround, or something like that. We discovered it was an exhaust resonance effect on that lighter body.'

The Esprit's Giugiaro origins are pretty well known, and today's production Esprits carry a motif of the Italian designer's imprint to remind one where this clean, and surprisingly wide body style came from. Kimberley took the time to show us around the second car that Giugiaro did for Lotus, the first being a pure show model cobbled around Europa chassis (widened) and a 2-litre engine. That first car was impractical for reasons such as production of glassfibre – 'We had to impress upon him that we must be able to withdraw complete panels from the mould,' commented Rudd – and the windscreen angle of that has been eased toward vertical by just over 2 degrees in the production model to provide safe vision. The red second show car was very close indeed to what has become the most exciting shape in British car production today. However one important point that was attended to was the removal of the petrol filler from the interior, where it would have been accessible through the o/s quarter panel glass to a more normal exterior position. The car was described fully in MOTOR SPORT for November 1975 by C.R. I will just explore the reasons for its belated appearance with Mr Rudd and how it felt to me.

Tony said, 'Well it was part of that master plan and there was a show car built first in 1972: if you ask Chapman he'll say it was 1969 because he thinks it all took too long! While Giugiaro worked with that show car we worked on the real thing and the question in my mind was, dare we throw away the traditional Lotus backbone chassis? I thought we could, but the boss said no, and we did have a job making it accommodate the engine.

'Then there was the Giugiaro body as

Flat rear lamps, plain back bumper in black and conspicuous under-bumper shielding identify the production Esprit S1.

By 1991, few original Esprit S1 examples remained on UK roads. This machine shows the period colours and overall lines (including 'blade' front spoiler) to perfection, but this example has S2 wheels, a non-standard glass sunroof and a sports steering-wheel.

S1 detailing included matt black wing mirrors . . .

The 'moquette' finish stands out on the door panel of a later Esprit S1.

. . . and period Lotus bonnet badge.

shown. We couldn't make that body, and we had to persuade Giugiaro to do it so that we could make the car in two halves on our equipment (this involved tidying up the roof panels where the rear window lifts, apart from the obvious top and bottom division) and all this used up most of 1973 and '74. With the Elite put into production, myself and a small team of engineers withdrew to make a running prototype into a working road car at the end of 1975.

'I reckon we solved 90 per cent of the problems, but others' – a wry smile once more featured from Mr Rudd, 'yes others, reckon I solved 10 per cent and they did the rest in production!'

Production in Lotus terms involves about 30 cars a week currently, sold through a small 35–40 strong band of British dealers. Naturally the Esprit only forms part of that total, which is why it will not become a familiar shape for some time.

As we climbed into the Esprit Rudd quipped, 'You pay £7,000 odd for the gearchange, the rest is free!' What startled me, and even won a measure of approbation from Jenks, was the interior. The fascia panel is surrounded by a restful brown suede, the forward vision is outstanding and the Veglia instruments rest smartly within light green faces, though Jenks did not like the 'wings' that extend out from either side of the flat instrument panel to carry the controls, and I think the man who did the black plastic steering wheel had no idea what they were going to do with the rest of the interior.

Driving the Esprit

I reflect as I select reverse without any difficulty that it is also nice to drive a Lotus where the handbrake is not designed as an integral part of one's shin. Reversing reveals the usual appalling rear vision, but as we set off in earnest on the track there can be no complaint about seeing where we should go.

Although we do but four or five laps in my hands, there are some revelant things to be said straight away. The plus points are that this British reply (or was it perhaps the instigator?) for the Ferrari glassfibre 308 GTB, which was tested in last month's MOTOR SPORT, contains the normal outstanding handling and ride combination. In other words I am able to push faster and faster into corners on short acquaintance, though I am disconcerted at the way the car will run wide into slower corners. Although the ride quality is good, there is a lot of bumping and thumping as we patter across a change in surface at 6,500rpm in second. The brakes are all that one could hope for in a car that you've known five minutes and that is being watched by its guardians as you apply the centre pedal vigorously from 100mph to 45.

The five-speed gearbox is good – it's a Citröen ID23 casing with Citröen Maserati ratios – but both Jenks and I miss gears on this first, hurried acquaintance. The ratios themselves are obviously good at Hethel, and the maximum engine rpm of 7,000 allows useful things like 60mph in second and a ready 100mph in fourth. Top speed is said to be 138mph with 40, 60, 90 and 125mph available in the first four gears.

The biggest snag we find with the car – apart from it prematurely passing away of fuel starvation caused by a sulking fuel pump – is noise. Now a bit of noise in a sporting car is usually very acceptable, but not when it's of the harsh 'four-banger' variety by your ear, and this aspect could stand improvement, especially for those who intend to drive far and fast: and you'll be able to travel far and fast when they change to Bendix fuel pumps! More seriously the car does reflect how Lotus have succeeded in creating a credible up-market two-seater. Now there really could be a day when Chapman's race-winning challenge to Ferrari is seriously repeated in exotic road cars, especially if Fiat continue with their policy of 'productionising' Ferrari.

Talking to Sir

Rather than formally interview Mr Chapman we were lucky to join in after DSJ and Tony Rudd had already secured his attention and a lively debate was ensuing over when, and if, Chapman had decided his present position as an international car manufacturer years ago.

Chapman twinkled as he told DSJ, 'It must have been at least 15 years ago when I talked with you in the Paddock at Monza and told you I was going to be a 'legit' road car manufacturer. You said I should make the 11, but I wanted to make a car specially for the road, not convert one: so you told me to go out and sell the 11 and buy a Porsche!

'I still work toward the Porsche ideal, but you have to do things in stages. We started in the business by making racing cars for at least the first three or four years, and nothing else. I carried on in the racing car business until the early 1970s – I mean the selling of racing cars as a business alongside our other activities – but when I started making racing cars it was a profitable business. Now, and especially when we made the decision to close the Lotus Components side of things, there are so many people competing for a share, and we simply could not make competitive cars profitably enough. No way I want to go back into that end of the business.'

I asked if he had gone as far as he wanted in the road car production side, or was there a lot more to come? Chapman smiled at the thought of doing a great deal more (those around him say he berates them for delaying his retirement by their slowness to act on his ideas!) and said, 'I think we're making almost too much of the car now, I mean, hell, we're even making the bloody air conditioning because the suppliers didn't want to know!

'Over the years it has been our policy to make as much as possible ourselves – bodies chassis, engines and so on, but air-conditioning, that's ridiculous. Actually it's not the whole unit of course, but we have been able to get over our particular problems of fitting a good package into a small size, and I think we can feel good about that.

'The thought of expanding my car business by, say 25 per cent, is not on. What I want to do for the next three years is make the models we are doing now, and concentrate on making them more efficiently with a longer list of options – in fact I have just laid down such a list that will include items like the Speedline wheels for Esprit, and so on.

'If you study our model numbers you will find that there are three more obvious numbers to insert. Those will be the V8 versions of the existing cars – which will probably go through minor production facelifts, but they will substantially be the same cars.

'We designed the V8 as a 4-litre for a market before the fuel crisis. It'll be all right though in a couple of years' time, we will be able to do it then. In the meantime we can just concentrate on making what we've got in bigger numbers and of increasing quality. Right at the moment we do not have the resources to put the bigger engine into production, but a better market . . . ' the eyes light up in anticipation, 'and the chance to earn some money and we'll be able to make the bigger engine.'

In a rare pause for thought Chapman added, 'By the way, a couple of minutes ago I heard from our men in California that the Esprit has passed its emission testing with flying flags for '77, which is terrific news.'

Discussing the V8 in a little more detail Chapman felt that it was going to cost about £1 million to put into production, wryly jibbing at Tony, 'and I don't suppose this fella will be able to find a way of getting the fuel in without injection . . . it's just impossible on that engine because a carburetter layout will not give us the sort of fuel distribution we need.'

We impolitely enquired how close Lotus had been to closing up shop and Chapman roared with laughter, replying in high humour, 'It's always the same, we totter from crisis to crisis. The fuel crisis hit us right after a six million pound investment programme, and we could have foundered for revenue as the volume dropped. About every six years we hit the brink and it's all a bit touch and go over the edge of a precipice: we had a strike in 1969 and other bad years I can recall were 1963 [Putting Elan into production? I can't remember. JW] and 1975, when we had nothing to sell but the Elite.' The confident grin returns, 'Yes, that means I've got five years 'til the next crisis.'

We discussed money as a natural adjunct to that and Chapman felt that the best years the company had ever enjoyed were the last three years of the '60s (he went public in 1968), while 1971/72 were described as, 'Not bad. I can't tell you what this year's results will be, but the half-year showed a modest £50,000 or so profit, and I must say the bank have been very good to us over the years.' If there is such an animal as a Chapman bank manager he must spend his life padlocked in a filing cabinet. To come out would invite the loan of large sums under skilled persuasion very swiftly.

A general headache in the 1970s has been safety expenditure and Chapman reported a conversation with Kimberley in which the two of them decided that the past five years had seen 80 per cent of engineering's effort devoted to safety and federal emission requirements. 'Now they can get on with production engineering,' said Colin with no small amount of satisfaction evident.

I asked about Chapman's mastery with glassfibre, what had led him into such close involvement with the production techniques of this useful material? He mused a moment before replying, 'Well it was such a messy unscientific business . . . all buckets and brushes. I decided I wanted to turn it into a normal industrial process and part of that scheme was to go ahead with a low-pressure injection moulding process. Another factor that helped a lot was the availability of polyurethane paints which can withstand the heat and stress of being in the mould and provide a good finish. For a quality car we needed a new process that was capable of giving good finish, both in itself and in paintwork, and that was repairable. I think we've achieved most of that, though it had its heartaches, like everything else,' he added a little ruefully.

I wondered if Champan had been sad to see the convertibles go? He looked a little surprised and replied, 'No, not really, I never really reckoned convertibles.' Jenks interjected saying that there was nothing like a proper open car. Chapman smoothly countered with the rejoinder that D.S.J. cannot have ever driven an air-conditioned Mercedes, adding, 'I always leap into that when I want to remind myself how good our air-conditioning has got to be!' Chapman also inclined to the view that Kjell Qvale's fascination for open cars led to some of Jensen's trouble, prosaically adding, 'Look at the cars on the street, the MG-Bs and things like that. They never have their hoods open anyway, even on sunny days,' mischievously grinning at D.S.J.'s protestations of the good open air life.

Discussing staff, Chapman made it clear that he does not want to grow much in employment – 'I'd like to add about 100 more to the present 500, but I would also like to increase from 30 cars to 40–45 cars a week when that has taken place. Increasing productivity can be achieved (perhaps 10–20 per cent) by buying new machinery like that profiler we have for reproducing shapes accurately.' He reflected earnestly, 'Do you know, we're lucky at the moment – there are plenty of semi-automated machines around that help people producing 2–4,000 cars a year.'

After telling us that the Research and Development department now had 27 people in, Chapman did put some general racing thoughts on the record ('There's an awful lot of ink going to be spilled over the new GP car, so we'll leave that out for the present,' he said). There are 43 staff on the racing side, which is located over the road from the factory.

In general terms Chapman feels that racing, 'must benefit Lotus Cars as well as the separate John Player team. Let's face it, Lotus would not exist if it was not for the sport. It gives people that little extra incentive to buy.

'I gave up sports car racing when they started fiddling about with the regulations. It's just about a full-time job keeping up with present day F1, and I have no desire to be involved in any other area of racing.

'I think there is a feed-back from F1 into the main factory, no doubt about it. When we win, like Japan, the men are all smiling and cheery in the plant, though I think before that recently the men were a bit grim, so it can cut both ways. The most important thing is a racing man's attitude to get on and do things quickly; that really has helped us actually get on and do things at Lotus. We did that certification programme on the new Esprit in three months flat, and that comes from a racing attitude to getting things done quickly, and so that they actually work when tested,' Chapman concluded.

It is time for us to close. Conversation on the return drag down to Oxfordshire is dominated by fascinating tales of the Lotus of yore. It hasn't changed that much in hectic, competitive spirit, but the products certainly have. We can see little chance of Chapman retiring before his 50th birthday, which at least means we can look forward to his original thinking for a year or two yet.

JW

FILM STAR

Right from the start, Lotus products had proved to have TV and film star quality. The 1957 Boulting brothers' film, *Brothers in Law*, saw the first appearance of the marque on the big screen and the Seven, prepared by Caterham Cars, became a cult car when two 1965 machines (registered KAR 120C) appeared in the sixties television series, *The Prisoner*. The Esprit S1 found its filming glory as a submarine and glamour wagon in the 1977 James Bond epic *The Spy Who Loved Me*.

Lotus devoted considerable effort to breaking into secret agent 007's glossy world and Lotus Public Relations executive Donovan 'Don' McLauchlan had to knock on a lot of studio doors. At the time, McLauchlan was trying to place a Lotus within another popular TV series, but the competition was tough, since mass producers could loan fleets of their vehicles for the months necessary to complete filming assignments.

Enter 007

The breakthrough came from Pinewood Studios, who reacted favourably to a 1975 preview of the new Esprit. The legendary Cubby Broccoli agreed terms with McLauchlan in late 1975 and Lotus were committed to the construction of two S1 Esprit road cars and five bodyshells – the spare bodies required to cover the explosive nature of the Bond story lines and the ingenious manufacture of a seven-knot submarine.

Whereas Lotus spent approximately £18,000 and a year of hard graft in placing the Esprit within *The Spy Who Loved Me*, the complicated 'submarinization' of the Esprit shells demanded more than $100,000 of the Bahama-based specialists Perrys. Lotus did some of the basic submarine conversion, concentrating on items such as the external fins, but the aerodynamics that made the Esprit such a success on the road did not take well to water. They still exerted a constant downward pressure that made it hard to keep the underwater Esprit from permanent internment on the Mediterranean sea bed.

Equipped with four electric motors, ballast

The Esprit continued the Lotus tradition of appearing on film. Here is the James Bond 007 machine used by Roger Moore in The Spy Who Loved Me.

tanks and joystick controls, the marine Esprits could manage about 7 knots – around 10mph (16kph). Whilst the two road cars (one was PPW 306R) dashed about in deeds of Bond derring-do, the spare bodies had an equally arduous film life. One was the recipient of a compressed air rocket motor, which launched it from the end of a Sardinian pier at more than 40mph (60kph) to join its submarine pals. (Underneath the Esprit outline was a simple space frame and locked steering.)

Although Lotus and the film-makers seemed happy enough with the results, only in the eighties did a Lotus reappear in a Bond movie. This time, the Turbo and Roger Moore starred, rather than the Esprit S1.

DEVELOPMENT DETAILS

Under the long-standing slogan, 'Lotus quality is everybodys' business', the company made a number of running changes within the S1 production span. Many of these concerned the body and its ancillaries, particularly the switch back to conventional spray-painting techniques.

It is worth noting that for the Esprits destined for the American market, steel was used to reinforce the cabin safety structures (rather than the Elite thin-wall aluminium techniques that were used in Europe). Naturally, there were impact bumpers on such cars, featuring a foam-filled rear bumper. Colin Spooner also recalled that they used plywood not just in the publicized centre cockpit bulkhead, but also to gusset the section between the headlamps on American-export Esprits.

Lotus tackled the seals around the glass hatch – customers had complained of leaks and fumes. They also ensured that the tailgate catches operated more efficiently. Inside the cabin, one obvious problem was the poor ventilation system. This was overcome by making air-conditioning available – the only solution in sunnier climes under that enormous 'greenhouse' pane of front glass.

As noted earlier, the S1 also changed over to a twin-motor headlamp retraction system. An access flap for oil and water checks was also incorporated in later Esprits, but a complete re-design was postponed until the S2 successor.

Most of the problems encountered by customers were not to do with the dramatic running gear failures of Lotus legend. When collecting engine data in 1990, I was surprised to realize that Lotus had built 50,000 engines by 3 May 1977. The bulk of that total belonged to the Lotus-Ford twin cam family, but the 50,000th motor was a 2-litre 16-valve Lotus 907 type that was duly installed in a Federal Esprit S1. From the customer viewpoint, the biggest change to the 2-litre engine occurred later in 1977 and affected both the S1 Esprit and the Elite/Eclat drivers, who had prompted a change in camshaft profiles.

Customer Complaints . . .

Tony Rudd recalled the development of the 'E' for 'Emission' overhead camshafts for the 907 motor:

We were getting feedback from Elite customers early on that they would forgo the 6,000rpm-plus performance levels in exchange for a bit more mid-range pull, effectively that between 70 and 90mph on the 3.7:1 axle ratio.

Working constantly on emission requirements in both America and Japan – Lotus was then one of the few places in Britain with such facilities on site – the company found a profile that benefited both emissions (its priority) and mid-range response.

The bonus mid-range pulling power was not quantified in either bhp or torque readings, but it remained welcome. It was especially notable between 3,000 and 5,000rpm.

Another landmark in terms of engine production was that of reaching 20,000 of the '9-series' DOHC 16-valve units. That unit (CDT 81 12 20000) was officially completed on 22 December 1981 and was installed in a British-specification Esprit Turbo. In fact, the 2-litre 907 engine (and its enlarged successors in normally-aspirated form) have proved durable, so long as they receive knowledgeable maintenance at the now unfashionably short periods recommended by Lotus. Similarly, there were no stories of sudden transmission failures, although the ID23 casting with Lotus selected ratios of Citröen-Maserati origin did show an appetite for second-gear ratios during the early days. These and other SM transference problems were sorted by Graham Atkin.

. . . and Lotus Remedies

So, Lotus were faced with a constant customer and press whine about body ancillaries and electrical quality, but it was a litany

Treating the factory road test Esprit as a hatchback. This S1 (RCL 377R) was assessed in the summer of 1977 and was also the Autocar *road test car. Performance was disappointing: top speed proved to be no more than an honest 125mph (200kph) and 0–60mph (0–100kph) took more than eight seconds.*

that centred on frequent minor failures and flaws rather than terminal failures.

To illustrate this point, the first S1 I drove (NCL 744R) at Hethel, lapsed into silence when the electrical SU fuel pump failed after less than ten laps. I was promised that production cars would feature Bendix pumping and concluded of those initial laps:

The Esprit does reflect how Lotus have succeeded in creating a credible up-market two-seater. Now there really could be a day when Chapman's race winning challenge to Ferrari is seriously repeated in exotic road cars, especially if Fiat continue with their policy of 'productionizing' Ferrari.

Thus it grieves me to recall that the second S1 I drove, the *Motoring News* banana-yellow test machine (RCL 377R) of August 1977, also suffered electrical tantrums. This time, it was the starter motor which simply clicked in contemporary Ford fashion instead of cranking up the slant-four. From Jaguar's front reception (embarrassing to ask their executives for a push-start . . .) to an ill-fated bump start in West London, I loved and hated that original Esprit with equal passion. I hope that part of my conclusion still gives a contemporary account of the car. Although I wrote this piece in the seventies, I think I would write the same today . . .

At present, Lotus are not into the West German detailing of a car. They make a very exciting car which performs well in everyday use, as well as with an enthusiast's flailing at the helm. Unfortunately, this will not ultimately be enough for the type of fastidious customer they are bound to attract. Many of them are Porsche people who want to buy British. They *must* be rewarded with inherent quality. That is not found in items like the skinny glassfibre engine cover – held down by bicycle clips and rubber bands – or rusting door hinges that look as if Bob-a-Job week passed their way. Lotus have produced a desirable car that is worth at least the same as many more prestigious names, costing a lot more. Now, all they have to do is to concentrate on the really fine details to establish their name right in the Ferrari/Porsche bracket . . .

Lotus have done a lot since then to improve on quality. Only the door locks sulked on 'my' 1990 Elan, but competitive quality remains a number 1 priority thirteen years after those words on the Esprit S1 were written.

4 Better, by the Number

'Careful development work had advanced the Esprit to the point where the only major drawbacks are those which it inherited from the imaginative pen of Mr Giugiaro.'

Motor, 22 August 1981

That quote was delivered in a generally complimentary test of the S3 Esprit, but it serves as a fair comment to all the normally-aspirated (i.e., non-turbo) models, whose development we chart in this section. As the numbers grew higher through the logical S2, S2.2 (bigger engine) and S3, so did customer and press satisfaction.

However, the growing effectiveness of the Esprit formula in the years 1978–1987 should not blind us to the rarity value of machines such as the S2.2. Lotus figures quote eighty-eight such Esprits made between February 1980 and March 1981. Neither can we ignore the collectable status of some limited editions, such as the distinctive Gold and Black John Player Special ('JPS') versions of the S2. This was pledged to a maximum of 100 such specials in each of the major Lotus markets. Therefore, there were no more than a hundred right-hand drive Esprit S2s originally manufactured amongst the 980 Esprit S2 models that Lotus recall making between June 1978 and January 1980.

It is relevant to note that all these low-volume Esprit derivatives preceded the current (1987 onward) 'soft shape' Esprit, and that the normally-aspirated model became history in September 1990. In that 1987–1990 new-look line, the normally-aspirated model was first confined to the UK, then dropped totally for autumn 1990. Since then, an all turbo-charged, all electronic ABS-braked Esprit range has been offered.

THE S2: MILD IMPROVEMENTS

On 27 July 1978, just two days before the annual factory holiday shutdown, Lotus decided to issue a press release detailing S2 modifications. That press release, however, was embargoed until '001 hours 16 August 1978' – a cunning move, as it meant that journalists could not get through to ask awkward questions, unless they called an unlisted direct line.

For publicity purposes, first in the queue for the new S2s were Team Lotus drivers Mario Andretti and Ronnie Peterson. The Italian-American and the British-domiciled Swede were then in the process of annexing the World Championship, benefitting from the Lotus breakthrough in ground-effect aerodynamics. That 1978 title would lead to the Esprit S2 celebration JPS model referred to in our introduction.

What did the Formula 1 drivers and showroom punters find altered over the original Esprit?

Externally, the sharp-edged lines were much the same as before, but some useful modifications had taken place. The front spoiler dropped the blade principle and wrapped around the under-bumper area instead. That was the reason why the company quoted the best original Esprit aerodynamic Cd factor on record: 0.335. The top speed claim remained at 138mph (220kph),

Performance: The Independent Story

Independent magazine test results did improve around the S2 demonstrator. *Motor* returned 130mph (210kph) as their maximum and 0–60mph (0–100kph) in 7.7 seconds. *Autocar* made it 135mph (220kph) by calculation (not timed) and 0–60mph (0–100kph) in 8 seconds dead, but both weeklies averaged only 19 and 19.2mpg which was getting on for poor in a 2-litre four.

Lotus themselves acknowledged the average fuel consumption problem, their test vehicles returning only 18.6 urban mpg in official tests, but cheered by 37.1mpg at 56mph and 31.3mpg at 75mph.

The *Autocar's* verdict on the S2 Esprit (compared with the Lancia Beta Monte Carlo, Maserati Merak, Ferrari 308 GTB, Porsche 911 SC and TVR Taimar) in January 1979 was:

The Esprit is the purist's car amongst the group – a beautifully balanced simple mid-engined driver's thoroughbred. However, it is terribly let down by boom and resonance periods that should be no part of a car in its price bracket. [The list price was then £11,754.]

If Europeans felt they had reason to grumble at the Lotus Esprit's performance, the Americans were still served by markedly inferior (save for the environment) emission-controlled models. The 1978/79 model year S2 was rated at 140bhp on 5,800rpm from the twin Zenith CD175 carburettor motor. Operating on a reduced (8.4:1) compression ratio, maximum torque was also reduced and reported as 140lb ft on 4,000rpm.

Since weight was up 196lb (90kg) from a European 2,248lb (1,020kg) to 2,444lb (1,108kg) – the effect on acceleration can be imagined. So far as fuel consumption was concerned, only 15.4 US city mpg were claimed in the 49-State Esprit and the Highway figure was 25.6mpg.

In fact, these figures were applicable only to 49 States, potential Californian buyers being forced to 'contact your local dealer' for details of the emasculation that was performed on the Sunshine State car.

but the most noticeable driving change was cross-wind stability – enhanced by the integrated front spoiler.

More 'air management' had been applied to the engine bay. Lotus had found that production cars did not equal the prototype's propensities to stay cool. Thus, a set of 'ears' sprouted around the side rear windows. They collected the air-stream for diversion to the engine induction (off side, or O/S), rear window demist and overheated luggage bay. The battery was moved from its S1 cabin location into 'the floor of the boot'. A matching ear on the near side (N/S) was simply listed as for cool air around the engine bay.

PERFORMANCE CHEEK

Lotus had the cheek to claim that: 'A further benefit from the cold air ram feed is to improve volumetric efficiency, giving 0–60 acceleration time improvements from 7.1 seconds to 6.8 seconds and 0–100 from 20.2 seconds to 19.4 seconds.'

In fact, Lotus originally claimed 6.8 seconds as the 0–60mph (0–100kph) capability with 0–100mph (0–160kph) in 20.7 seconds – figures that independent magazine tests in

(Overleaf) The wedge profile of the 1975–1987 Esprit was the originally distinctive product of two show cars created by the Italian Giugiaro design centre and Lotus personnel, headed by founder Colin Chapman.

Britain failed to match. It is worth recalling that the E-camshaft had been installed during the late-1977 section of the S1 run (allowing much stronger 'real world' mid-range performance) and continued into the S2. Official output figures were not altered, but a new exhaust system promised more peaceful durability with an intermediate silencer and aluminium spray finishes.

Metal and Rubber

Aside from the aerodynamic changes, the most striking external alterations came from the fitment of Speedline alloy wheels. Manufactured in Italy by the company that was also supplying the all-conquering Lotus 79 Grand Prix equipe, the new wheels were designed by Lotus at the personal behest of Colin Chapman. The main benefit of the silver enamel-coated 7JK × 14in front and 7.5JK × 14in rear rims was that a 1in (25mm) increase in track could be claimed. According to my brochure figures, this hub offset and rim increase only applied at the back, where the total track was given as 60.5in (1.54m). Tyre specification had also altered: 205 section rubber was listed front and rear. The variation in effective height was obtained by using 60 profile front tyres and slightly taller 70 per cent aspect ratio rubber for the rear. The spare was a fully functional alloy, but it retained at 13in (330mm) diameter and carried a 185/70 HR tyre (usually by Dunlop).

Other external changes included the use of black chip-resistant paint treatment to the spoiler, sills and rear valance. Given the width of an Esprit cabin, remote-control door mirrors became a vital accessory, and electric operation of such mirrors was introduced for the S2. (Concours competitors may care to note that the early S2 carried an upright chrome stem to the mirrors, but the subsequent S2 and even the S3 employed matt black stems.)

Double coachlining was employed from nose to tail with 'Esprit S2' identity decals appearing alongside the fuel filler caps. From the rear, a most notable alteration was the incorporation of ridged Rover 3500 tail lamps, which encompassed high-intensity fog warning lamps.

INTERIOR BENEFITS

The external changes paled by comparison to those within. The instrument cluster retained the jet fighter pod appearance, but the black-and-white dials to replace the vague Veglia originals came from Smiths and were clearly marked. The major dials retained a 160mph (260kph) speedometer and an 8,000rpm tachometer, now supported by clearly calibrated oil pressure, battery volt, water temperature and fuel tank gauges. The switchgear also underwent fundamental changes, including the adoption of 'paddle' switches for the dashboard controls (they replaced the previous rocker action). Switch functions were identified by individual graphics, illuminated via fibre optics. Similarly, the electric window switches were moved from the beefy centre tunnel to a position aft of the gear lever. The ashtrays were also modified: smaller trays were now mounted in the door sills.

A digital clock arrived in the roof lining. Mounted between the sun visors, it predicted how and where Lotus would eventually mount a complete sound system!

Luxury and Practicality

Interior trim lost its original green tinge and replaced it by a suedette finish to the fascia and much of the door trims. A leather trim option was priced around £200 and the JPS Celebration model also featured a wider use of leather within.

More practically, the fixed-back bucket seats became 2in (50mm) wider and incorporated new foam foundations that effectively increased headroom by an inch.

JPS: A Special Esprit S2

'Even by today's standards the handling and roadholding are brilliant.'

These were the words used by the doyen of road testers, Roger Bell, when summing up the John Player Special (JPS) Commemorative Edition of the Esprit S2 for *Super Car Classics* in June 1990.

At the time, JPS colours were the height of British automotive chic, as Lotus had pulverized the Grand Prix opposition with the ground-effect 79s of Mario Andretti and Ronnie Peterson. The company took commercial advantage of these results by planning the production of 100 such black and gold Esprits for each major market: UK, USA and 'rest-of-the-world' export Esprits.

The differences over standard S2 specification were in the trim, not mechanical.

Externally, the gold-and-black JPS themes were overblown to the point of emblazoning 'World Champion' along the golden double coachline that adorned each black flank. Even the black forward Lotus badge was embraced by a loving gold garland.

The four-spoke alloy Speedlines became gold and each JPS Esprit bore a decal adjacent to the fuel filler cap that said, 'COMMEMORATIVE EDITION No . . . ' filled with relevant production number within the 100-off schedule.

Gold lining to brightwork was applied inside and out, framing the front and rear glass, or the fascia and central transmission tunnel divides.

The interior wore a fine three-spoke leather-rim wheel in place of the exceptionally nasty standard two-spoke moulding. Leather was also applied to the gear lever, its gaiter and sections of the interior trim, including the edges of the ripe corn-coloured cloth seat panels and centre tunnel.

The net result was a more valuable limited edition that tempted Lotus into repeating the slick marketing trick on the slightest pretext.

Over the years, we have had many more limited Edition Esprits. Unfortunately, Lotus have not had reason to celebrate another Grand Prix World Championship since 1978, never mind the 1–2 result that Mario and Ronnie scored in that glorious season.

Access to the engine bay was considerably improved. The engine cover was re-designed, with a Britool tool kit, wheel brace and jack on top, and there was also an access hatch for oil and water checks towards the rear of the cover. Within was a fitted dam to separate the hot and cold sides of the engine bay – part of the search for improved starting manners from hot. The cover's appearance was slightly improved, partially by finishing it in Hammerite, and then covering much of the *ensemble* with carpeting.

The S2 also had to incorporate the air-intake system for the carburettors, whilst hot air from the engine bay was extracted thermally to exit via the right-hand external 'ear'. American Esprit S2s had an electric motor that fan-assisted hot air extraction.

THE COST OF COSMETICS

The S2 was primarily a machine of greater creature comfort, rather than of improved performance, but the inflationary car pricing climate of the period saw its price acclerate as fast as the vehicle . . .

Launched at £11,124.37p, the S2 reached £12,000 within months of its debut, albeit in leather trim specification. When it went out of production in December 1979 – leaving some S2 models still to be registered in 1980 – the Esprit S2 was priced from £14,175. A giddy rise compared with those 1975 'about £4,500' estimates, and getting on for three times as much as the initial production price in less than three selling years!

The ultimate hatchback? Despite the frequent need to resort to the production parts bin of what has become Rover Cars, the Esprit continued to impress from front to back. The area behind the side rear window sported many different air intake and extraction systems to serve the hothouse environment of the mid-mounted Lotus 16-valve engine; this S2 has a simple intake scoop.

Square rear, and we can see the Rover 3500 ridged tail lamps as well as the wide use of Lotus vacuum moulding to provide bumpers and even the number plate surround.

Lotus wheel design replaced the first Wolfrace aluminium units for the S2 of 1978.

Factory badging is complemented by an owner's stark warning against using methanol on one glass-fibre filler cap.

'Hatch' raised, but glassfibre engine cover in place, the Esprit's layout was not conceived as a model of practicality. Note the glazed protection of the window dividing engine from cabin, and note also that the cover itself was changed almost as often as the model designations.

The wood-capped gear lever controlled a Citröen-based transmission action that was actually more positive, but heavier, than that of the current Esprit and its Renault-sourced transaxle.

Fixed-back seats were a long-term fixture in the Esprit, yet all but the tallest drivers could usually find an effective, albeit literally 'laid-back' driving position.

Trouser snapper! The right-hand location of the fly-off handbrake has trapped many a startled driver by the trouser leg . . .

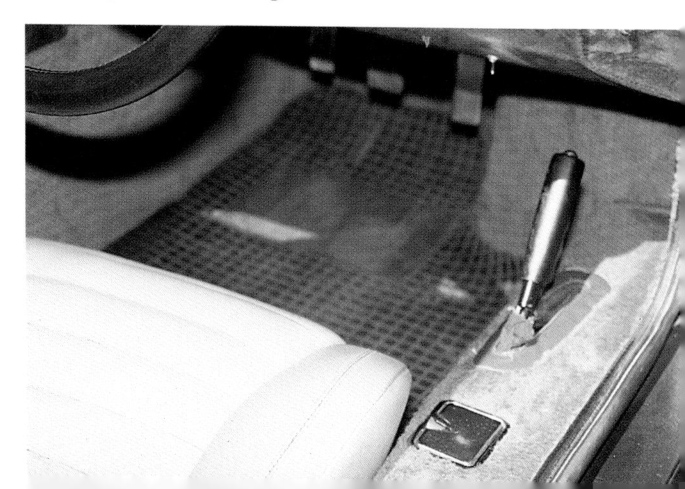

S2.2: BIGGER ENGINE, RARITY VALUE

A distinct one-year-and-one-month production stop-gap, the Lotus Esprit S2.2 brought some important changes to Esprit engineering; changes that have been kept in the nineties: 2.2-litre Lotus engines and chassis galvanization.

Both these improvements were sold under the slogan 'When you arrive in a Lotus – you've arrived!' The launch cost during May 1980 was £14,951. The last recorded list price (in 1981) was £15,270. That was in line with the normal Lotus practice of pitching their Esprit wares in the price region of the classic Porsche 911. In 1981, the (then) West German coupe was under £1,500 more.

Introduced as the 'Lotus 2.2-litre series', the larger engine was installed for the front-engine Eclat, and Elite, as well as the Esprit S2.2. Individually badged as 'Esprit 2.2', but dressed in pure S2 clothing – right down to the Dunlop-shod Speedlines – the interim Esprit carried Lotus between the seventies' generation of Esprits and the new generation of Turbo and S3 models in the eighties.

Esprit 2.2: Lotus Claimed Performance

(All on 4:1 final drive rather than 4.375:1 of S1)

Maximum speeds in gears

First	40mph (65kph)
Second	60mph (100kph)
Third	88mph (140kph)
Fourth	120mph (190kph)
O/D Fifth	138mph (220kph)

Acceleration
(Compared to Lotus S2, figures supplied by Lotus)

mph	***(kph)***	***S2.2 – secs***	***S2 – secs***
0–30	(0–50)	2.4	2.6
0–40	(0–65)	3.5	3.7
0–50	(0–80)	5.0	5.6
0–60	(0–100)	6.7	7.3
0–70	(0–110)	8.9	10.1
0–80	(0–130)	11.3	12.8
0–90	(0–145)	14.8	16.3
0–100	(0–160)	19.2	21.5

Flexibility (Fourth gear, Lotus figures)

30–50	(50–80)	6.8	9.0
40–60	(65–100)	5.6	8.3
50–70	(80–110)	5.5	8.5
60–80	(100–130)	5.4	8.6
70–90	(110–145)	6.1	9.3
80–100	(130–160)	7.1	10.6

Flexibility (Fifth gear, Lotus figures)

30–50	(50–80)	13.0	14.4
40–60	(65–100)	7.5	13.6
50–70	(80–110)	8.4	12.9
60–80	(100–130)	9.3	13.8
70–90	(110–145)	8.3	15.7
80–100	(130–160)	8.6	16.6

Facts and Figures

Initially, Lotus reported an output of 86 such Esprit 2.2 vehicles, but in January 1982 they supplied new written totals that included only 46 Esprit 2.2. This was amended to 88 examples in 1990/91 company research findings supplied to the author.

While cross-checking with an overall production summary (May 1990) supplied by the company, I found that 1980 was the lowest production year at Lotus since 1966. They reached just 383 cars, 246 of them Elite and Eclat. It therefore seemed possible that the Esprit 2.2 reached only 46 units, for overall normally-aspirated Esprit output is listed at just 80 for 1980. Then, the new Turbo of that year (in limited edition Essex-decalled status) gathered only 57 copies.

RECIPE FOR ENLARGEMENT

The starting point for an enlarged Lotus DOHC, 16-valve unit was an early example of Lotus Engineering consultancy. The clients, Chrysler UK, were working on a project to produce a high performance basis

Stretching a Lotus Engine: Statistics

The 2.2-litre 912 replaced the 2-litre 907 in 1980, when 'over 18,000' of the 2-litre units had been made. There were the following dimensional changes, all according to Lotus official material issued at the time:

Capacity 2,174cc (was 1,973cc)
Bore × stroke 95.29 × 76.2mm (was 95.29 × 69.2mm)
Compression 9.4:1 (was 9.5:1)
Peak horsepower 160bhp @ 6,500rpm (was 160bhp @ 6,200rpm)
Peak torque 160lb ft @ 5,000rpm (was 140lb ft 4,900rpm)
Fuel consumption
Urban: 19.7 mpg (703km/100l)
S2 was 18.6mpg (664km/100l)
56mph (90kph) – 38.7mpg (1,382km/100l)
S2 was 37.3mpg (1,332km/100l)
75mph (120kph) – 33.3mpg (1,189km/100l)
S2 was 31.3mpg (1,117km/100l)

for a World Rally Championship contender when they sold out to Peugeot and Citröen. Peugeot inherited the Talbot badge and the finished car thus became a Talbot Sunbeam Lotus – it also carried a 2.2-litre stretch of the Lotus 2-litre that was coded 912.

This 2,174cc unit retained the usual 95.2mm bore but relied on a new crankshaft and associated reciprocating components to lengthen the stroke to 76.2mm in place of the 69.2mm of the previous 1,973cc. Incidentally, that stroke was shared with a now long-obsolete Vauxhall slant-four of 2.3 litres – the unit that originally inspired Lotus along the slant-four racing and production trail.

Ingredients

Inherent changes in transforming a 2.0-litre type 907 into a 2.2-litre type 912 included:

1. Thin disc flywheel.
2. Replacement sump to suit Sunbeam hatchback saloon.
3. Uprating of main bearing support panels.
4. Replacement of camshafts.
5. Re-jetted Dell'Orto DHLA 45E twin-choke, downdraught carburettors.

Operating upon a marginally lower compression than the previous 2-litre, the 9.4:1 compression ratio Sunbeam Lotus unit was rated at 150bhp at 5,750rpm and 150lb ft of torque at 4,500rpm. For competition, over 240bhp and 8,000rpm were available and the car proved capable of winning both a marque and driver's world title for Talbot Lotus in 1980/81.

Lotus adapted the 2.2 litres for their own dual production purposes:

1. A turbocharged engine to replace the planned V8 (*see* Chapter 5).
2. A long-lived, normally-aspirated 2.2 that served the Elite, Eclat, Excel and Esprit through the eighties.

The dimensions of the engine were as for the Chrysler/Sunbeam, but it gained 10bhp and 10lb ft of torque by comparison. The torque bonus was particularly useful. It was up by 21 per cent at a low 2,400rpm and, at that point, it yielded 140lb ft – the first Esprit had achieved that same figure at 4,900rpm. Such comparisons emphasized how far the Lotus '9-series' engine had come since its debut.

Method

Lotus stressed that this was not the same unit as had been contracted to Chrysler, citing the following changes in specification:

1. Carburation.
2. Ignition (infra red-triggered, no contact points).
3. Oil system.
4. Main bearings casting.
5. Wet sump design.

The front compartment is not the answer for those who have used up the rear luggage stowage, although a limited amount can be squashed in around the spare wheel, headlamp power-lifting mechanism and hydraulic cylinder.

Twin tail pipes terminate a system that introduced a secondary silencer in 1978. The system underwent several modifications, including stainless steel construction and ball joints for durability purposes.

For the Esprit, it is worth knowing that clutch diameter went up an inch. The diameter now stood at 9.5in (24cm), and this from the S2.2 onward. Specifically, Colin Spooner recalled:

The clutch diameter increase also demanded that we alter the casing. Then, the exhaust system had to be changed if we were going to get the best out of the bigger engine, so that demanded another system with the appropriate bore sizes and free-flow characteristics to get over any increase in back pressures. Then, there was the engine itself. There were real NVH roughness problems [Noise Vibration and Harshness, a Ford multi-purpose expression] with the extra stroke of the later motor, and we tried to get over these with new mountings.

Since the S2.2 did *not* feature the Turbo/S3 chassis features – but did introduce the galvanization process to the Esprit – any change in engine mountings had to be viewed with caution, in case the handling was upset.

Tony Rudd had reverted to pre-World War II expertise in the use of a flexible fly-wheel to help damp out some of the inherent vibrations of a larger four-cylinder unit. Lotus, however, also had to 'face a number of airborne resonances in the cockpit and tackle these with a change in sound-deadening materials' (in the words of Colin Spooner).

In public use, the S2.2 was not sold widely enough to gain significant feedback, but there was no doubting that the 2.2-litre engine matched the Esprit's handling and cornering ability at prodigious rates with a lot less fuss than the original layout.

S3: AN ALL-ROUND ADVANCE

The date 22 April 1981 was the official birthday of the Esprit S3, a product that owed its propulsion to the 2.2-litre engine of the S2.2, but whose chassis and substantially revised running gear came from the February 1980 Lotus Essex Turbo Esprit. The £13,461.23 Esprit S3 was (as for a simultaneously-launched lower-cost production Turbo) one of the most sensibly priced, (on a pound-to-striking-performance basis) Lotus designs ever offered.

The S3 was born of the need to meet a far grimmer national and international car market. Lotus had just gone through that appalling 1980–1981 production low-point against a very dark background. Britain was in recession and the American market had ceased to exist. A Lotus and Rolls-Royce deal in America failed to produce any orders in 1981, as the two sides proved incapable of any sales liaison in the USA. Employment at Hethel was at an all-time low: just 385 workers made 345 cars for 1981. That was a depressing figure that dropped even lower at the time of the traumatic switch from the Elan and Europa to the new-generation Elite. Still, at least they were now making up to 76 per cent of the Esprit in-house.

In fact, it looked as if the Elite were the root-cause of the problem, since in that period between 1980 and 1981, production of that particular model was still in its infancy. The Eclat proved no sales miracle either, so we saw the Esprit and its recent Turbo brother propping up the public sales side of the Lotus Group with 301 of those 345 production orders.

Remarkably, the traumas wrought by Colin Chapman's death and the subsequent ownership machinations until the arrival of GM never managed to slash Lotus production to such low levels again, so that from 1981 onward, things gradually improved. Lotus made over 500 cars in 1982 and the 1,000 mark was comfortably passed in 1988, by which time the Esprit derivatives accounted for all but 244 cars of 1,302 manufactured.

THE RATIONAL SUPERCAR

By the time the S3 was announced, Lotus could boast of the Esprit concept that it was 'the only practical mid-engine 2-seat sports car' made in Britain and that 'over 3,000 units' had been sold world-wide since its introduction. I made it 2,179 Esprits from the 1975 launch to the end of 1981, but Lotus publicity always was a law unto itself.

The important point in 1990 was that the S3 proved by far the best Esprit to appear in normally-aspirated guise and original outline. Picking up on the Turbo chassis meant vast gains in torsional rigidity, while the suspension systems were tailored to the car rather than unhappy legacies of either past traditions or adapted production components.

A five-year warranty was offered to support the galvanized finish of the later steel chassis. Shared by the S3 and the Turbo, the principal identification point was a wider front box section to accommodate the suspension system that was 'adapted from the Elite', according to Lotus publicity material.

That meant it was also shared with the Eclat and offered a 1in (25mm) spread in track via upper wishbones, single lower link, anti-roll bar and slightly softened (over Turbo) Armstrong damper and coil spring layout – the spring ascribed with a 10 per cent lowering in wheel rates. However, many insiders and Lotus specialists agree that even this Elite/Eclat front-end was far from perfect. Few have a good word for the Triumph GT6 vertical link components that were used until 1985.

The rear suspension now gained the short top links that it had always needed, leaving the plunger-type driveshaft to now accommodate changes of geometery. Track was increased by nearly an inch – 0.7in (18mm) – and aluminium hub carries remained in use. The eighties rear-end layout was officially described as, 'unequal length, non-parallel transverse links with radius arms.'

ROAD TEST
Lotus Esprit S3

Reproduced from *Motor*
22 August 1981

A dream car at a budget price, the latest 2.2-litre Esprit is a much improved car, combining superb performance and road manners with outstanding fuel economy and significantly reduced interior noise; inherently impractical, but very exciting.

The most a car body stylist has any right to expect from a way-out styling exercise is that it will persuade a manufacturer to utilize his services for the production or development of more mundane vehicles. However, the mid-engined Lotus Esprit sprang from just such a 'concept car' built by Giorgio Giugiaro for the 1972 Turin Show, and nine years later more than 3,000 Esprits have been sold throughout the world.

The first Esprits, which appeared at the end of 1975, suffered from many detail faults; all-round visibility was disastrous, the build quality was poor, the noise level was too high, and even the handling was not as sharp as many people had hoped. It was an interesting car to drive, but we considered at the time that it would not be a pleasant one to own.

Lotus introduced a revised version, the Series 2, in 1978; while this gave much better steering response and handling, its engine was still almost intolerably boomy, and questions about quality control remained. Last year, the engine capacity was increased from 1,973cc to 2,172cc, and the Esprit Turbo 'supercar' also made its debut.

Earlier this year, the Series 3 model was introduced. With a great many modifications aimed not only at reducing production costs but also at improving quality, it is a much better product all round, and a testimony to Lotus's development abilities. Not before time, there appears to have been a realization that a quality price must be matched by a quality product. As one of our more senior testers wrote, 'If only the Esprit had been like this from the start . . . '

This is not to suggest that the Esprit is – or ever can be – a particularly practical car: it can accommodate only two people, and those preferably of average height or less, while luggage space is scarcely worth mentioning. Despite the use of excellent door mirrors, visibility remains poor: parking this wide monster (it is only 1in narrower than a Rolls-Royce!) is by no means easy, and even the forward vision is less than perfect, as the offside windscreen pillar is directly in the driver's line of sight when negotiating right-hand bends.

Furthermore, we wonder just what sort of market there is left for ostentatious cars such as this, though you do not have to linger long in London's West End or the South of France to realize that even these days there are still plenty of people with enough money and inclination to pay £13,461 for a wedge-shaped glass fibre two-seater.

In fact, at that price, which is actually £1,800 lower *than an S2 cost in January, the Esprit S3 probably gives the best value of any model in the Lotus range, and it shapes up well in terms of price against the opposition, though apart from a couple of obvious contenders, like the Porsche 924 Turbo (£13,998) and 911 SC (£16,732), it is difficult to define exactly what that opposition might be. Lotus claim, perhaps rather unkindly to AC (whose £13,238 ME3000 trickles along at a production rate of one car per week) to be 'the only British manufacturer whose model range includes a practical mid-engine two seat sports car' and there is not much direct competition of this nature from anywhere.*

If you are intent on having a mid-engined car, there are two cheaper rivals, the Fiat X1/9 and Lancia Montecarlo, but neither offers anything like the performance of the Lotus. Further up the price range we find the De Tomaso Pantera GTS (£17,940), Maserati Merak SS (£18,986) and the Ferrari 308 GTBi (£21,810). More likely alternatives than any of these are BMW's 628 CSi (£16,635) and the TVR Tasmin (£13,824).

'Rationalization' of Esprit production now means that the Esprit 3 utilizes the galvanized Esprit Turbo chassis with its wider front box section and improved engine mountings; the chassis is guaranteed for five years against rot 'subject to normal use'. The bodywork also incorporates many features which first appeared on the Turbo, including wrap-around bumpers, re-styled sill panels with anti-chip primer, air scoop/extractors behind the rearmost side windows, and modifications to the airflow under the car (claimed to give the Esprit a drag coefficient of 0.33).

The front suspension of all models in the Lotus range is now very similar, with upper wishbones, a single lower link, an anti-roll bar and coil springs, while at the rear, the Esprit is now fitted with the Turbo-type suspension, consisting of double unequal-length non-parallel transverse links with radius arms (the driveshafts no longer form part of the location); new aluminium hub carriers are used, and the springs are slightly softer than those of the Turbo.

The fore/aft mounted 2.2-litre engine, designated 912, is based on the 907 two-litre, of which more than 18,000 were produced. Though it shares the same basic design as the Sunbeam-Lotus (911) engine, it has different carburation, ignition, oil system, main bearing casting and sump design. In the Esprit 3, this 16-valve dohc unit develops 160bhp at 6,500rpm, and peak torque of 160lb ft is developed at 5,000rpm; perhaps more impressive than this is that 140lb ft is on tap at a lowly 2,400rpm.

We were unable to check Lotus's claimed maximum speed of 138mph, but feel this to be slightly on the optimistic side, 135mph being a more likely figure; even so, we cannot think of any car costing less than the Esprit which has a higher top speed.

The first, and best known, Esprit limited edition of the early years was referred to at Lotus as 'Special' or 'Commemorative' and even simply as 'Black' but to the public in Britain, it always seemed to be 'JPS'. The latter is a reference to the gold on black colour scheme that will be forever linked with images of Lotus Grand Prix contenders of the ground-effect era.

From the front, the standard Esprit S2 outline was little affected by the special edition colour scheme, but note the golden laurel wreath around the Lotus badge.

Our interior views highlight the startling effect of the golden cloth upon the generally overcast interior of the first limited edition Esprit. The most practical addition was the sports three-spoke steering-wheel in place of the standard plastic horror.

The gold theme extended even to framing the windscreen of the special edition S2 Esprit.

A numbered rarity, this John Player Special was thc 20th of a planned 100-off production run for Britain.

Limited edition details included finishing the standard Lotus alloy-wheel design in gold. Another detail was to frame the bonnet badge with a wreath that reflected the success of the World Championship winning type 79 Grand Prix cars.

Its acceleration is just as impressive, 60mph coming up from rest in only 6.5sec and 100mph in 19.0sec, which says a lot for the efficiency of this engine with its twin sidedraught Dellorto carburetters. In its high fifth gear (24.2mph/1,000rpm), it will pull respectably, the important 50–70mph increment taking 9.3sec; drop down to fourth, and the flatness of the torque curve is shown by the fact that all the steps between 40 and 60mph, 50 and 70, 60 and 80 and 70 and 90 take less than 6.5sec.

Not only are these figures much better than those of the S1 and S2, but they are no longer accompanied by deafening engine booms, and although the occupants will always be aware that the engine is sitting just behind their shoulders, its note is no longer irritatingly intrusive. The engine is a little fluffy at first when started from cold (even with the aid of the manual choke). Once running, it is very smooth all the way to its rev limit.

Lotus have consistently aimed for lightness and efficiency in their cars, eschewing the notion that any disadvantage in weight or aerodynamics may be overcome by horsepower; as a result, their cars are not only quicker than might be expected from their power outputs, but also more economical than their performance would suggest: despite some very hard driving, the Esprit returned an outstanding 23.1mpg in our hands, and we imagine that some owners would be able to better our computed touring consumption figure, 24.5mpg, by two or three points. The Esprit 3 has twin tanks (with both fillers lockable) which can take a total of 15 gallons of four-star; this allows a sensible range of over 350 miles, considerably greater than in most cars in this class, with the exception of the Porsche 924 Turbo.

The Esprit's stubby gearlever and narrow gate permit very rapid movements between the very well spaced ratios, with the aid of a progressive clutch, but the change itself is a little heavy, and there is more spring bias than we would like towards the 3rd/4th plane. At 7,000rpm (just before the rev-limiter cuts in) this permitted maxima in our test car of 37, 67 and 97mph in the three lowest gears, though examples fitted with the standard-size wheels and tyres will be somewhat lower-geared.

Ever since the S2 was introduced, we have been immensely impressed not only with the sheer grip and traction of the Esprit, but also with its ability to instil confidence at high speeds on twisty roads. With the S3 on its optional (and attractive) BBS alloy wheels and Goodyear NCT tyres – 195/60 VR 15 at the front and 235/60 VR 15 at the rear (standard fitting is 205/60 VR 14 and 205/70 VR 14) – Lotus have taken a step further towards the ultimate driving machine.

Apart from the astonishing roadholding, there is so much feel, via both the steering and the chassis, that even a very experienced driver is rarely likely to reach the car's exceptionally high cornering limits. In medium and fast bends there is barely a trace of roll, no tyre squeal whatever, and terms like 'understeer' and 'oversteer' are largely redundant. Lifting off or even the ill-advised practice of braking in mid-corner merely tighten the car's line, and barely any movement of the strongly self-centring steering is required to change direction.

If the car has any shortcomings in its cornering ability, they are to be found in tight low-speed bends, where the tendency of the front wheels to slide on the limit becomes more apparent, and where the steering (on more lock than is usually required) has a strange overcentre feel to it. But this is a very minor criticism of a car which makes many of its rivals seem, by comparison, almost medieval. Owners would, however, be well advised to remember that not only are they driving a very wide car, but also a car which makes most of our rural speed limits seem more absurdly low than ever.

To match straightline and cornering performance of this magnitude, a highly efficient braking system is required. Lotus's long-term assessments have led them to the surprising conclusion that ventilated discs gave neither the feel nor the longevity required for the car, so larger (10.5in diameter) plain discs have been used at the front than were fitted to the S2; the 10.8in rear discs remain unchanged. The system is servo-assisted and the circuits are divided from front to rear.

We found that the efficiency of the brakes was more than adequate, and that pedal operation was both light and progressive. We would not quite award full marks though, because we found them less stable during heavy applications than we had hoped.

Despite its very long doors the overall height of less than 44in makes getting in and out of an Esprit easier for athletic types. Once inside, drivers of average height or less will find themselves in a snug and generally comfortable environment, but might wish for some extra pedal space. Anyone of more than about 6ft in height will find that headroom is severely restricted. The seats, despite having no backrest adjustment, are fairly comfortable but could do with more lumbar support.

The pedals, as stated, are in a cramped footwell, but are ideally placed for heel-and-toe gearchanges for those with dainty right feet, and the arrangement of all the major controls is very good indeed. Less impressive, indeed fiddly, are the minor switches, grouped around the sides of the instrument binnacle. The instruments themselves are plentiful in number and well marked, but these virtues are of little value since the minor dials are often obscured by the steering wheel and all the faces suffer badly from reflections in sunlight. A further criticism of the interior, which will affect some owners, is that the ashtrays seem to have been designed by a crusading non-smoker.

Most awkward of all the controls are those for the heating and ventilation, two stiff slides which govern temperature and direction. While heat output is fairly good, we found some difficulty in achieving and maintaining a stable temperature.

Without fan boost, the flow of ambient air into the cockpit is mediocre; with the fan on its lower (and acceptably quiet) setting, it bcomes reasonably strong, and is also easily regulated.

Our noise-meter readings confirmed our subjective impressions that the latest Esprit is significantly quieter from the inside than were its predecessors, thanks partly to the better engine mountings and partly to a special sound insulation barrier. At a steady 30mph (perhaps because of tyre roar rather than any mechanical thrash) it is slightly noisier than the average car; at 50 and 70mph it is very close in noise output to the average of all the cars we have tested in the past couple of years, while at high engine speeds in the gears it is no noisier than many saloon cars. There is still room for improvement here, particularly in the suppression of wind and road roar, but the important fact is that the overall noise level is no longer a major deterrent to enjoyment of the car.

The finish of early Esprits was little short of a disgrace, but Lotus have made great efforts since then to improve their cars both in appearance and quality. Not everyone likes glass fibre bodywork, but if you are buying a car made of that material, a modern Lotus is among the best, and the latest Esprit's exterior is immeasurably neater in detail than the early examples. Not all our testers liked the bright red interior of our test car, but all were agreed that it was well put together, while the finish of the luggage area these days is very smart; this fact may not, of course, do a lot to compensate those who actually wish to carry some luggage in it . . .

The improved layout of the engine bay allows much easier access to the fillers for

Lamps up or down, this 1985 (S3) example of the Esprit underlines the considerable refinement gained by Lotus over the original model – even though the machine looked ostensibly the same as it had on its announcement, a decade previously.

Externally, the needle-nose profile of the Esprit was maintained in S3 guise, but beneath, a galvanized new chassis with extensive engine bay cradle and stouter front end are found.

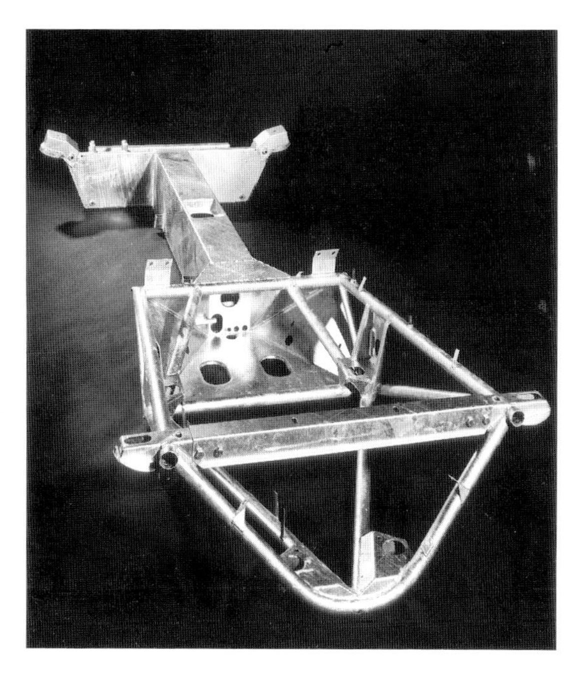

Interior gains on the S3 included fussy but comprehensive black and white VDO instrumentation and a more elegant leather rim, two-spoke steering-wheel of Turbo origin.

The engine was left at the usual 160 normally-aspirated bhp for the life of the S3, but access and service durability were improved within the confines of a mid-engine design.

Luggage space, such as it is, concentrates on the rear compartment rather than under the front bonnet. We can see the reason why in this picture: the forward engine water radiator and a spare wheel need to be accommodated.

PERFORMANCE

CONDITIONS

Weather	Wind 5–20mph
Temperature	58°F
Barometer	29.8 in Hg
Surface	Dry tarmacadam

MAXIMUM SPEEDS

	mph	kph
Estimated	135	217
Terminal Speeds:		
at ¼ mile	92	148
at kilometre	113	182
Speed in gears (at 7,000rpm):		
1st	37	60
2nd	67	108
3rd	97	156

ACCELERATION FROM REST

mph	sec	kph	sec
0–30	2.2	0–40	1.7
0–40	3.4	0–60	3.1
0–50	4.7	0–80	4.7
0–60	6.5	0–100	7.0
0–70	8.5	0–120	9.9
0–80	11.1	0–140	13.4
0–90	14.3	0–160	18.9
0–100	19.0	0–180	25.5
Stand'g ¼	15.0	Stand'g km	27.9

ACCELERATION IN TOP

mph	sec	kph	sec
30–50	10.5	60–80	6.7
40–60	9.9	80–100	5.6
50–70	9.3	100–120	6.1
60–80	9.7	120–140	6.2
70–90	10.2	140–160	8.2
80–100	12.4		

ACCELERATION IN 4TH

mph	sec	kph	sec
20–40	7.6	40–60	4.7
30–50	6.9	60–80	4.0
40–60	6.2	80–100	3.8
50–70	6.2	100–120	4.2
60–80	6.4	120–140	4.4
70–90	6.5	140–160	5.3
80–100	8.0	160–180	6.3
90–110	9.7		

FUEL CONSUMPTION

Touring*	24.5mpg 11.5 litres/100km
Overall	23.1mpg 12.2 litres/100km
Govt tests	19.8mpg (urban) 38.7mpg (56mph) 33.2mpg (75mph)
Fuel grade	97 octane 4-star rating
Tank capacity	15.0gal 68 litres
Max range	368 miles 592km
Test distance	764 miles 1229km

*Consumption midway between 30mph and maximum less an allowance of 5 per cent for acceleration.

NOISE

	dBA	Motor rating*
30mph	68	14
50mph	70	16
70mph	76.5	25
Max revs in 2nd	81	34

*A rating where 1=30 dBA, and 100=96 dBA, and where double the number means double the loudness.

SPEEDOMETER (mph)

Speedo	30	40	50	60	70	80	90	100
True mph	32	42	52	63	73	83	94	105

Distance recorder: 3.5 per cent slow

WEIGHT

	cwt	kg
Unladed weight*	21.0	1,067
Weight as tested	24.7	1,255

*with fuel for approx 50 miles

Performance tests carried out by *Motor*'s staff at the Motor Industry Research Association proving ground, Nuneaton.

GENERAL SPECIFICATION

ENGINE

Cylinders	4 in-line
Capacity	2,174cc (132.6cu in)
Bore/stroke	95.29/76.2mm (3.75/3.0in)
Cooling	Water
Block	Aluminium alloy
Head	Aluminium alloy
Valves	Dohc
Calm drive	Toothed belt
Compression	9.44:1
Carburetters	Two Dellorto DHLA4SE side draught
Bearings	5 main
Max power	160bhp (DIN) at 6,500rpm
Max torque	160lb ft (DIN) at 5,000rpm

TRANSMISSION

Type	5-speed manual
Clutch dia	8.5in
Actuation	Hydraulic

Internal ratios and mph/1,000rpm

Top	0.76:1/24.2
4th	0.97:1/18.9
3rd	1.32:1/13.9
2nd	1.94:1/9.5
1st	2.92:1/6.3
Rev	3.15:1
Final drive	4.1:1

BODY/CHASSIS

Construction	Glass-fibre reinforced plastic body; steel backbone chassis
Protection	Chassis hot-dip galvanised (five-year guarantee)

SUSPENSION

Front	Independent by upper wishbones, lower transverse links, coil springs, anti-roll bar
Rear	Independent by non-parallel unequal-length double transverse links, radius arms, coil springs

STEERING

Type	Rack and pinion
Assistance	None

BRAKES

Front	Disc, 10.5in dia
Rear	Disc, 10.8in dia
Park	On rear wheels
Servo	Yes
Circuit	Duals, split front/rear
Rear Valve	Yes
Adjustment	Automatic

WHEELS/TYRES

Type	Light alloy BBS 7J × 15in (F); 8J × 15 in (R) (optional extra: *see* text)
Tyres	Goodyear NCT 195/60 VR 15 (F), 235/60 VR 15 (R) (optional extra: *see* text)
Pressures	21/25psi F/R

ELECTRICAL

Battery	12V, 44 Ah
Earth	Negative
Generator	Alternator, 70A
Fuses	8
Headlights	
type	4 × 5in sealed beam
dip	220 W total
main	240 W total

Make: Lotus. **Model:** Esprit S3
Maker: Lotus Cars Ltd, Norwich, Norfolk NR14 8EZ
Price: £10,805 plus £900.42 Car Tax plus £1,755.81 VAT equals £13,461.23. Extras fitted to test car: stereo radio/cassette player with four speakers and power aerial (£392.44); 15in BBS wheels with wider tyres (£85.96); Price as tested: £13,939.63.

oil and water, and for some service work, but even so any major attention must be awkward with the engine in situ. *It appears to us that Lotus have made a major effort to improve their cars' reliability (our own long-term Elite became very costly indeed in the later stages of its time with us), and we would be interested to hear from current owners whether or not they have succeeded.*

For its price, the Esprit is moderately well equipped, including items like electric window lifters and a passenger door mirror (remotely adjustable, as is the driver's door mirror). Most owners will want to have the sort of stereo radio/cassette player with four speakers and a power aerial which was fitted to our test car (£392.44 extra), while other possible options include air conditioning, hide interior trim, and metallic paint finish. The BBS wheels fitted to our test car add £85.96 to the price (and this includes the extra cost of the larger tyres).

Careful development work has advanced the Esprit to the point where its only major drawbacks are those which it inherited from the imaginative pen of Mr Giugiaro – and the normal demands of practicality do not really apply to this sort of 'fantasy' purchase.

Questions and Answers

At the back, much of the increased torsional strength (a whopping 50 per cent bonus was claimed) could be credited to the tubular cradle that was developed for the engine and transmission. There were also additional cross-bracing tubes that had been required when Lotus had run prototype V8s (to 1979) and the replacement 2.2 Turbo power train. It all added up to such an improvement in foundation to the Esprit formula that one was tempted to ask why the company had not done it that way in the first place?

The answer to that question appears to be a combination of tradition (the original Esprit rear-end was pure Chapman theory and practice), cost-cutting and lack of facilities.

So what did Lotus have in the eighties that they lacked in seventies? Answer: a lot of basic automotive engineering equipment, such as a stress rig to analyse chassis loads – items which the De Lorean cash (and experience) allowed Lotus engineers to use on their own products.

During this Turbo/S3 development period, Lotus also had the opportunity to assess the long-term merits of ventilated disc brakes for the Esprit. The company reported that:

> After long-term assessment and running chassis evaluation, ventilated disc brakes were found lacking in feel and longevity and were therefore discarded in favour of larger, solid front discs than that employed on the S2. The rear-brake assembly used on the S2 has been retained.

Notice that there is no mention of the S2.2, which immediately preceded the S3. Notice also that Lotus failed to add that the move from a 9.7in (25cm) front discs to 10.5in (27cm) was also accompanied by the use of a vacuum servo.

FASHIONABLE OPTION

Theoretically, S3 wheels and tyres remained the same Speedline 7 and 7.5in rim with the 205/60 and 205/70 aspect ratio combinations of the S2/S2.2 Esprits. Yet, the most photographed and frequently encountered combination was the optional BBS aluminium 'spider web' pattern alloy wheels (£85.96, according to *Motor*). These offered a taste of Turbo motoring (and gearing) by a 1in (25mm) increase in diameter, measuring 7 and 8J × 15in to carry 195/60 and 235/60 VR NCT rubber.

Now, Lotus followed their Grand Prix inclination and switched over to Goodyear, developing a relationship that is still in

The Rivals

Other possible rivals include the BMW 635 CSi (£18,950), De Tomaso Pantera (£17,950) and Porsche 3.3 Turbo (£27,950)

LOTUS TURBO ESPRIT — £20,900

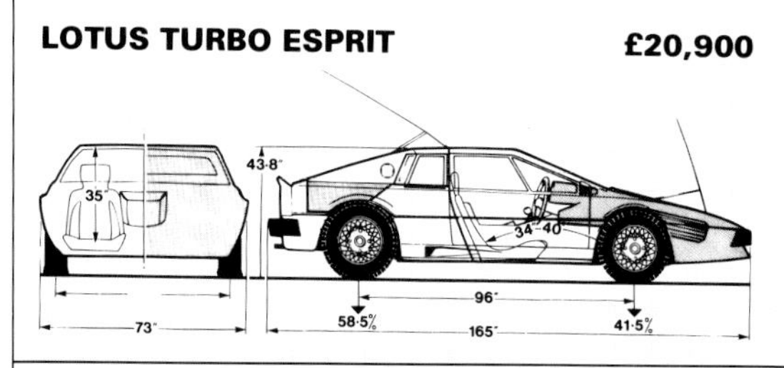

Power, bhp/rpm	210/6–6,500
Torque, lb ft/rpm	200/4–4,500
Tyres (F/R)	195/60 VR 15; 235/60 VR 15
Weight, cwt	22.6
Max speed, mph	152*
0–60mph, sec	5.6
30–50mph in 4th, sec	6.2
50–70mph in top, sec	8.0
Overall mpg	18.5
Fuel grade, stars	4
Boot capacity, cu ft	3.5
Test Date	28 March 1981

*estimate

Turbo power promotes Lotus towards the top of the first division in the high-performance league. Stunning acceleration from smooth and viceless turbo-charged 'four', allied to perfect ratios, strong roadholding, superb handling and tireless braking, all add up to a driver's car *par excellence*, with good economy and a comfortable ride as icing on the cake. But some Esprit shortcomings remain: poor heating, awkward visibility, bad pedal layout and lack of space for tall drivers.

FERRARI 308 GTB — £20,127

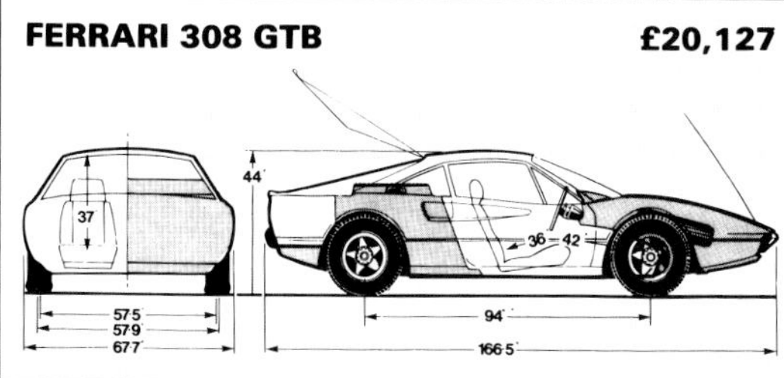

Power, bhp/rpm	255/7,700
Torque, lb ft/rpm	210/5,000
Tyres	205/70 VR 14
Weight, cwt	26.0
Max speed, mph	150*
0–60mph, sec	6.6
30–50mph in 4th, sec	5.5
50–70mph in top, sec	7.5
Overall mpg	13.8†
Fuel grade, stars	4
Boot capacity, cu ft	not measured
Test Date (GTS)	26 August 1978

*estimate
+Twin test

Arguably the most beautiful of modern supercars, the strictly two-seater mid-engined 308GTB uses Ferrari's delectable quad-cam 3-litre V8. A genuine 150mph car, its through-the-gears acceleration is outclassed by the Lotus', but it is well made and handles and holds the road like a true thoroughbred, as well as providing a comfortable ride; though engine noise levels are high, and fuel consumption is not as good as the Lotus' or Porsche's.

JAGUAR XJ-S — £19,763

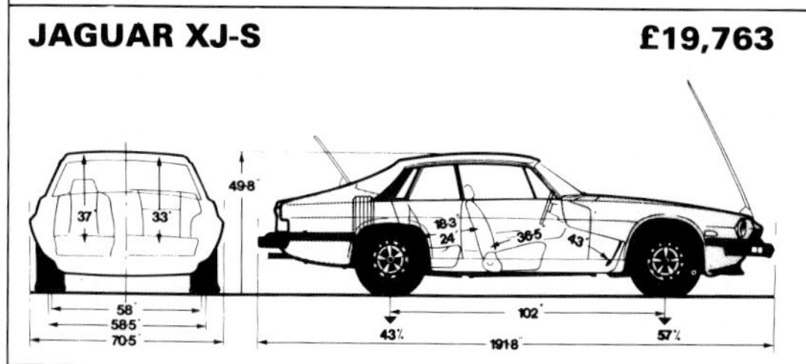

Power, bhp/rpm	296/5,400
Torque, lb ft/rpm	318/3,900
Tyres	205/70 VR 15
Weight, cwt	34.3
Max speed, mph	145*
0–60mph, sec	7.6
30–50mph in k'down, sec	2.8
50–70mph in k'down, sec	3.5
Overall mpg	13.5
Fuel grade, stars	4
Boot capacity, cu ft	8.4
Test Date	25 October 1980

*estimate

Now available only in automatic form, the XJ-S continues to provide an exceptional blend of performance, refinement and comfort at a competitive price. Economy recently improved, but still a thirsty car. Styling hasn't improved with familiarity, and cramped in rear, but if you can afford the fuel bills the XJ-S remains one of the world's finest and most desirable cars.

MASERATI MERAK — £18,986

Power, bhp/rpm	220/6,000
Torque, lb ft/rpm	199/4,500
Tyres (F/R)	195/70 VR 15; 215/70 VR 15
Weight, cwt	27.0
Max speed, mph	150*
0–60mph, sec	7.8
30–50mph in 4th, sec	7.2
50–70mph in top, sec	10.8
Overall mpg	13.3
Fuel grade, stars	4
Boot capacity, cu ft	not measured
Test Date	24 September 1977

*estimate

V6-engined Italian supercar with (very) occasional rear seats, recently much reduced in price. Good performance at the top end, but acceleration outclassed in this company, as is fuel consumption. Excellent handling and adhesion, but the ride is rather harsh; reasonably good gearbox, heavy clutch. Noise suppression good, ventilation and finish poor. More legroom than in most Italian cars and fair luggage space.

PORSCHE 924 CARRERA GT — £19,211

Power, bhp/rpm	210/6,000
Torque, lb ft/rpm	203/3,500
Tyres (F/R)	205/55 VR 16; 225/50 VR 16
Weight, cwt	—
Max speed, mph	150*
0–60mph, sec	6.5
30–50mph in 4th, sec	7.9
50–70mph in top, sec	9.5
Overall mpg	22.2
Fuel grade, stars	4
Boot capacity, cu ft	4.8
Test Date	7 February 1981

*estimate

Limited edition, competition-orientated version of the 924 Turbo, of which the entire right-hand drive allocation has been sold, but worth mentioning as it too has a turbocharged 'four'. Excellent performance on boost, delivered with remarkably good fuel economy. Fine handling, gearchange and brakes all help make this is a splendid driver's car, though ride and noise suppression could be better, as could the ventilation and the low speed torque.

PORSCHE 911 SC SPORT — £18,179

Power, bhp/rpm	204/5,900
Torque, lb ft/rpm	195/4,300
Tyres (F/R)	185/70 VR 15; 215/60 VR 15
Weight, cwt	22.9
Max speed, mph	148*
0–60mph, sec	5.7
30–50mph in 4th, sec	6.3
50–70mph in top, sec	8.9
Overall mpg	20.4
Fuel grade, stars	4
Boot capacity, cu ft	9.8
Test Date	15 November 1980

*estimate

Even faster and substantially more economical than before, the latest 911SC is without question one of the world's most satisfying (as well as sensible) supercars. Superb handling and roadholding and exceptionally high standards of build and finish remain traditional facets, as do a firm ride, hard-to-control heating and strong road noise. In all, though, a true gem among supercars.

force for the Esprit at the time of writing. Part of the reason for that loyalty continues to be the kind of service that produced twelve months' development work by Goodyear, who have tailored the rubber compounds and sidewall configuration to suit the handling and suspension characteristics of this new model.

COSMETIC CHANGES

The East Anglian air of Norfolk is bound to be changeable as it flits over so many acres of flat lands. Indeed, it brings with it a new Esprit interior virtually every time we look around. The nasty two-spoke plastic mouldings of the earlier Esprits was forsaken for a neat leather-rim device of small diameter, while the black-and-white instrumentation now picked up all but the boost gauge of the Turbo, including a 170mph (270kph) speedometer.

The seating went through another trim transformation (but retained fixed back rests) to complement new foam foundations. 'Cropped velour fabrics' were the official standard finish, but optional leather treatment proved popular, either as a full leather cladding option, or as hide with velour inserts peeking shyly at the customers who liked to sit on the trimming fence.

Lotus claimed that: 'A new sound insulation barrier around the cockpit area has resulted in a 50 per cent reduction of interior noise levels.' Certainly, the cabin was a much more peaceful place, but a lot of the improvement came from the fact that Lotus could now adopt more sound-absorbent engine and transmission mountings, because such mountings no longer had to restrain the power train, thanks to the replacement rear suspension.

What mattered to the customer was that noise levels had now dropped to the levels of popular mass production saloons.

EXTERNAL CHANGES

Exterior changes for the S3 were less dramatic than for the Giugiaro-modified Turbo, but were quietly effective none the less.

The previous matt black areas, such as the front spoiler and side sills, were colour-coordinated into the body, which took on the glassfibre bumpers of the Turbo model, complete with a proud LOTUS logo at the back.

The air scoops behind the rear side-glass also took on a colour-matched hue – the same as the main bodywork. Those 'ears' were confirmed in their 'air management' role, taking in cold air to the carburettors and extracting engine-bay heat via the counterpart ducting.

Overall finish improved dramatically during this period, even the luggage bay was nicely trimmed and the single-piece engine cover allowed better access to an engine layout that was never designed with DIY in mind. In Lotus's words, the battery had now gone walkabout to a 'rear corner (RH) behind the wheelarch'. Meanwhile, the exhaust system featured flexible down-pipes that looked, according to one insider, 'like giant Aeroquip lines'. These down-pipes were ball-jointed before another flexible section led to the silencer.

Although there was no change in power quotes for the S3, contemporary road test data from *Autocar* revealed that performance of the normally-aspirated car had now come right into line with Lotus expectations of 1976. Full details are given in our accompanying road test data and the current *Autocar & Motor* title, but the essentials were a reported 135mph (220kph) maximum speed coupled to an independently-timed 0–60mph (0–100kph) average of 6.5 seconds and an excellent 23.1mpg (825km/100l) overall.

Truly, the S3 was by far the best Esprit yet, but it never really received the sales recognition it should have enjoyed, as the Turbo stole so much of the limelight. More about *that* in our next chapter.

5 The Performer . . . Esprit Turbo

'Anywhere I would be doing 90mph and happy in the Esprit 2, the Esprit Turbo is doing 110mph with the same happy feeling.'

Roger Becker, 1980

Another significant comment about the Esprit Turbo came from Hugh F Kemp, director of Powertrain Engineering. In 1990, he said: 'The development of the engine has been focused on specific output and refinement.' These quotes emphasize the two enormous gains that were immediately apparent in the turbo-charged Esprit: 150mph (240kph) performance to match the styling, and a chassis to match the Lotus reputation.

Initially, the Turbo model was a 100-off limited edition in the Essex petroleum colours of a then current Lotus Grand Prix sponsor, but it rapidly developed into the mainstay of Esprit production. It was a significant flag-waving success, and it was a significant success too in terms of sheer engine and chassis speed. By 1982, Turbo production exceeded that of the Esprit S2 by 45 units, and that of any other Lotus model by a larger margin. From 1982 to 1986 an Esprit Turbo derivative was the most popular Lotus, then the Excel was the single biggest volume product, by just three units! Increasing American Esprit exports and the availability of many more variants of the Esprit Turbo (especially the charge-cooled SE) took it back past the Excel for 1988/89.

Hopefully, for future Lotus credibility, the Elan will have surpassed all other output during 1990. For the Elan is set on a course that is anticipated to yield 3,300 units a year, whereas the 1988 record for Esprit output was 1,058 examples, and all but 90 of those were turbo-charged.

TORTUOUS TURBOCHARGER TRIALS

Development of the turbo-charged (Type 910) Lotus started in May 1978. By this time, Lotus already had the basis of the enlarged (Type 912) 2.2-litre engine to use as a foundation on which build their most powerful four-cylinder. By the end of 1978, Lotus also had an agreement with Essex to support some of the launch costs. This resulted in an enormous public debut at the Albert Hall, where some 700 VIPs were serenaded by Shirley Bassey.

Initially, engine development progress was slower than you might have expected. The project was delayed by internal politics, as the much postponed V8 was favoured by many senior Lotus management. The V8 project did continue until 1979, alongside the Turbo. Indeed, there is every reason to think that the Esprit owes that V8 project a large vote of thanks for the quoted 50 per cent gain in torsional chassis strength. The V8, after all, had been engineered with the objective of accommodating 4-litre V8 torque and weight.

Tony Rudd reported:

Really, the car that turned out to be the Essex Turbo could have been the M71 Esprit V8. Look at the chassis cradle for the engine – you will see it has got space for another bank of exhausts. Nobody comments on that,

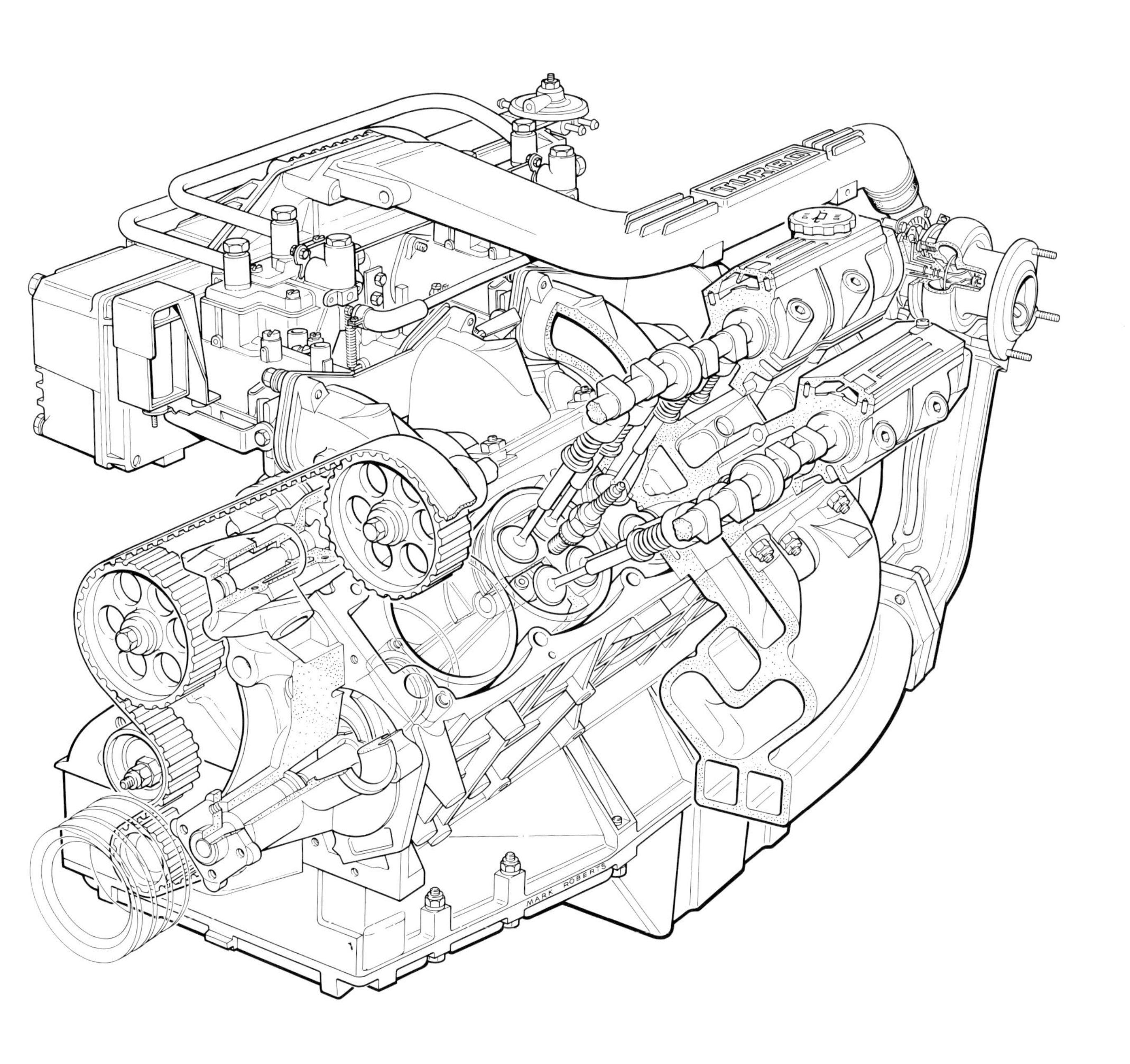

The first Lotus production turbo motor retained its DOHC valve gear with prophetic quadruple-valve combustion chambers. The sidedraught carburettors were successfully prepared to meet the incoming charge from the aft-mounted Garrett AiResearch turbocharger. The result was a tractable 210bhp from 2.2 litres.

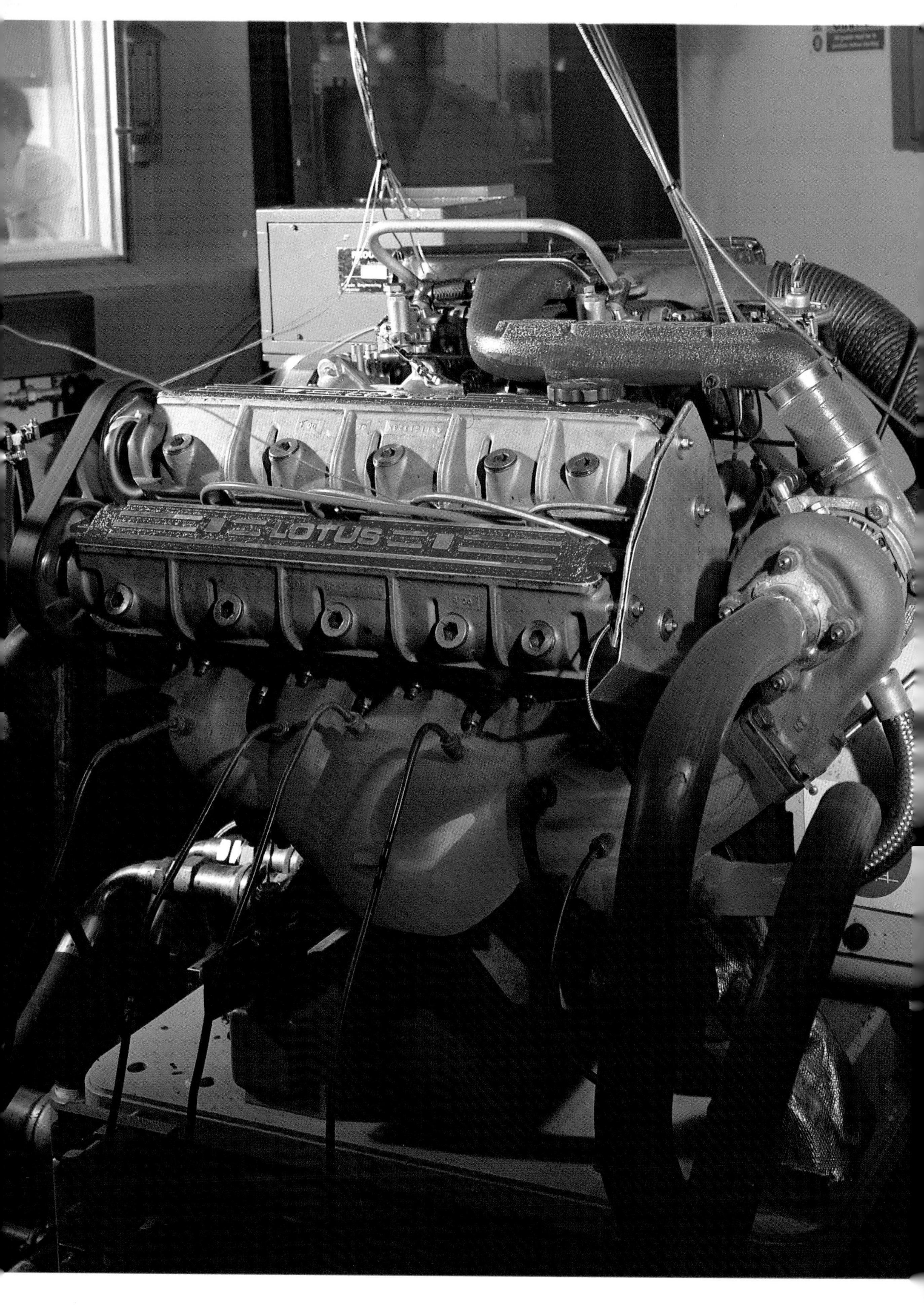
LOTUS

Original Lotus Essex Esprit livery was vividly extrovert and cost over £20,000 in 1980. Lotus sources say that less than sixty were constructed. This is one of the earliest, wearing Compomotive alloy wheels rather than the later BBS fitment.

but I promise you that is what the extra space is for. The idea of slotting on another cylinder bank had always appealed to Colin Chapman.

Turbo Drama

Researching in 1982, former Powertrain engineering manager Graham Atkin gained the credit for fighting the Turbo project through against many heavyweight managerial guns, and he was also the source of Citröen transmission knowledge when I conducted my 1990 question-and-answer session with current Powertrain chief, Hugh Kemp. All were very helpful, in typical forthright Lotus engineering tradition, but it was an anonymous insider who really gave the flavour of the Turbo project in a chance aside. This began:

Red hot, quite literally. The turbocharged version of the DOHC Lotus 16-valve engine also exploited a 2.2-litre capacity. It developed little short of 100bhp per litre with friendly, and widely acclaimed, power delivery characteristics.

The turbo taught us *not* to do a new engine and vehicle together again! It was the most miserable development time I have seen, because we were learning the hard way. What other manufacturers would take five

Three-quarter view reveals decal details of the first turbocharged Lotus production car.

years to do we did in five *months*. And so, there were many blow-ups and fires, sending four pages of reports to management about our progress, or lack of it.

It has to be remembered that when Lotus did get to the heart of sorting out their dramatic turbo project, the result was universally hailed as a major advance in turbo enginering, particularly in the absence of lag from the non-intercooled and carburated unit of comparative simplicity.

My candid informant continued:

Initially, it was a stop-start kind of programme; part of the time we'd be working alongside the demands of the De Lorean project. Then, there was at least a year's delay, as up to 118 engineers were crammed into Hangar 3 chasing the De Lorean timetable for a January 1981 launch [it emerged in March of that year]. Our engine people were flat out on the V6 that was in the De Lorean, and when we did get to look at the Turbo again, it was much more complicated than you might imagine . . . particularly as we left the electrics on the basis of a sweeping up job at the end of the programme.

Drastic Change

Writing with the benefit of hindsight, one fundamental aspect of the Turbo programme was altered during production and needs underlining. It was only the initial batch of Esprit Turbos – by far the majority would

Lotus did not intend onlookers to miss the badges . . .

Later (1982) Esprit Turbo livery accompanied significant price drops, but the addition of optional equipment often put customer delivery prices back in the £20,000 bracket.

have been in Essex colours – that were produced with the original dry-sump oil lubrication. Following a 7 February 1980 press embargo, production commenced in June 1980. Twelve months later, this Esprit joined its carburated cousins in utilizing wet-sump principles. What lay behind the about-turn in such a fundamental aspect of engine durability and reliability?

Why had Lotus adopted the dry-sump system (in which oil is separately carried in an external tank, rather than in the 'wet' sump

Leather-clad and wearing its in-car entertainment upon the roof panel, an original Lotus Essex Esprit Turbo poses outside the factory.

Side view of the original production Turbo reveals Compomotive wheels at rest, extensive aerodynamic revisions and the feeling that 150mph (240kph) from 2.2 litres was a fitting achievement for Britain's most successful motor racing/road car marque.

of an engine cylinder block) for the Esprit Turbo? 'For the long distances and high speeds that are possible with the Turbo', was Tony Rudd's predictable reply.

This oil system is applied to all forms of competition engine, where the regulations allow it. The engineer, and customer, gains in the freedom from oil surge within the sump and better control of lubrication demands under duress. There are snags, however, and these were explained by Tony Rudd and amplified by Lotus engineer Ken Sears.

'Quite honestly it is not necessary to dry-sump, unless you are really thrashing the motor,' opined Rudd. He added: 'It grieves me to see the oil cooler virtually bulging on a dry-sump system when it is being started from cold.' Ken Sears confirmed:

There was an initial development problem with coolers splitting in cold conditions. That was overcome by using thermostatic control, but in service the tedium of explaining to customers how to check dry-sump oil level – on a flat surface of course – far outweighed any theoretical service advantages. For example, every variation in temperature led to a different oil-level height being recalled on the dipstick, leading to understandable confusion.

Thus the wet sump reappeared in June 1981 and any Esprit equipped with an original dry sump has to be regarded as a comparative rarity.

POWERFUL DEVELOPMENT

The principal engineer on the turbo project was Martin Cliffe, but even the directors at Rudd and Kimberley's level were involved, as Lotus took their crash course in turbo technology. Primary objectives were to trade ultimate horsepower for accessible pulling power and here the company had the positive advantage of an efficient 16-valve, DOHC, power unit as the basic foundation.

As cost and time constraints ruled out the usual fuel-injected, electronically-managed approach, Lotus were forced to re-think the turbo-charger installation around their traditional twin-choke Dell'Orto carburettors and to dispense with the usual intercooler. Instead, they arranged that the Dell'Ortos be re-equipped to stand the rigours of ingesting air and fuel under pressure from the single Garrett AiResearch turbocharger. A Lucas pump and pressure regulator were asked to supply fuel at 4.5lb in over tick-over pressure. The significance was that pressure was always that much above that required throughout the rpm range. Additionally, the fuel was kept in constant (cooling) circulation by means of a return line, as you would find on a fuel-injection layout.

Extra Touches

Lotus contributed some original thought on feeding pressurized air from a turbocharger outlet to the plenum chamber of the carburettors. This was done via ridged alloy tubing that dispersed heat (a cheaper intercooler action), whilst changing section from circular to oval section in a flared pattern that slowed gas speeds, but allowed enhanced pressures.

Another clever development touch was the inclusion of divided exhaust tracts in the molybdenum iron exhaust manifold that led straight into the turbocharger intake flanging. Together with an exceptionally short path between inlet manifolding and valves, the result was exceptional engine response to the throttle.

The turbocharging installation featured replacement camshafts that supplied extra lift (0.380 versus 0.358in of the 'E-Cam') and a marginal 6deg alteration was made in the timing of inlet-valve closure and exhaust-valve opening.

John Miles, now working at Lotus as an engineer but then writing for *Autocar*, reported in June 1980:

If you want to be cruel, the engine is willing to lug from as low as 1,000rpm without snatch or jerkiness. On full throttle in fifth, boost begins to build up from as low as 1,900rpm. You are well into the torque at 2,500rpm.The revs are rising far more rapidly now and by the time the engine is turning over at 3,500, virtually full boost is being developed – the real push in the back starts. There are none of the usual turbo drawbacks.

Ancillary engine work tackled in the engine conversion naturally included the cast-alloy dry sump, which was of ladder construction and carried the main bearing caps integrally. Compression ratio went down from 9.5:1 to 7.5:1 with an enlarged combustion chamber. Major specification alterations for the low-volume bowl of the pistons, which also carried 'new skirt profiles', while 'the ring pack was lowered relative to the piston pin', according to Lotus.

The heated demands of turbocharging were met by substantial changes to engine-compartment ventilation and the inclusion of sodium-filled exhaust valves that ran in Stellite seats. A bonus in water-pump capacity was included, and the water passages through the head gasket were diverted to ensure that 75 per cent of the increased water flow came in the environs of the exhaust valves.

DETAIL GEARING CHANGES

The transmission remained on a Citröen base. A new alloy bellhousing for the 2.2-litre turbo application and accommodation of a 9.5in (24cm) diameter clutch – up by 1in (25mm) – were the principal changes. Gear ratios were as for all Esprits thus far, but the overall gearing was altered by the adoption of bigger wheels and tyres, raising top gear to 22.6 from 22mph (36 from 35kph) per thousand rpm. In practical terms, that meant the 149mph (240kph) that *Autocar* timed represented 6,593rpm, over the power peak, but well within safe engine speed limits.

Peripheral modifications encompassed replacement plunging action driveshafts to co-operate with the new top-link rear suspension. As on the S3 also, were replacement four-point mountings for the engine and gearbox that were biased toward eliminating harshness rather than compromised in the old handling/anti-vibration role.

LIFE IN THE FAST LANE

Back to John Miles and *Autocar* for an imaginative and knowledgeable insight as to how that 912 turbo motor felt at higher rpm in a 1980 context:

The build-up of power is smooth and strong – without peak – to the safe limit of 7,000rpm, launching us to an indicated 130mph on quite a short straight.

Lotus 912 Turbo Engine Statistics, 1980

4 cylinders in line, inclined 45deg to left.

Bore 95.25mm
Stroke 76.20mm
Capacity 2,174cc
Compression ratio 7.5:1
Fuel requirement 98 RON leaded
Fuel intake Pressurized Dell'Orto DHLA 40H carburettors, 35mm chokes, Lucas fuel pump set 4.5lb in surplus pressure.
Turbocharger Garrett AiResearch T3
Maximum boost 8psi
Peak turbine speed 110,000rpm
Dry sump: via Toothed-belt oil pump, driven at 0.69 of crankshaft rpm; two scavenge pumps.
Camshaft timing
Inlet opens 28 BTDC
Inlet closes 58 ABDC
Exhaust opens 58 ABDC
Exhaust closes 28 ATDC
Camshaft lift 0.38in
Spark plugs NGK BPR7EV
Emissions certification ECE 15

PEFORMANCE
210bhp DIN at 6,250rpm
200lb ft DIN at 4,500rpm

Only a few days previously [Roger] Becker had returned from the Nardo high speed track in southern Italy, where the Esprit Turbo had been lapping consistently in the 145–155mph bracket.

Incidentally, the Esprit suffered a front tyre failure at full speed on the Italian track and came to rest stably on three tyres. Unfortunately, the same could not be said of the other development car . . .

The second incident took down a hedge and a 4in girth willow tree just outside Mike Kimberley's office . . . errant Esprit disappearing in a shower of glassfibre and hedge clippings into the moat that runs behind the said hedge.

There were no injuries; the incident was caused by a vehicle parked on the correct line as the test Esprit made its 140mph (225kph) approach and so was instantly forced to alter its course.

ROAD TEST

Lotus Turbo Esprit

Reproduced from *Motor*
28 March 1981

Since its launch in 1975 signalled the completion of the new Lotus range of up-market prestige cars, Britain's sole mid-engined sportster has existed in a kind of limbo. It was always too quick and too expensive to be classified among upper bracket 'ordinary' sports cars like the Porsche 924 or Datsun 280ZX, yet with only a 2-litre four-cylinder engine – albeit an exceptionally efficient one – simply not potent enough to be a serious alternative to established exotics in the Ferrari, Porsche and Lamborghini mould. In a sense, its flying-wedge Giugiaro styling and superb road manners created expectations that it was unable to fulfil.

But all that changed in February last year when Lotus unveiled the Turbo Esprit which, in one fell swoop, presented the men of Modena, Stuttgart and Sant'Agata with a high-performance rival that could confidently take them on at their own game, and *stand a good chance of winning. At last the Esprit had the urge to go with the image.*

It also acquired a lavish appointments list – including such luxuries as air conditioning, a four-speaker digital stereo radio/cassette player, electrically-adjustable door mirrors, electric window lifters and full leather trim – and an appropriately exotic price.

At £20,900, the Esprit's most obvious rival – also mid-engined and a strict two-seater – is the Ferrari 308GTB which costs £20,127. But there are quite a few others of similarly exotic image and price, not least of which are a pair of Porsches, the 911SC in Sport form at £18,179, and the limited edition (and fully sold-out) 924 Carrera GT at £19,211. Other Italian contenders include the Maserati Merak (£18,986) and the de Tomaso Pantera (£17,950), while British opposition is provided by the somewhat more svelte and spacious, automatic-only Jaguar XJ-S at £19,763.

All of which makes the Lotus the most expensive car in its class; but if performance is to be the yardstick – as inevitably it must – then the Esprit still offers sound value, since it is also by a small margin the quickest car in its class. What's more, its straight-line potency is matched by powerful and tireless braking, prodigious roadholding, and handling which is as forgiving as it is rewarding. In short, it's a driving machine par excellence, *and that virtue alone should be sufficient to sway many a potential buyer, (not least existing Esprit owners wanting to climb further up the performance ladder), with a remarkably comfortable ride and a moderate thirst being thrown in as something of a bonus. But while Lotus has also been very successful in improving the Esprit's previously poor mechanical refinement, there are other long-standing weaknesses that have remained uncorrected in*

PERFORMANCE

CONDITIONS

Weather	Wind 0–15mph
Temperature	35°F
Barometer	29.5 in Hg
Surface	Dry tarmacadam

MAXIMUM SPEEDS

	mph	kph
Banked Circuit	*See* text	
Terminal Speeds:		
at ¼ mile	97	156
at kilometre	118	190
Speed in gears (at 7,000rpm):		
1st	41	66
2nd	62	100
3rd	92	148
4th	125	201

ACCELERATION FROM REST

mph	sec	kph	sec
0–30	2.1	0–40	1.7
0–40	3.0	0–60	2.7
0–50	4.3	0–80	4.3
0–60	5.6	0–100	6.0
0–70	7.4	0–120	8.4
0–80	9.4	0–140	11.5
0–90	12.2	0–160	15.2
0–100	15.4	0–180	20.9
0–110	19.7	0–200	—
0–120	28.4		
Stand'g ¼	14.4	Stand'g km	26.7

ACCELERATION IN TOP

mph	sec	kph	sec
20–40	—	40–60	—
30–50	—	60–80	—
40–60	8.5	80–100	5.2
50–70	8.0	100–120	4.9
60–80	8.1	120–140	5.4
70–90	8.4	140–160	5.6
80–100	8.9		
90–110	10.7		
100–120	—		

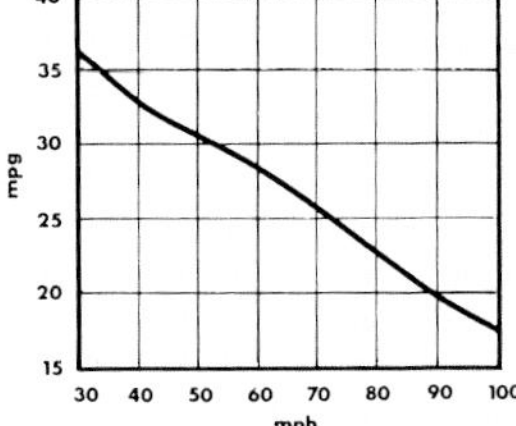

ACCELERATION IN 4TH

mph	sec	kph	sec
20–40	8.2	40–60	4.9
30–50	6.2	60–80	3.6
40–60	5.5	80–100	3.4
50–70	5.2	100–120	3.2
60–80	5.2	120–140	3.4
70–90	5.5	140–160	4.0
80–100	6.1		
90–110	7.8		
100–120	—		

FUEL CONSUMPTION

Touring*	18.7mpg 15.1 litres/100km
Overall	18.5mpg 15.3 litres/100km
Govt tests	19.7mpg (urban) 38.7mpg (56mph) 33.3mpg (75mph)
Fuel grade	97 octane 4-star rating
Tank capacity	19.0gal 86.0 litres
Max range	355 miles 571km
Test distance	714miles 1149km

*Consumption midway between 30mph and maximum less an allowance of 5 per cent for acceleration.

NOISE

	dBA	Motor rating*
30mph	70	16
50mph	74	21
70mph	78	28
Max revs in 2nd	86	48

(1st for 3-speed auto)
*A rating where 1=30 dBA, and 100=96 dBA, and where double the number means double the loudness.

SPEEDOMETER (mph)

Speedo	30	40	50	60	70	80	90	100
True mph	29	38	48	57.5	67	77	87	97

Distance recorder: 3.5 per cent fast

WEIGHT

	cwt	kg
Unladed weight*	22.6	1,148
Weight as tested	26.3	1,336

*with fuel for approx 50 miles

Performance tests carried out by *Motor*'s staff at the Motor Industry Research Association proving ground, Nuneaton.

GENERAL SPECIFICATION

ENGINE

Cylinders	4 in-line
Capacity	2,174cc (132.6cu in)
Bore/stroke	95.29/76.20mm (3.75/3.00in)
Cooling	Water
Block	Aluminium alloy
Head	Aluminium alloy
Valves	Dohc 16-valves
Cam drive	Toothed belt
Compression	7.5:1
Carburetter	Two Dellorto 40CDHLA and AiResearch T3 turbo-charger
Bearings	5 main
Max power	210bhp (DIN) at 6–6,500rpm
Max torque	200lb ft (DIN) at 4–4,500rpm

TRANSMISSION

Type	5-speed manual
Clutch dia	9.5in
Actuation	Hydraulic

Internal ratios and mph/1,000rpm

Top	0.76:1/22.7
4th	0.97:1/17.8
3rd	1.32:1/13.1
2nd	1.94:1/8.9
1st	2.92:1/5.9
Rev	3.46:1
Final drive	4.375:1

BODY/CHASSIS

Construction	Glass-fibre body on fabricated steel chassis
Protection	Chassis dip-galvanized: 5-year guarantee

SUSPENSION

Front	Independent by upper wishbone, lower transverse links, fore-aft location by anti-roll bar; coil springs
Rear	Independent by single upper and twin lower transverse links and radius arm; coil springs.

STEERING

Type	Rack and pinion
Assistance	No

BRAKES

Front	10.44in discs
Rear	9.7in discs, inboard
Park	On rear
Servo	Yes
Circuit	Split front/rear
Rear Valve	No
Adjustment	Automatic

WHEELS/TYRES

Type	3-piece, 15in diameter
Tyres	Goodyear NCT 195/60 VR 15 front, 235/60 VR 15 rear
Pressures	21/25psi F/R

ELECTRICAL

Battery	12V, 44 Ah
Earth	Negative
Generator	Alternator 70amp.
Fuses	8
Headlights type	4 circular halogen, retractable
dip	210 W total
main	240 W total

the Turbo: in particular, its awkward visibility, meagre ventilation and stuffy heating, poor pedal layout and wretched discomfort for very tall drivers. Such failings of day-to-day practicality are by no means unique in this class but that doesn't make them any more excusable. As for whether they are sufficient to outweigh the Turbo's strengths in other areas, that is something that only the individual purchaser can decide. All we can say is that while you can *buy supercars that are more practical, more comfortable and more civilized, we doubt if you can buy a superior* driving machine *for under £25,000.*

To the naked eye the Turbo is distinguished from the 'ordinary' S2 Esprit by a deeper front spoiler, a rear spoiler and a subtle lip across the roof's trailing edge. These are not mere cosmetic add-ons but strictly functional, combining with deepened door sills (reminiscent of Grand Prix cars' side skirts) and an undertray beneath the engine, to reduce aerodynamic lift front and rear and endow the Turbo with a slippery 0.35 drag coefficient. Other external body changes include NACA air ducts in the door sills and a slatted-louvre (in place of glass) tailgate panel, which together improve the flow of cooling air through the engine bay. The picture is completed by three-piece composite alloy wheels shod with massive ultra-low profile Goodyear NCT covers – 195/60 VR 15 at the front and 235/60 VR 15 at the rear.

Beneath-the-skin changes are similarly comprehensive and wide-ranging. The Turbo's steel backbone chassis is wider and stronger, and the all-independent coil spring suspension is substantially revised. In place of the S2's Opel components at the front there are Elite-derived upper wishbones and lower transverse links triangulated with the anti-roll bar. At the rear, the S2's fixed-length drive shafts (which double as upper suspension locating members) are replaced by plunging shafts, and new upper transverse links complete the location; the non-parallel lower transverse links and longitudinal trailing arms remain as before, as do the inboard rear brake discs. The front discs are enlarged (but still solid, not ventilated) and a larger master cylinder and servo are provided.

The theme continues with the engine itself, Lotus having chosen not so much to adapt a turbocharger to its 16-valve four-cylinder engine as to redevelop the engine to suit a turbocharger. As with the rest of the car, the story behind its development has been thoroughly chronicled in previous issues (w/e 16 February and 5 April 1980), but it is worth detailing some of the lengths Lotus went to in order to ensure not only the engine's strength and reliability (dry sump lubrication, revised cooling system, a stiffer bottom end, sodium-filled exhaust valves and stronger dished pistons) but also to minimise the loss of torque at low revs which usually characterizes turbocharged engines. Central to the achievement of this aim were an increase in capacity from 1,973cc to 2,174cc and the adoption of a 'blowthrough' turbocharging arrangement which allowed the carburetters (fuel injection was ruled out on grounds of cost and excessive development time) to be located as close as possible to the cylinder head for prompt throttle response. Additionally a great deal of fine tuning was carried out on manifold design and the positioning of the boost pressure sensor, and the valve lift of the camshafts was increased.

As a result, Lotus are able to claim that despite its 7.5:1 compression ratio the Turbo produces more torque at 2,000rpm than the naturally-aspirated 2-litre achieves at its peak of 5,000rpm, and it goes on to reach a maximum of 200lb ft at between 4,000 and 4,500rpm. Equally impressive is the maximum power: 210bhp (DIN) at 6,000–6,500rpm, a full 50bhp more than the naturally-aspirated unit produces.

By absolute standards even the standard Esprit is no mean mover, but turbo power promotes it into an altogether different league where it can confidently tackle the heavyweights of the performance world with no allowances needed for its comparatively small four-cylinder engine, as a test track session against the clock soon revealed.

As usual, we had taken Lotus' own claimed 0–60mph time (in this case 5.55sec) with a large dose of salt, and after a few practice runs to determine the ideal standing start technique we were more than satisfied to achieve 0–60mph in 6 seconds dead and 0–100mph in a shade under 16 seconds. Admittedly the rev-limiter cutting in at 6,700rpm (instead of 7,000) had prevented us reaching 60mph in second gear, but the figures we had achieved were still sufficient to rank the Turbo Esprit convincingly among the upper echelons of superquick supercars. We were happy to call it a day.

Not so Lotus. No sooner did they hear about the over-eager rev-limiter than senior development engineer Roger Becker was hot-footing it across from Norwich to MIRA with a replacement that would allow the engine full rein. By the time he arrived it was late, we were tired and the light was fading – but we tried again.

It was worth it. With the engine now free to spin all the way to 7,000rpm or beyond and bringing 60mph within the compass of second gear, the gear-change saved made all the difference. Sixty came up in 5.6 seconds, 100mph in 15.4, 120 within the half-minute.

They simply don't come much quicker than that. From a standing start the Turbo Esprit will leave a Maserati Merak floundering in its wake, show a clean pair of heels to a Ferrari 308 GTB, and just about hold off the latest Porsche 911SC up to 110mph.

Unfortunately our all-too brief tenure of the car precluded any attempt to verify the maximum of 152mph that Lotus claim to have recorded at Italy's Nardo test track, but our own experiences suggest that such a figure is not unduly optimistic: even along MIRA's short straights we touched 140mph. More importantly, we lapped MIRA's banked circuit for 40 miles or more at speeds of never less than 120mph, often approaching 140mph, and the engine felt content to maintain such speeds all day – as did the driver and passenger.

It's an engine that impresses not just in what it does, but the way it does it. At one extreme it will accept full throttle from 1,000rpm in fourth, or 1,500rpm in fifth; at the other it will soar to 7,000rpm with the power there all the way and absolutely no sense of strain. In honesty the engine cannot be described as quiet, but it does have a remote, muffled quality – free from mechanical thrash and harshness – that renders it inoffensive, and a purposeful, aggressive note that was liked by most of our testers. Moreover, the near-intolerable booms that marred earlier Esprits have all but disappeared.

The achievement of which Lotus can be most proud, however, is its success in not only reaping all the customary benefits of turbocharging – as evidenced by the standing start figures, or the ability in fourth gear to cover each 20mph increment between 40mph and 90mph in 5.5 sec or less – but also in minimizing the technique's traditional bugbears. For a turbo, it has an unusual amount of bottom end torque, reflected in 20–40 and 30–50mph times in fourth of 8.2 and 6.2sec, which are significantly superior to those of turbocharged rivals and can even stand comparison with those of the naturally-aspirated ones. Best of all though, is that in the Esprit the transition to full turbo-boosted potency is so gradual and so progressive that without keeping an eagle eye on the boost gauge it is impossible to specify any particular point at which the turbo 'comes in'. Where the achievement of positive boost in most rivals takes the form of a sudden, dramatic and potentially embarrassing rush of power, the Esprit delivers a sustained, relentless yet gentle surge that starts at below 2,000rpm and

The Rivals

Other possible rivals to the Esprit include the very rare AC 3000 ME (£13,238), the BMW 628 CSi (£16,635), the De Tomaso Pantera (£17,940) and the Porsche 911 SC (£16,732).

LOTUS ESPRIT S3 — £13,461

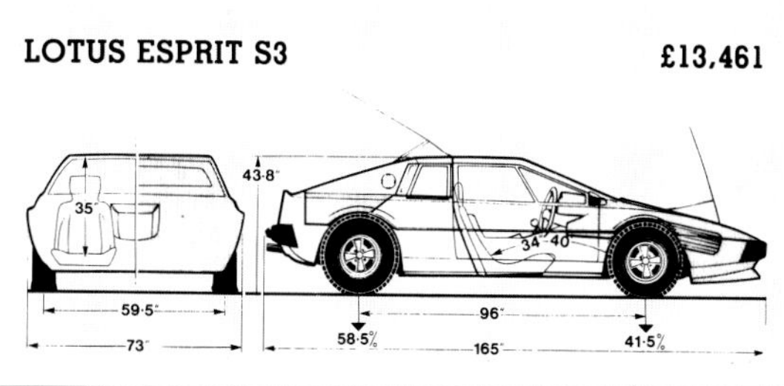

Power, bhp/rpm	160/6,500
Torque, lb ft/rpm	160/5,000
Tyres (F/R)	195/60 VR 15 (f); (optional extra) 235/60 VR 15 (r)
Weight, cwt	21.0
Max speed, mph (estimated)	135
0–60mph, sec	6.5
30–50mph in 4th, sec	6.9
Overall mpg	23.1
Touring mpg	24.5
Fuel grade, stars	4
Boot capacity, cu ft	6.6
Test Date	22 August 1981

A very much improved car in its latest Series 3 form, with outstanding handling and roadholding and a comfortable ride. Excellent performance backed up by impressive economy, safe brakes and a reasonably good gearchange. Greatly reduced noise levels make it much more pleasant to drive, but very poor visibility (worsened by stray reflections on instrument panel and glass division) is an inherent fault. Fair accommodation for two people with soft luggage.

FERRARI 308 GTBi — £21,810

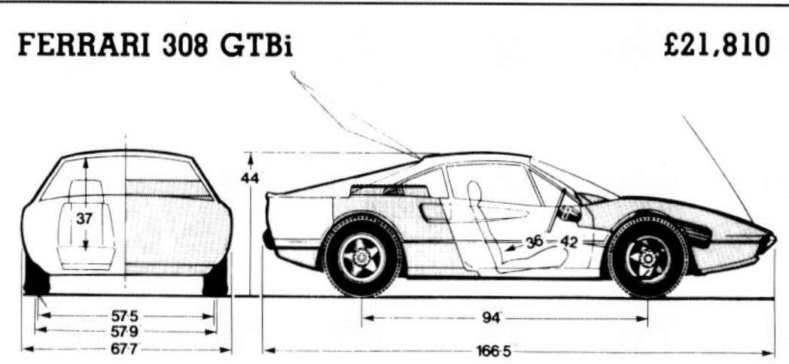

Power, bhp/rpm	255/7,700
Torque, lb ft/rpm	210/5,000
Tyres	205/70 VR 14
Weight, cwt	26.0
Max speed, mph	150*
0–60mph, sec	6.6
30–50mph in 4th, sec	5.5
Overall mpg	13.8†
Touring mpg	—
Fuel grade, stars	4
Boot capacity, cu ft	not measured
Test Date GTS	26 August 1978

**estimate † Twin test*

Arguably the most beautiful of modern supercars, the strictly two-seater mid-engined 308 GTB uses Ferrari's delectable four-cam 3-litre V8. Since our test, this has switched from four Webers to fuel injection, and is apparently no longer as fast as the figures quoted here. It has the roadholding and handling of a true thoroughbred combined with a comfortable ride. Engine noise levels rather high, and fuel consumption heavier than average.

MASERATI MERAK SS — £18,986

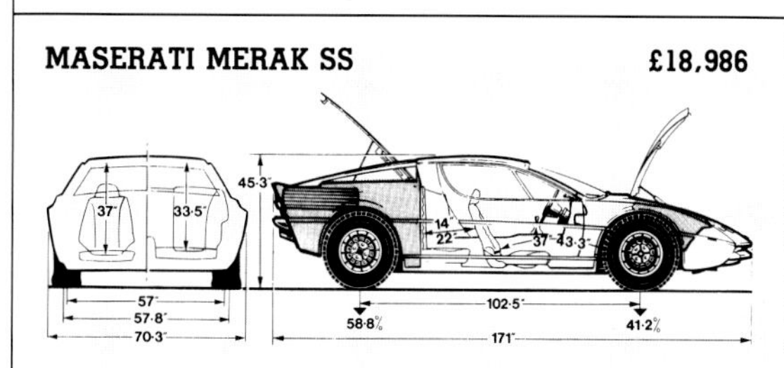

Power, bhp/rpm	220/6,500
Torque, lb ft/rpm	199/4,500
Tyres (F/R)	195/70 VR 15/ 215/70 VR 15
Weight, cwt	27.0
Max speed, mph	154*
0–60mph, sec	7.8
30–50mph in 4th, sec	7.2
Overall mpg	13.3
Touring mpg	—
Fuel grade, stars	4
Boot capacity, cu ft	6.6
Test Date	24 September 1977

**Manufacturer's Figure*

V6-engined Italian supercar with (very) occasional rear seats. Excellent performance (particularly at high speed) but overall consumption is high; at steady speeds it is reasonable. Excellent handling and adhesion, but the ride is rather harsh. Reasonably good gearbox, but the clutch is heavy. Noise suppression good, ventilation and trim finish poor. More leg room than in most Italian cars, and fair luggage space.

PORSCHE 924 TURBO — £13,998

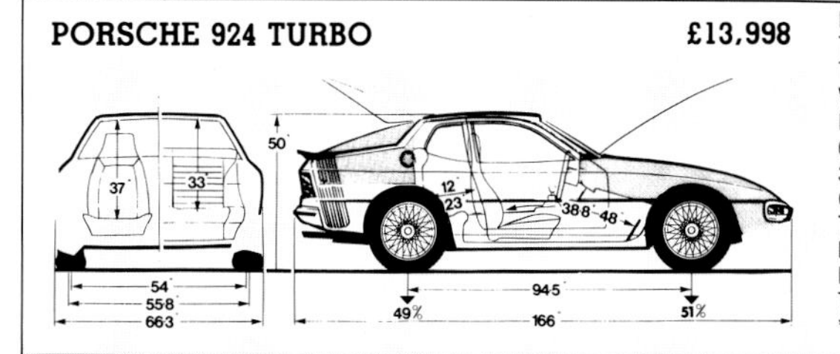

Power, bhp/rpm	170/5,500
Torque, lb ft/rpm	181/3,500
Tyres	185/70 VR 15
Weight, cwt	23.7
Max speed, mph	140†
0–60mph, sec	7.0
30–50mph in 4th, sec	8.8
Overall mpg	21.0
Touring mpg	—
Fuel grade, stars	4
Boot capacity, cu ft	4.8
Test Date	26 January 1980

**Estimated*

Turbocharged version of Porsche's 2-litre, four-cylinder, front-engined but rear wheel drive 924. Performance when the turbocharger is on boost is in supercar class, but is poor at low speeds and revs. Considering performance available, fuel consumption exceptional. 1981 models claimed to be even better. Too much road noise and poor ventilation, low-speed handling and gearchange are minor flaws in an otherwise superb machine.

AUDI QUATTRO — £14,500

Power, bhp/rpm	200/5,500
Torque, lb ft/rpm	210/3,500
Tyres	205/60 VR 15
Weight, cwt	24.8
Max speed, mph	138*
0–60mph, sec	6.5
30–50mph in 4th, sec	8.2
Overall mpg	19.9
Touring mpg	—
Fuel grade, stars	4
Boot capacity, cu ft	7.6
Test Date	21 March 1981

Whether or not its unique format – ultra-high performance and 4-wheel-drive – starts a new trend, the Audi must be considered a milestone in car design simply because it is stunningly good. It combines phenomenal handling and roadholding with performance, refinement, economy, comfort and accommodation in a way that has no equal, against which its weaknesses (poor ratios, unprogressive heating, sparse instrumentation) are minor.

TVR TASMIN — £13,824

Power, bhp/rpm	160/5,700
Torque, lb ft/rpm	162/4,300
Tyres	205/60 VR 14
Weight, cwt	21.5
Max speed, mph	128*
0–60mph, sec	7.8
30–50mph in 4th, sec	8.9
Overall mpg	22.4
Touring mpg	—
Fuel grade, stars	4
Boot capacity, cu ft	3.5
Test Date	18 April 1981

**Estimated*

Plugging the gap between ordinary and exotic sports cars, TVR's latest is all that a real sports car should be, with strong performance and roadholding, powerful brakes, comfortable interior for two and satisfying transmission. Plush finish, good ventilation and respectable ride are evidence of TVR's increasing maturity. Weak points include too much steering kickback, excessive hood-up wind noise, finicky instruments, small boot. Quoted figures are from less expensive convertible version.

continues unabated to the 7,000rpm rev limit. For sheer all-round driveability, this turbo sets new standards.

Considering the shorter-than-usual test mileage of which performance testing consequently represents a greater-than-usual proportion, our overall fuel consumption of 18.5mpg is a creditable result for a car of this performance, though it's bettered among our chosen rivals by both the Porsche models. In conjunction with the Esprit's twin-filler 19-gallon fuel tank this should allow it a useful range of at least 350 miles on each filling of 4-star.

Apart from a larger-diameter clutch and bigger bellhousing to accommodate it, the Esprit's Citröen SM-derived gearbox is unchanged, providing a fine set of closely stacked ratios that keep the acceleration flowing beautifully. The effective gearing is slightly raised, though, by the Turbo's larger wheels and tyres, to give 22.7mph/1,000rpm in fifth and 41, 62, 92 and 125mph at 7,000rpm in the lower gears. As before, the gearchange is conventionally arranged (fifth on a dog-leg to the right and forward) and is extremely positive, with short throws and strong spring-biasing towards the 3rd/4th plane. But although fairly quick, our Turbo's shift quality was not as featherlight as in other Esprits we've driven, some testers commenting on some stiffness in the lever movements. Certainly you need to use the full travel of the clutch to do the gearchange justice, and the clutch itself was criticised for its somewhat woolly and indeterminate – albeit progressive – point of engagement.

No such criticisms can be levelled against the steering. True, the effort is quite high at parking speeds and the front tyres tend to scrub across the surface during low speed manoeuvres, but on the move the mechanism is sharp, direct and amply endowed with feel. It displays the kind of precision that faithfully translates the slightest movements of the wheel – needing no more than a slight flexing of your wrists – into just the desired change of direction, yet without being responsive to the point of twitchiness.

So it is too with the behaviour of the chassis, which combines finesse and a sense of balance with a poised forgiving nature in a way that makes the Esprit one of the easiest of supercars to drive at its limits; even though those limits are prodigiously high.

The basic characteristic is just sufficient understeer to inspire confidence and ensure predictability, backed by just the right amount of lift-off tuck-in to let you tighten the car's line without unsettling its composure at the rear. Indeed, so forgiving is it that even by braking hard and deep into a bend you are unlikely to unleash a full-blooded tailslide. If the bend is tight enough and the gear is low enough, you can use the throttle positively, to influence the car's attitude, balance out the understeer or even, ultimately, to power the tail out into a gentle and easily held tail slide, confident that it is still you, and not the car, that remains in charge.

And if you need to slow down or stop in a hurry, the Lotus still won't betray your confidence in it. The brakes are quite simply superb, combining stability with tremendous stopping power, and progressive responses to a nicely weighted pedal action.

As a driving machine, then, the Turbo Esprit is a masterly effort by the Lotus development team, but it is only when you pause to consider the car's ride that you appreciate the full measure of their achievement. For a sporting car that handles this well, the ride is astonishingly good. It's firm at town speeds but by no means uncomfortably so, and once you get moving on the open road it displays a level of suppleness, firmly controlled by perfect damping over humps and undulations, that could hardly be matched by the most comfortably sprung of luxury limousines.

Equally worthy of a limousine is the

sumptuous treatment of the interior, featuring extensive use of Connolly hide trim, with deep pile carpeting and cloth headlining taking over where the leather leaves off at floor and roof level respectively. To the naked eye the standard of assembly is immaculate, though the smell of resin is offensive to sensitive noses.

The cockpit layout is as before, apart from some detail changes. The instruments – generous in number and crisply labelled, but still prey to stray reflections – have been cunningly repositioned to make space for a boost gauge. At the same time, they remain unobscured either by the wheel or the driver's hands.

The seats have been reshaped with some success, and drivers up to about 6ft in height found the low-slung seating position comfortable despite the lack of backrest recline adjustment. But our tallest tester (6ft 3in) was desperately uncomfortable, complaining of poor legroom, totally inadequate headroom and bodily contact between the facia and his knee when changing gear.

Drivers of all *shapes and sizes were critical of the layout of the pedals, which are just too close together, so that unless you drive shoeless or have unusually small feet there is a risk of catching on the throttle when braking, or on the brake when declutching. The wheel and gear lever fall easily to hand, however, as do the column stalks, and the minor switches and heating/ventilation controls, which are now all back-lit at night.*

The latter are now positioned conveniently on the centre console. February temperatures provided little opportunity to test out the air conditioning which is fitted as standard, but soon revealed that while the heater is undeniably powerful it is also hopelessly difficult to control, with no apparent progression between 'Hot' and 'Cold'. The consequent stuffiness is aggravated by the meagre trickle of air provided through the central fresh air vents when the heater is in use. Ironically, a much better throughput is provided by the side window demister vents, but these cannot be directed towards the occupants' faces.

As already discussed, the level of engine noise in the Esprit is acceptable for the type of car, and a fair bit of road noise is probably inevitable; but it's a shame that Lotus have been unable to suppress wind noise, which is the dominant noise source at the sort of cruising pace that would otherwise be encouraged by the Esprit's mechanical effortlessness and outstanding directional stability at three-figure velocities. Under the category of noise must also fall the number of creaks and rattles that accompany progress on bumpy roads, though the basic structure feels admirably strong and rigid.

There is one other long-standing Esprit failing that remains uncorrected in the Turbo. Despite two excellent electrically-adjustable door mirrors, it is an exceptionally difficult car to see out of, due to the combined effects of a low seating position, heavy front and rear pillars, the louvred tailgate, and sundry reflections off the screen at night. And in tight spaces the problem is aggravated by the sheer width of the car, and the way the nose drops right out of the sight of any driver of less than average height. In the face of such problems, the effectiveness of the wipers and the power of the headlamps provides little compensation.

UPRATED BODY AND CHASSIS

The single most important – and long-lived – component in the Esprit Turbo was not the engine, but the galvanized steel chassis. As explained for the S3, the five-year warranted backbone was credited with a 50 per cent boost in torsional stiffness via replacement (and wider span) frontal box section and the re-jigged rear-end cradle. Front and rear

*Roger Moore in his second Bond epic (*For Your Eyes Only*), starring the Esprit as well as himself. Although complete in non-Essex Turbo livery this factory machine retained Compomotive wheels for its explosive role.*

For Your Eyes Only

The second Bond movie to use an Esprit was the early eighties epic, *For Your Eyes Only*. The star was Roger Moore once again and the venues were Corfu and Cortina D'Ampezzo rather than the underwater world.

A pair of Esprit Turbos were prepared: OPW 654W and OPW 678W. The lower number had seen limited service as a road test vehicle (Doug Nye, *Sporting Cars*, June 1982) whilst the higher digits did service both as a white car in Corfu and a bronze 'hero' machine in Cortina.

In theory, OPW 654W was the victim of a characteristic Bond explosion – in fact they built a car as close to reality as possible and then destroyed it.

Presumably, companies other than Lotus have bid for the right to place their product in subsequent Bond epics, for the Esprit has been replaced by all sorts of machinery in later adventures.

track increases were 1in and 0.7in (25 and 18mm) respectively.

Also worth noting was the presence of a 'full-width increased capacity radiator and oil cooler' across the front of the chassis and comprehensive suspension changes. At the back, there were 'new double unequal length non-parallel transverse links with radius arms', while, 'plunging driveshafts are used with new aluminium hub carriers' all this in Lotus's words.

Also shared with the S3 was the deletion of the old Opel Ascona wishbones at the front in favour of a common Lotus (Elite) suspension system. That system worked on the unequal-length wishbone principles and carried a slightly smaller anti-roll bar than the S2 specified. Shock absorbers were by Armstrong, Lotus dismissing gas damping at this stage in Esprit turbo development.

BIGGER BRAKES, WHEELS AND TYRES

Bigger does not usually mean better to Lotus engineers brought up in the original Chapman weight-saving religion, but the Esprit's 31 per cent growth in power demanded some constraint in other departments.

Most obvious were the three-piece alloy Compomotive alloy wheels of 15in diameter and 7in front rim width versus 8in breadth aft. These wheels did not make much more than initial production, for the S3 and the Esprit Turbo grew to share a BBS cast alloy of the same dimensions. The car was developed using Pirelli P6 as a benchmark, but Lotus's co-operation with Goodyear allowed a unique NCT-branded cover – one whose VR-rated characteristics were said (by Lotus) to draw 'heavily from Goodyear experience in producing successful Formula 1 rain tyres.'

Lotus engineering antipathy to the adoption of ventilated disc brakes (and their frequent service vibration problems) led them into specifying solid discs of the same increased dimensions as those of the Esprit S3. That meant less than an inch gain over the S2 to a total 10.5in (250mm) and the usual 10.8in (270mm) inboard rear discs. Both master cylinder vacuum servo assistance wore enlarged components.

The Esprit was not raced very often in British production form, but when it was tried in the early eighties (using the standard of Rouse preparation that yielded four British national titles for proprietor Andy Rouse in saloon car events), the weak point was found to be the brakes. This deficiency was particularly traced to overheating of the inboard rear units, so they did have distinct limits . . .

AERODYNAMIC STYLE

'Giorgetto' Giugiaro re-enlisted as the interior and exterior designer on the blown Esprit, but functional aerodynamics had some inevitable effects upon the exterior. The prime decisions to consider concerned cutting high-speed lift, and ensuring that the engine bay was well ventilated. The latter point was vital, since the bay had to cope with 200°F (90°C) and more of surplus heat shed by the turbo-charged engine – a unit for which exhaust temperatures beyond 950°F (510°C) were possible under sustained full boost.

The most extrovert moves were the full-width front spoiler, balanced by an imposing rear air dam that curved around the three-quarter rear panels to meet the side extensions of the rear bumper. The aerodynamic drag factor was variously quoted between 0.35 and 0.37, significantly up on earlier Esprits with less elaborate bodywork. That, however, was not the driving and durability point.

Those front and rear spoilers, assisted by a vestigial lip above the rear window, cut lift at 100mph (160kph) and beyond by more than half and put the Esprit into a state of high speed balance that is rarely achieved by showroom cars. Even Lotus publicity material misquoted the advances that had been made, so it is worth stating that front-end lift was slashed from 58 to 28lb (26 to 13kg), whilst the back benefited from a similar percentage reduction, descending from 63 to 26lb (28.5 to 12kg).

There was plenty of other aerodynamic work to appreciate in 1980. For a start, the car's underbody had been attended to, a logical step in view of Team Lotus's work on ground effects and subsequent flat-bottom vehicles. The front spoiler under-section was boxed in and a tray under the engine compartment allowed the continuance of the flat underbody characteristics for much of the under-body area.

So successful was this production flat-bottom manoeuvre in reducing turbulence beneath the Esprit Turbo that NACA air scoops had to be let into the extended and concave 'side skirts' to collect engine-bay air. This air was then deflected upward by a collector 'door' in the engine under-tray, in line with the beginning of the rear wheel-arches. Such airflow was directed up past the engine (relying on convection at rest) and exhausted through vents in the engine-bay cover and the rear window slats.

The overall efficiency of suspension, giant Goodyear tyres and conscientious aerodynamics could be appreciated in a steady-state cornering prowess of just over 1G for the Turbo, versus 0.9G for an Esprit S2.

Roofed Stereo and Others

The replacement Giugiaro interior was further influenced by the personal foibles of Essex Petroleum's David Thieme. He specified the flashy complexity (and £1,000-plus cost within the overall price) of a Panasonic IC Hi-Fi Stereo system that was mounted in the roof and played via a quartet of standard speakers.

More conventional interior revamps extended to a central boost gauge and 170mph (270kph) speedometer, both now lit in green. Air conditioning was standard, the controls had moved to the centre console and its switches illuminated whenever the Esprit lights were on. Seating came in for some fundamental alterations with yet more foam foundations and replacement head rests, but it was for the showroom appeal of thin leathers stitched with ruche abandon that the Esprit begun to reinforce the 'Medallion Man' reputation that was so evident on the gaudy Essex exterior.

EXPENSIVE START, FOLLOWED BY BETTER VALUE

At launch time, the Essex Commemorative Lotus Esprit Turbo was a £20,950 compilation of the features described. Then, the 2.2 Esprit was still in its brief model span and cost £14,951, but neither turbo-charged nor normally-aspirated models did much business in the 1980 launch year.

Lotus met 60 advance orders for the Turbo with a production figure of 57 units and the S2/S2.2 sold a combined 80 units, making it the second worst production year on record for the Esprit, the lowest being the 134 made in the first (1976) twelve months.

Lotus did not ignore the commercial lessons of 1980. On 15 April 1981, the company were free to promote a 'bargain basement' turbo, which dived triumphantly beneath the £17,000 barrier. To achieve such a comparatively low cost, the standard fancy stereo, air conditioning and standard leather were placed on the option list. If you were cynical enough to add such items to the £16,982.23 Turbo tag, the 1981 model, *sans* Essex livery after the initial 100 run, was priced at a total £18,840. A figure which was still a bargain for a 150mph (240kph) mid-engine machine in 1981.

Immediately, sales rose and production

more than doubled in 1981. Former Lotus sales director (later recruited by Jaguar) Roger Putnam smiled happily and reported:

For the first time in two years we have a monthly increase in production . . . That elusive glimmer of light at the end of the tunnel has stopped flickering and is becoming brighter here at Lotus.

Brave words in the redundancy and recession stricken period of the early eighties, but it was fair to say that the Esprit did sell at much higher volumes through the decade, and much of the improvement came from the original turbo and its sharp-edged derivatives.

Naturally prices increased, reaching £24,980 in October 1986, but Lotus did recognize that the public would not sustain the initial stance of pricing the Essex-limited edition *beyond* the Porsche 911. It is only on the more recent Turbo derivatives that the Esprit Turbo SE has escalated to within a £1,000 of Porsche 911 starting prices.

RUNNING CHANGES

The most obvious running change was the transition from Essex livery to 'Lotus Turbo Esprit' general availability, formally released to the press in April 1981. Even though the Esprit S3 wore BBS Mahle cast-alloy wheels for the shiny brochure presentation, its red-and-gold turbo-charged counterpart remained on the Compomotives.

However, the split-rim wheels which proved unsatisfactory in service were replaced by the BBS Mahle one-piece cast alloys during the summer of 1981, so it is worth keeping a razor eye open for this aspect when buying second-hand.

Another thing to check in the same period (March–September 1981) is whether dry- or wet-sump lubrication is installed – the dry-sump system being served by a separate external oil tank and dip-stick. On the transmission side, the Citröen gearbox remained, its ratios only modified in as much that bigger wheels and tyres altered the mph per 1,000rpm figure marginally. The figures now stood at 22.7mph (36.5kph) instead of 21.85mph (35.15kph) per 1,000rpm of the first Esprit.

However, the gearchange quality was better, thanks to a two-section linkage along the right-hand side of the S3 or turbo motor, compared to the three-section which went to make up the linkage along the left side of the S1, 2 and 2.2 Esprits.

For 1984 the Esprits, including the Turbo, gained the option of a 'Lotus-designed, tinted glass, two-tilt, removable sun-roof'. The option price was £335 and the option list was still quite extensive. Items like leather trim (£820) and air conditioning (£740) added to a basic cost of £19,980 in that model year. The S3 was £3,995 less in April 1984.

Both inside and outside the company, I have heard that Esprits – and all other Lotus models in production at the time – benefited from the Toyota influence and shareholding (Toyota holding 16.5 per cent of Lotus in December 1984). In the case of the Esprit, the tangible benefit in 1985 was a better front-end suspension layout, which finally dispensed with some Triumph components that had clung on when the Opel Ascona early front-suspension layout was dismissed.

Specifications

By October 1985, the Esprit S3 was retailing from £17,980 and the Turbo was now priced at £23,440. Specifications were not significantly changed at this point, although there had been an opportunity to update the S3. (The Excel SE was announced at this point, bearing 180bhp and 165lb ft of torque in place of a standard Excel/Esprit S3 160bhp and 160lb ft.)

If you are interested in how extra power was achieved upon the Excel SE, the answer

In 1984 Lotus offered this tilt/detachable glass sunshine roof as an extra option, at additional cost.

was principally in raising the compression (10.9:1 on the SE) on replacement forged-alloy pistons. These operated in association with revised inlet camshaft profiles (increased lift and duration), plus enlarged cross-section to intake porting. Both valve sizes and exhaust camshafts were left untouched, but diameters of the inlet valve throats were increased.

Incidentally, the stiffer die-cast camshaft housings of the Turbo were transferred to the normally-aspirated SE motor. It is also worth noting that the 1976–1987 non-Turbo Esprits were never offered with the 180bhp SE specification, which may tempt the ingenious to do what the factory never found the need to complete and convert their Esprit S3 to 180bhp specification. Because of exhaust restrictions, peak power will be less than on the Excel.

MORE TURBO POWER

The high-compression route for the normally-aspirated SE was a hint of how the final turbo models ran out of production, prior to the October 1987 adoption of a completely new and much more rounded outline for the Esprit.

The Esprit turbo HC (High Compression) appeared at the October 1987 Motor Show in London. That occasion was also used to unveil another limited edition, based on HC running gear, that was intended to celebrate twenty years of Lotus in Norfolk and up the price per Esprit.

Sharing the limited Earls Court stand space in the autumn of 1986 were two versions of the HC, both offering 215bhp at an unchanged 6,250rpm (a 2.5 per cent bonus in

Side sill extensions, NACA air inlet ducts and 1984–1985 badging are clearly displayed.

(Right) You can see why the factory do not issue pictures of the Esprit with headlamps raised, but the full frontal view of the turbocharged Esprit remains daunting.

(Left) White was the colour-coded theme of the mid-eighties and this privately owned Esprit Turbo shows that even an individual choice such as the Esprit may be further tailored to customer choice. Note the factory sunroof.

power). Torque (the power to pull you through mid-range blues) was more urgently tweaked: 220lb ft at 4,250rpm representing a 10 per cent elevation, and a 250rpm drop in peak torque engine revs.

Also on that 1986 stand were an automatic transmission Excel SA, Excel SE (180bhp), Esprit S3 and John Player Special 98T Grand Prix car. The 160bhp Lotus Excel was omitted due to lack of space. It did, however continue in production – a machine vastly underrated both by its makers and the sporting public.

Under the skin of the earlier Lotus turbo Esprit in left-hand-drive trim, we can absorb details such as the twin-tone horns and laid back front radiator as well as the advanced chassis that served the Esprit into the nineties.

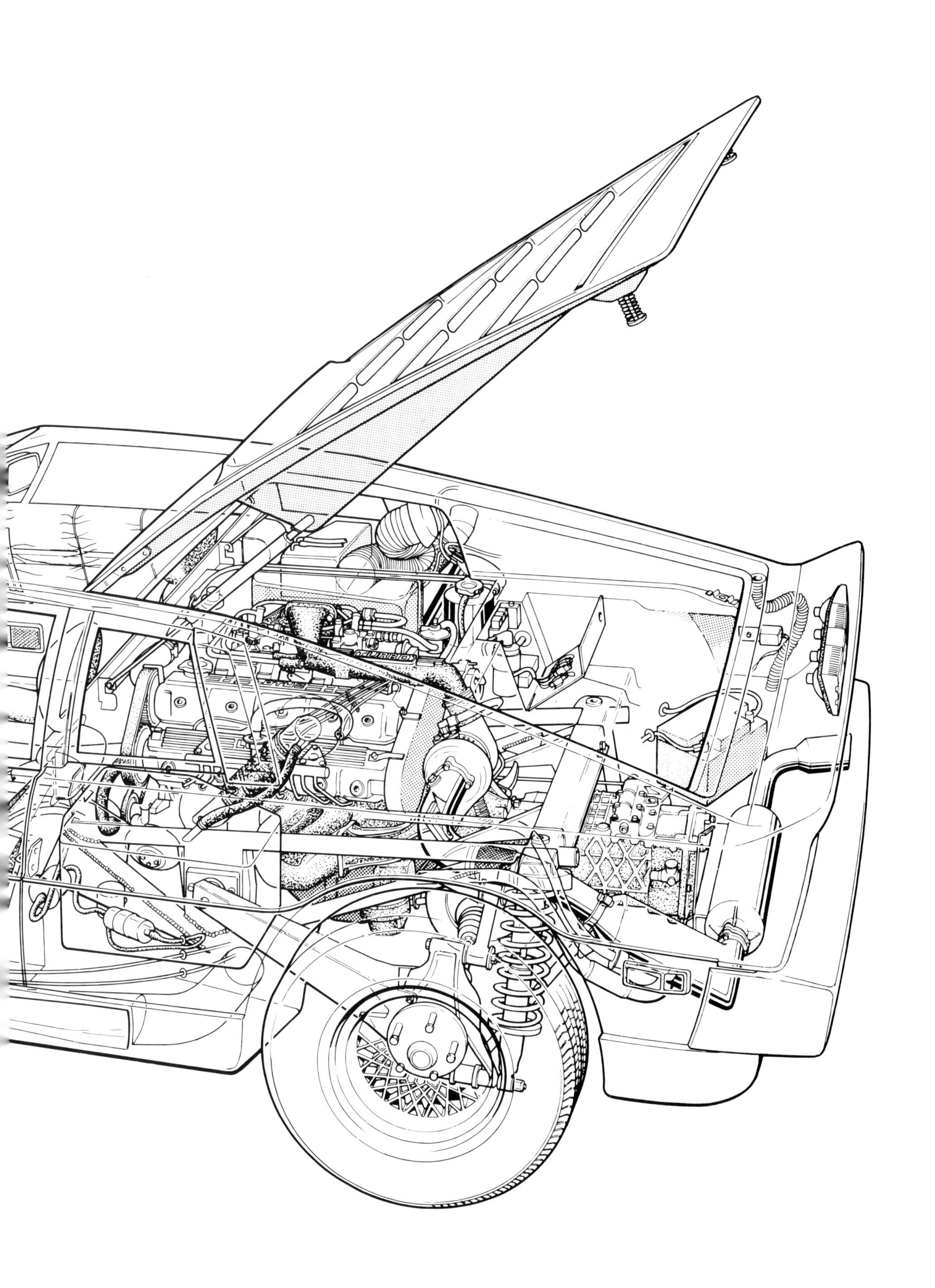
TURBO

The clarity of Giugiaro's styling vision is emphasized by this 'white-out' of Esprit Turbo lines . . .

. . . in private ownership.

The engine bay became a little more cluttered with the addition of a Garret AiResearch turbocharger, but a gain of 50bhp was more than adequate compensation for Esprit Turbo customers.

The extended front spoiler left the Goodyear tyres partially exposed.

Performance

Just how quickly the Turbo accelerated, and its genuine ability to exceed 150mph (240kph), was the subject of many motoring magazine articles, but an independently-timed UK test of the 1980–1987 Esprit turbo that had verified the 150-plus Lotus figure is a rare bird.

Compare the performance tables (what Lotus claimed and a sample of magazine test results on the popular 0–60mph (0–100kph), overall mpg, and maximum speed runs).

Also note the results of contemporary *Motor* road test and register that the acceleration runs were recorded after a test track visitation from Roger Becker, when testing was delayed sufficiently to make a top-speed run impossible.

Lotus Turbo Esprit HC: Statistics

4 cylinders in-line, inclined 45deg to left.

Capacity 2,174cc
Bore 95.25mm
Stroke 76.20mm
Compression ratio 8:1
Fuel requirement Min. 98 RON unleaded
Fuel intake Twin Dell'Orto DHLA 45M carburettors with balance pipe.
Turbocharger Garrett T3 turbocharger with downsize casing and increased boost.
Max. boost 9.5psi instead of 8psi
Lubrication Wet sump
Performance 215bhp at 6,000rpm; 220lb ft at 4,250rpm.
Cooling Higher fin density and increased air flow for oil and water radiators. Extra engine bay air-intake. Higher capacity water pump.
Electrical Mechanical overboost dump valve (exhausting straight into the silencer) replaced by electrical overboost switch that responds to excess boost by cutting ignition.

Engine Boost

To make an Esprit HC yield another 5bhp and an additional 20lb of torque, Lotus had utilized some Excel SE engine techniques. Compression could not escalate beyond 10:1 with a turbocharger huffing in its four-valve-per-cylinder ears, but 8:1 was then reasonably advanced, especially given that this was not an electronically-managed fuel injection engine. In fact, Lotus increased the size of the carburettors (specifying Dell'Orto DHLA 45M), specified a balance pipe and ensured that the intake tracts were modelled on those of the Excel SE.

Mahle-forged pistons brought the increase in ratio from 7.5:1 to 8:1; Nikasil process for the liners was specified once more. Lotus rather reluctantly joined the European low-lead petrol age stating: 'The new Lotus turbo engine can be safely operated on unleaded fuel (minimum 95 RON). We recommend 4 star (98 RON) for maximum engine durability.' In other words, 'don't call us if it pinks a piston to death . . . '

Other fundamental changes to the engine at this point included new cast-iron manifold castings 'to improve gas flow' and a replacement casing for the Garrett AiResearch T3 turbocharger. Lotus also allowed the boost to increase from 8psi to 9.5psi, which was approaching boldness, given the increase in the compression ratio.

Full performance results, according to Lotus, are given below, but can be summarized as offering a lot more mid-range acceleration (plus 20 per cent, said Lotus). Maximum speed was unaffected; fuel consumption was improved at constant speeds, and acceleration was just fractionally better than the already sensationally rapid 0–60mph (0–100kph) time of 5.5 seconds achieved by the 210bhp turbocharger.

Interior improvements on all Esprits now included adjustable rake for the seat backs (it only took a decade . . .) and you could release the rear 'hatch' from within via remote control.

Lotus mph and mpg figures: Turbo/HC

Mph	(kph)	1980–1986 Seconds	1986–1987 Seconds
0–30	(0–50)	2.05	
0–40	(0–65)	2.85	
0–50	(0–80)	4.20	
0–60	(0–100)	5.55	5.35
0–70	(0–110)	7.35	
0–80	(0–130)	9.25	
0–90	(0–145)	11.85	
0–100	(0–160)	14.65	

Standing ¼-mile: 14.4 seconds at @ 98mph

FIFTH GEAR ACCELERATION

Mph	(kph)	1980–1986 Seconds	1986–1987 Seconds
50–70	(80–110)	8.0	6.35
70–90	(110–145)	8.4	6.5

GEAR SPEEDS (at 7,000rpm)

First	41.2mph (66.3kph)	
Second	62mph (100kph)	
Third	91.1mph (146.6kph)	
Fourth	123.5mph (198.7kph)	
Fifth/OD	152.0mph (244.6kph)	152.0mph (244.6kph)

FUEL CONSUMPTION

	1980–1986	1986–1987
Urban	15.7	15.7
56mph	28.4	35.6
75mph	24.1	28.8

Press Extracts . . .

Motor March 1981
0–60mph: 5.6 seconds
Test mpg: 18.7
'We touched 140mph'

What Car? July 1982
0–60mph: 5.8 seconds
Test mpg: 17.8 to 22.1
Lotus 152mph max. speed quote

Motor Trend USA, November 1983/July 1984
0–60mph: 6.11 seconds
Test mpg: 14 (City)
'One good flying lap . . . recorded 152.0mph,' then suffered piston crown/plug electrode failure during 1984 session.

Car & Driver USA, November 1983
0–60mph: 6.4 seconds
Test mpg: 14
Maximum: 141mph

Road & Track USA, December 1983
0–60mph: 6.6 seconds
Test mpg: 17.5 US mpg
Reported 148mph at @ 6,550rpm

Autocar, November 1985
0–60mph: 6.1 seconds
Test mpg: 17.6
138mph at @ 6,100rpm, but 'pop-up headlamps raised.'

Motor, July 1986
0–60mph: 5.6 seconds
Test mpg: 21.3
Maximum: 140.9mph

ANOTHER ANNIVERSARY

The 1986 High Compression unit was accompanied by a 1966–1987 celebration of twenty-one years in Norfolk. (Yes, it did say twenty years on other publicity material; that is Lotus!) The customer paid £31,000 and received the standard cabin comforts that were optional, or not available, on the less expensive Esprits Turbos. Air conditioning, Connolly leather hide; suedette rim steering-wheel (still two-spoke); removable glass sun-roof; six-speaker Clarion E980 stereo and three-piece* 'Designer luggage set' hinted that Lotus had seriously begun to set their kit-car days aside.

Only three colours were offered: red, metallic blue or metallic grey. No maximum production number is specified in the Lotus material, but the following was promised:

* The colour pictures firmly showed *five*-piece luggage set in red-edged fawn, posed outside the main entrance doors.

Factory fresh: 1986 Esprit Turbo interior in the optional full leather suit.

This superb chassis study of the 1986 Esprit Turbo was – as for so many other Hethel illustrations – the work of local concern Focalpoint.

Each vehicle built will carry a signed and numbered certificate of authenticity and will also be individually sign written and carry its appropriate identity number, denoting its exclusivity, both on the exterior and on a specially commissioned engraved silver plaque mounted on the leather dashboard.

Yes, lack of punctuation and all, that is exactly how Lotus promoted a very expensive Esprit in 1987.

THE FEDERAL FUTURE

For Americans and, subsequently, in a radically uprated engines engineering package for Europeans, the switch to fuel injection brought benefits far beyond improved emission control, as well as superior economy. But first, the company rebels had put together another Esprit body that reflected the spirit of the nineties and produced another leap in quality that made the car almost unrecognizable in comparison to the original.

6 A New Suit for the Esprit

'The Esprit has become the *supercar bargain.'*
Motor, 1988

The first major alterations to the Giugiaro/ Chapman Esprit outline did not occur until October 1987, when approximately 4,700 of the original Esprits had been manufactured*. After that twelve-year span, the revamp was carried out with a management instruction to 'remain faithful to within an inch to the original dimensions'. Yet, the result was a *very* different product, and one from a very different Lotus car company.

The vital overhaul of body lines was to dispense with the 'Medallion Man' paper-dart image of sharply creased edges. The deletion of the central raised seam (marking the point at which the two body halves marry) was accompanied by equally important running changes.

Before we discuss the background to this evolutionary Esprit, however, it is worth knowing that the October 1987 Esprit was available at less than £30,000 in both turbocharged and normally-aspirated trim (215 and 172bhp).

Whilst the 16-valve 2.2-litre Lotus engine remained as in the preceding Esprit, significant mechanical changes were implemented. These included the adoption of a Renault 25-based transaxle and clutch; outboard placement of the rear disc brakes and a replacement wiring harness that accompanied a total rethink of the previously rather 'fussy' instrument and control binnacle.

*Mike Kimberley told the author in 1988 that production of the old model actually ceased on Friday 31 July 1987.

EXTERNAL RE-DESIGN

The Esprit revamp was almost an underground activity. It was carried out over a period of months rather than years by Lotus loyalists Colin Spooner, Peter Stevens and Ken Sears. It should be noted, however, that Peter Stevens was usually employed by Lotus as a freelance consultant.

Spooner, Stevens and Sears used the local facilities of the company's modelling shop at Dereham and design director Colin Spooner told me in 1990: 'We were delighted with the results, but with so few of us on the project, it was a job to cope with all the business of production needs.'

The successful 'off-site' creation of what was effectively a new Esprit – Lotus only claimed it was a 'stepping stone' evolution – should remind us that Lotus were now a very different company to the one that had produced the 1975 Esprit. Colin Chapman's death in 1982 had obviously rocked the company to the core, but the founder's preoccupations in later years had returned to the race track and the separately funded and structured Team Lotus. The team working under Michael Kimberley at Lotus Cars had therefore become used to a degree of autonomy that most certainly did not exist when Chapman and Giugiaro were creating the original Esprit – or when Chapman was busy poking around the prototype Esprit suspension and demanding to know why extra parts had been added against the Lotus creed of 'Lightness is next to Godliness'.

Peter Stevens (1943–)

A founder member of the west London based Royal College of Art (RCA) degree course on automotive design, the black moustache and perkily intelligent features of Peter Stevens are familiar throughout a spectrum of motoring.

Peter's personal enthusiasm has taken him into weekend voluntary jobs assisting World Championship racing teams and on to regular attendance at international Motor Shows.

His design portfolio is enormously varied. Best known for his work on overhauling Lotus bodies in the eighties and nineties (Eclat into Excel, then the post-1987 Esprit) his Hethel monument will probably always be the new Elan. In that period, he was a full-time employee at Lotus and left to work as studio chief on the design of the nineties McLaren supercar, just as the Elan was reaching production maturity.

During a busy design career, Peter Stevens also worked on such diverse projects as ERF commercial vehicle cab and exteriors (nine years); what became the Jaguar XJR-15, and many other Tom Walkinshaw Racing (TWR) competition and performance projects. These included the sporting style of some subsequent Jaguar Sport machines (particularly XJR-15) and most of the aerodynamic Mazda body components on sale in the late eighties. At McLaren in late 1990, Peter Stevens commented:

I also worked with Trevor Fiore on the Alpine 5 (Renault 5 GT Turbo in UK), plus the pretty A310 coupe. My first association with Gordon Murray was as a consultant at Brabham. I worked on all the Parmalat Brabham-Alfa Romeos through to the 'lay down' Brabham-BMW, responsible for all the graphics and team identity.

It is good to be back working with Gordon Murray again, but I certainly will not forget Lotus; it was a very important period in my working life.

Thus concluded one of Britain's most influential designers and a key figure in extending the commercial life of the Esprit.

THE GM EFFECT

The Lotus company of 1987 had evolved under approximately one year of GM ownership into an outwardly far more confident organization. Michael Kimberley continued to head up the main Lotus Group, the umbrella organization to Lotus Cars, Lotus Engineering and the American Lotus Cars Inc. operation. The latter was most recently captained by ex-Porsche North American boss, Ronald T Foster.

Our old friend and Esprit *raconteur* Tony Rudd was now chairman for Lotus Engineering, with former Motor Industry Research director Cedric Ashley as his managing director. I say that the company was 'outwardly far more confident', because this was the carefully fostered image of stability now being presented. That image went alongside the widely-quoted figure of £55m invested by General Motors in Lotus over a five-year plan (which included £20 million for Lotus Engineering).

Within Lotus there was, and remains, a lot more dissension over 'The GM effect'. Most dissatisfaction emanates from the creative departments – creativity being, after all, what makes up much of Lotus's reputation. Others, but by no means all, feel that 'all these big company paperwork and reporting systems are stifling that quick creative spark that is Lotus. If that goes, you really have to ask yourself, what remains?'

In 1988, in an interview that reflected on the successful launch of the new Esprit, Mike Kimberley said:

The 'soft' look for the Esprit arrived in 1987 and has boosted the life of the turbocharged models into the nineties.

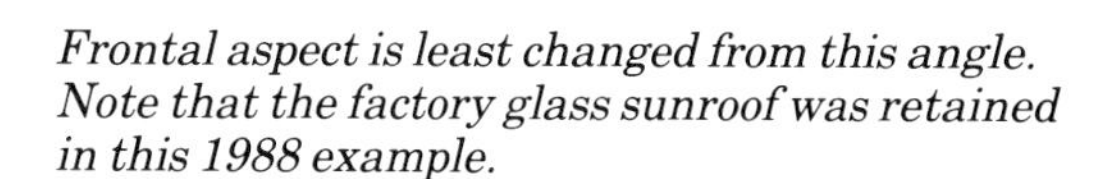

Frontal aspect is least changed from this angle. Note that the factory glass sunroof was retained in this 1988 example.

Given the 'jellymould' treatment typical of the eighties' concern with aerodynamics, the Esprit displayed an exceptionally uncluttered profile. Note the post-1987 alloy wheels from Lotus and Speedline.

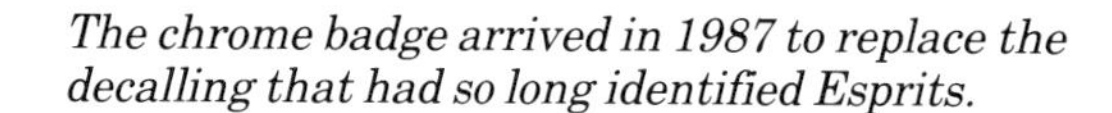

The chrome badge arrived in 1987 to replace the decalling that had so long identified Esprits.

Spot the difference? This factory press picture of an 'Esprit' plated example is the rare, normally-aspirated variant, which is principally identified by the lack of a rear glass shield between the flying buttress panels.

The commodity we most value at Lotus is our employees, particularly the engineers. As a breed, they are not easy to recruit, but we currently have some 900 staff, about 460 of them engineers for the Group, or Lotus Engineering. That compares with employment for 704 in our first year [1987] with GM and a plan to employ more than 1,000 in 1988.

Such confidence was based on an exceptionally successful launch for the re-shaped Esprit. Michael Kimberley recalled: 'As at the 22nd of October 1987, just a day after the official Motorfair debut of the car in London, we had orders for $8.2 million covering 371 Turbo Esprits, and it was obvious we would have to recruit another 80 production staff to cope.'

Such figures were not PR hype; a look at the 1988 versus 1987 Esprit production output shows over 100 extra normally-aspirated Esprits in the new shape, whilst the Turbo gained 498 units over its predecessor.

Lotus Product Planning manager Peter Riddle reported in December 1990:

It is difficult to precisely quantify the sales gain that the X–180 coded new Esprit created, because production varied under the influence of the Elan and Esprit launches in subsequent model years. Remember, the Elan launch in 1989 involved major restructuring of Lotus production facilities. Nevertheless, the comparison between 1986 (454 Esprits) and 1988 (1,058 Esprits) demonstrates how successful the X180 re-engineering programme has been.

EXPANDED FACILITIES

At this stage, Lotus acquired another 55 acres and could boast two emissions laboratories as well as nine computer-controlled engine test beds. Lotus emission work was, and remains, up to international standards, with Japanese and American certification obtained in addition to other varied standards gleaned across Europe and Australasia.

As stated earlier, Lotus Engineering also work for outside clients and this generally benefits their own products. In the case of the Esprit, the company's Noise Vibration and Harshness (NVH) laboratory should be particularly nominated, as should the chassis torsional 'torture test' rigs, whose employment has brought remarkable improvements in the feeling of quality and durability that has accompanied the introduction of the later shape Esprit.

BODY WORK

Officially, design director Colin Spooner's brief was that: 'A more modern and sophisticated shape [was required], but with no need for change to the basic mechanicals. This is always a tough proposition, but in this case was aided by the excellent proportions of the basic design.' In fact, the fifteen months from concept approval to production period seems to have begun as an unofficial 'let's see what we can do with Esprit' by the Spooner-Stevens alliance, but once management saw its potential, a lot more support was forthcoming.

One primary benefit was that the basic body could serve so many markets, all resting on a common steel chassis and sharing the majority of panels, something that was not always true of the earlier Esprit. Another item shared, this time, by all post-autumn 1987 Esprit types, was a new set of Lotus design alloy wheels. These 15in diameter units were 7in wide at the front, 8in at the rear. They asserted a loyalty to the Goodyear Eagle NCT, which has been a characteristic of later Esprits. The Goodyears themselves, however, have evolved around Lotus demands and extensive testing, particularly in the case of the later 'Eagle Chassis' (*see* Chapter 7).

Colin Spooner commented in 1990:

It was one of the most difficult developments in the Esprit's life. We were set the brief of not going inside the original Esprit dimensions and also had to keep every major dimension within that one-inch growth figure. We were simply told 'don't deviate from that and get rid of those table-top straight lines!' So we drastically changed the body within very tight constraints; certainly its integrity was vastly improved, but we needed to take on three new sets of mould tools after we tackled the basic question of front-screen curvature. Of course, this had been at the heart of the Chapman-Giugiaro conception and Chapman would not allow any subsequent A-pillar changes, but we needed to increase the apparent screen curvature to cut wind noise and to fit in with the theme of a softer, more rounded, and current design. Modern glass helped us in the new Esprit, but we brought both base and top screen lines forward as well.

More Bodywork

Other glazing changes for the later body embraced the side glass and the use of double seals to steel window frames in a further, successful, diminishment of wind noises. A removable panel in the roof was supplied either in composite Nomex honeycomb or as a tinted glass sun-roof.

The Turbo and normally-aspirated models were distinguished front and rear by the use

Production Technique

Body construction for the new Esprit started to reflect Lotus Engineering research. Lotus utilized Kevlar sections to provide roll-over hoop protection within the cabin, but the proven marine ply rear bulkhead remains in production. Other key body manufacturing elements were the use of the Lotus Vacuum Assisted Resin Injection (VARI) moulding, the glassfibre-reinforced strategically via polyurethane foam formers and Continuous Filament Mat (CFM). In order to create a strong side sill for maximum accident protection performance, foam inserts were placed in the mould reinforced by a glass-based CFM.

The production process begins when a 'female' mould is covered by Gelcoat, but instead of the traditional layers of woven mat and resin, just the dry reinforcement materials are placed on the mould, together with any of the formers or CFMs required.

When all the reinforcement materials are in place, an inner male mould with a peripheral air-tight seal is brought beneath the female mould and bolted into place. Then, polyester resin matrix materials can be added. Under vacuum conditions, resin is drawn into the mould cavity and is distributed evenly; the resin is injected at low pressure and also serves to clamp two sections together.

That operation naturally cut manufacturing times compared to the previous hand-laying process and there was a notable gain in panel quality, due mainly to uniform panel thickness.

The complete moulding process takes from a matter of minutes for a minor panel to an hour or so for the two major (upper and lower) halves of the body shell. Incidentally, both halves are joined by epoxide structural adhesives on the overlapping joint that is now largely hidden on the re-styled Esprit.

The body is painted via a two-pack polyurethane paint, cured in the Lotus ovens at a heated 176°F (80°C). Special paints, like the pearlescent white that has proved so popular on recent Esprits, notably add to the production time and Lotus probably undercharge the extra fuss involved with these gleaming treatments.

The body bolts on to the now traditional galvanized steel backbone chassis (warranted against corrosion for eight years) and unchanged over the earlier Turbo/S3 lineage.

Even the adoption of some time-saving processes in body construction failed to cut total production time below a Lotus-quoted 'three months and over 500 man hours'.

At last! The adjustable backrest arrives within the optional plush leather of a post-1987 Esprit. The Lotus emblem was incorporated in the handwheel that controls the limited rake adjustment.

of a single glazed pane between the uprights of the 'Flying Buttress' rear-end, the said aft pane being deleted on the lower-powered model. At the front, the Turbo carried standard fog lamps and subtly re-contoured panels to allow extra air induction.

Air management was generally far cleaner than in the original. Flaps for the fuel fillers sank those out of sight on the hindquarters. The old air induction slots around the enlarged rear windows were masked smoothly into the overall contours, although the lower-side sill intakes lived on. The overall aerodynamic drag factor was quoted as 0.35Cd for the double-glazed Turbo and 0.36Cd on the slower Esprit, not so significantly different as one would guess from the revised post-1987 Esprit lines.

Overall body weight was up by an amount that would have caused Chapman to frown, but the result was a genuinely smoother to drive vehicle, with cabin noise neatly contained, especially for the turbo variants. Compared with the first Essex Turbo, the autumn 1987 turbo was just 99lb (50kg) up, which seemed a fair price to pay for the extra refinement. In the later car, that 2,789lb (1,265kg) was distributed as a predictably tail-heavy 1,192lb (540kg) front, 1,597lb (720kg) aft.

INSIDE STORY

The cabin remained strictly that of a two-seater, but marginally more interior space was found. Headroom was increased by 0.9in (22mm) and the seat/toe box pedal width was increased by 0.10in (25mm). The most

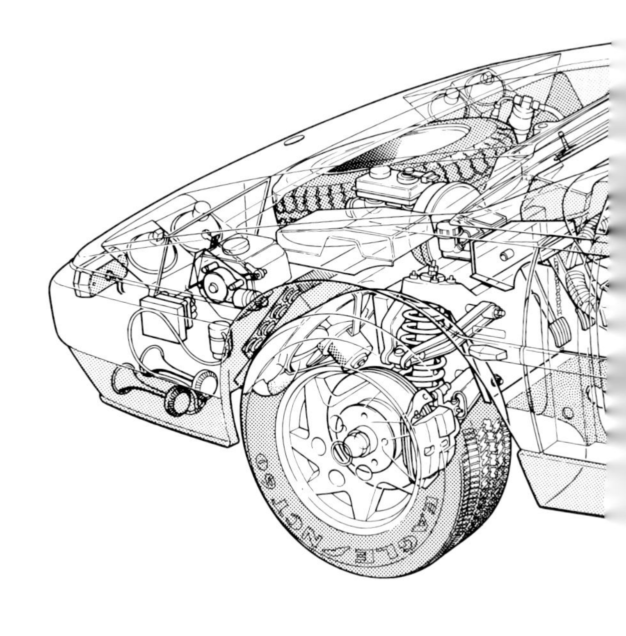

practical change within concerned the instrument panel 'boomerang', which now contained six-dial 'black and white' VDO instrumentation and push-button switches that were a lot less fiddly than the earlier rockers and sliders.

The seating gained increased back-rest rake angles with full leather trim and an initial £660 option over a mixture of tweed and leather. Minor alterations were aimed at the door trim and a change in that massive central transmission tunnel outline. The Turbo Esprit put on a 14in (355mm) leather-bound wheel of three spokes, whilst the normally-aspirated model had to make do with the plainer two-spoke item that had featured on the S3.

RUNNING CHANGES

There were some detail changes to the turbocharging ancillaries around the 2,174cc Lotus 16-valve motor, but the major mechanical changes centred upon the transmission.

Graham Atkin had managed to keep the Lotus-Citröen transaxle alliance alive through service difficulties with second gear durability and increasingly restricted availability. Finally, Citröen were only

Andrew Dibben created this conscientious cut-away of the 215bhp Esprit turbo in its new suit. Running gear was largely unchanged, except for the introduction of a Renault five-speed transaxle to replace the original Citröen unit.

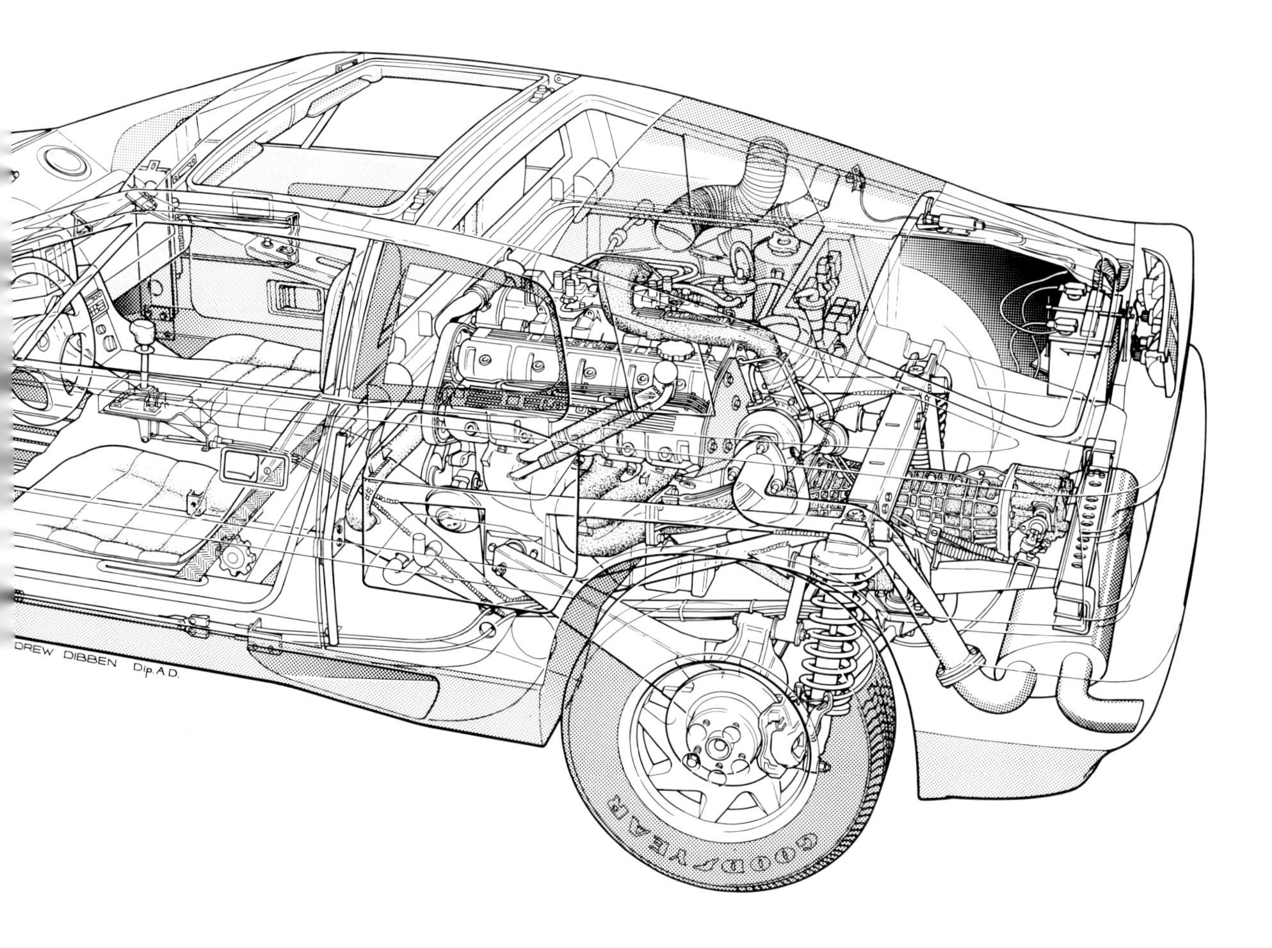

manufacturing the basic hardware for use in light commercial vans!

A perusal through the possible sources of a transaxle to accommodate a Lotus power train was made. That transaxle had to have turbo-charged potential for extra power durability (there was no formal intercooler until the 1989 Esprit SE) and the best co-operation turned out to be from Renault and their specialist car division, Alpine of Dieppe. Initially, Lotus were interested only in the production fitment. Later, however, contacts were made with Alpine (who use Renault transmissions at the rear of their pretty and effective V6 2 + 2 GT) to produce closer competition ratios.

French Connection

The production five-speed that Lotus chose used common ratios in the 110 or 125bhp four-cylinder Renault 25 (then badged 25TX and GTX). It is worth noting that V6 Renaults and Alpines did not share ratios with Lotus, although the Alpines had all but the same fourth gearing. For the record, the old and new Lotus ratios, and their effect on overall mph per 1,000rpm are placed in our adjacent specification panel.

Along with the new gearing came a 235mm single-plate diaphragm spring clutch from Renault and a new gear linkage. This was a controversial and literal change from rod links to a cable mechanism that Lotus described as 'low inertia'. Whilst the change *was* lighter than for previous Citröen transaxle Esprits, the mechanism could be unreliable (the test SE for this book was stuck in third after less than a week) and the shift quality itself could be described as vague alongside that of its predecessor.

Other Changes

A new generation of water-cooled casings concentrating on cooling around the bearing housings) had arrived from Garrett AiResearch since the advent of the original Esprit Turbo. Lotus specified the T3 updated derivative and mated it to a complete stainless-steel exhaust layout. Carburettors remained Dellorto twin-choke and side-draught. (Dellorto spelling was now anglicized for easier UK trading.)

In a 1988 interview, Mike Kimberley revealed that fuel injection and intercooling would be coming for the Esprit in Europe. (Only the Federal American Esprit specification then were available with standard fuel injection.) The Lotus director admitted that the cost per car of going from their traditional Italian twin-choke carburettors to fuel injection was 'rather expensive – over £650 per unit, and intercooling will probably account for another £300.'

Power (215bhp at 6,000rpm) and torque (220lb ft at 4,250rpm) remained exactly as for the preceding Esprit Turbo HC, as did all the principal dimensions of the now established wet-sump engine, including the 8:1 compression ratio. The normally-aspirated unit remained similar to that of the 180bhp Excel, yielding 172bhp at 6,500rpm and 163lb ft of torque on 5,000rpm. The safe maximum advised for both engines was 7,000rpm.

Lotus sources revealed engine building time as 'two full weeks' in this period and went on record with the following technical tidbits:

Pistons are balanced within 3 grams tolerance. Valves are diligently lapped by hand. The crankshaft, flywheel and clutch assembly are balanced as one unit. And every engine is individually hot-tested for one-and-a-half hours before being fitted . . .

THE PRICE OF PERFORMANCE

The new Esprits were launched at £22,950 for the normally-aspirated 1988 model year Esprit and £28,900 for the Turbo. Both

Renault Ratios

The swap to Renault gearbox in 1987 meant that the Esprit, turbo-charged or normally-aspirated, had perceptibly taller gearing (the mph generated per 1,000rpm are shown after each internal ratio given below) and new peak gear speeds. The latter were obtained courtesy of *Autocar & Motor* for their issue of 20 April 1988.

Internal ratios	**Post-1987**	**Pre-1987**
Fifth	0.82:1/23.7mph (38.1kph)	0.76:1/22.7mph (36.5kph)
Fourth	1.037/18.7mph (30kph)	0.97/17.8mph (28.6kph)
Third	1.38/14.1mph (22.7kph)	1.32/13mph (21kph)
Second	2.059/9.5mph (15.3kph)	1.94/8.9mph (14.3kph)
First	3.364/5.8mph (9.3kph)	2.92/5.9mph (9.5kph)

Peak gear speeds, post-October 1987

First	41mph (66kph) @ 7,000rpm
Second	67mph (108kph) @ 7,000rpm
Third	99mph (159kph) @ 7,000rpm
Fourth	131mph (211kph) @ 7,000rpm
Fifth	153mph (246kph) @ 6,450rpm

Performance, post-October 1987

'The first roadgoing Lotus to top the magic 150mph figure'. This statement introduced *Autocar*'s full test in 1988, and *Motor* also agreed with Lotus that a genuine 150mph (240kph) was on; no quibbles. Here is a compendium of the 1988 Esprit Turbo test results from the two British weeklies of the period. Separate cars were tested (E444 PPW and E324 TAH). A record of Lotus claims is also included.

Lotus Claim	***Autocar***	***Motor***
Max speed, mph (kph), 152 (244) @ 6,300rpm	153 (246) @ 6,450rpm	154.3 (248.3) @ 6,510rpm
0–60mph (0–100kph), secs. 5.3	5.4	5.0
0–100mph (0–160kph), secs. 14.7	13.3	12.6
Fuel consumption, mpg (km/100l)		
—	19.6 (700)	21.6 (771)

Lotus official mpg (km/100l)

Urban	16.4 (585)
56mph (90kph)	33.9 (1,211)
75mph (120kph)	26.6 (950)

Note Lotus claims for the 172bhp 'starter' Esprit were largely unchanged over the S3, viz a top speed of 138mph (222kph) 5,600rpm; 0–60mph (0–100kph) in 6.5sec; 0–100mph (0–160kph) in 18.8sec. Unratified fuel consumption figures were:

19.3mpg (689km/100l), urban
39.8mpg at 56mph (1,421km/100l at 90kph)
33.3mpg at 75mph (1,189km/100l at 75mph)

Such claims are really the only guide we have to later Esprit performance without a turbocharger, as the magazines were not offered a chance to independently test such an Esprit.

asking prices reflected an increase of some £3,000 over their predecessors. It is significant that no commentators criticized Lotus for this considerable increase, by far the majority highlighting the Turbo model as *the* supercar bargain of the period.

As the range settled into the market, it became apparent that the Turbo was still a bit too reasonable, so Lotus had increased its cost to £29,950 by spring of 1988. For

(Left) On the line at Hethel in 1988, the benefits of the new body had already increased production rates.

Critical moment: the Esprit turbo chassis and glassfibre body are united in 1987.

comparison purposes, the benchmark Porsche 911 was then £36,358; a Ferrari 328 GTB was £42,732 and the pretty Renault Alpine GT Turbo V6 (which, as noted, shared some Esprit transmission technology) was £26,990.

The normally-aspirated Esprit remained a comparatively rare bird for UK market consumption and sold just 90 copies amongst 787 turbo models made in 1988. Nevertheless, the 172bhp Esprit remained in the range until the autumn of 1990. The last list price stood at £30,700 – but then the most expensive turbo derivative (SE) was nearly £45,000 . . .

This meant that both Esprits types were present for a mild modification session in the show season of 1988. Embargoed until 29 September 1988 was the announcement of the return of the 'classic Colin Chapman styled logo, originally introduced in 1950' and some detail Esprit range changes. These included electrically-heated door mirrors that Lotus also felt were more aerodynamic, central locking and electric operation to release the fuel-filler flaps.

Turbo cradle: how the Lotus high compression turbo lay within the chassis is well depicted in this 1988 factory photograph. It emphasizes both the cogged belt drive to dual overhead camshafts and the tight radius needed for the top exhaust manifold curves.

The vented disc brake was not a production fitment on the Esprit prior to the 1987 face-lift. Note the sturdy box section lower link of the front suspension arm and the similarity of the upper wishbone to the original Opel fitment.

Esprit de corps, *as a covey of Lotus mid-engine machines head for the final assembly stages at the close of 1987.*

7 The Fastest Esprit ... Turbo SE

'This is the most exhilarating Lotus I have ever driven.'
Michael Kimberley, 1989

The charge-cooled SE Esprit derivative has been the most powerful variant with the most accelerative power and the fastest-selling Esprit to date, with 264bhp and 0–60mph (0–100kph) in under 5 seconds. From its formal unveiling on 10 May 1989 to the close of its debut year, the 160mph (260kph) Lotus Esprit Turbo SE recorded production of 563 units. This figure handsomely exceeds the production level of any previous Esprits, save that of the S1 in 1977, and then, there were no alternative Esprit models to distract customers.

Naturally, this was the most expensive Esprit to date. The SE was launched in May 1989 at £42,500, which was then a bold thrust that took them closer to the 'starter' Porsche 911s than for many years. The price tag reflected that Lotus overheads were constantly increasing, as they staffed and invested for the 1990 Elan.

Some 600 engineers were listed on the payroll of Lotus Engineering or Lotus Cars at this time; just thirty of them worked for less than twelve months on the development of nine prototype Esprit SE vehicles. More were employed on increased-durability trials, which now equated to the GM 100,000-mile procedures on any new product. Of specific test interest to Esprit SE customers were a 400-hour time of dynamometer tests in America and Britain and two 36,000-mile harsh durability trials at the now Lotus-owned Millbrook facility in Bedfordshire. This facility covers a 2-mile speed bowl, and durability and handling courses.

GMP4 SPEC

At the British press launch, Powertrain engineer Simon P Wood (later a group leader on the Lotus Omega/Carlton project) explained that the SE owed its existence to the 1988 'GMP4-coded Esprit' variant. The latter was the second fuel-injected Esprit in emission cleansed trim, and one that, like the SE, 'runs only unleaded 95 RON fuel in conjunction with a catalytic convertor exhaust system'.

In case you are wondering, the first fuel-injected Esprit was created in October 1985 for the American market. It was superseded by the GMP4 (a coding referring to GM-sourced fuel injection and engine management system) in September 1988, after 881 had been manufactured in HC power trim.

In Europe, the GMP4 specification (rated at 228bhp) was also available in strictly emission-controlled markets from December 1988, and was also superseded by the SE. The SE had thus become a Lotus 'world car', sold in much the same catalytic convertor trim for all markets – a considerable relief after years of fiddling around with varying carburettor and exhaust specifications.

Logical Steps

Lotus Powertrain director Hugh Kemp recalled the logic behind the further development of the aluminium 16-valve Lotus engines of the mid-eighties and beyond:

The 1989 Lotus Esprit Turbo SE was immediately identified by its raised rear wing and revamped aerodynamic appliances, including the air management systems of the front spoiler.

Originally, we had a chassis that contributed to an apparent lack of refinement in the engine installation, but when we switched over to the Turbo/S3 chassis, we could then soften off the engine mounts and concentrate again on attaining better refinement with higher, specific power outputs.

In normally-aspirated terms, our biggest noise and vibration problem had been the switch from 2 to 2.2 litres. The chassis helped for the S3, but not as much as we would have liked in comparison with the turbo, which was a *lot* better from the start.

We pursued two main engine development routes. On the normally-aspirated motors we did pursue the higher compression that was first seen in the Excel at 180bhp instead of 160. However, in the Esprit there was not so much space for the exhaust system. It became rather convoluted, and there was not the sheer volume of space for the silencers, so we ended up with just over 170bhp, rather than the 180 of the front-engine Excel.

Even in the later specification, we did not ever engineer the normally-aspirated Esprit engine into catalytic convertor form, so it always stuck with carburation rather than fuel injection, and it really became a UK-only engine option in Esprit.

However, the high compression route did have a turbo application too. Naturally, we did not go to the heights of a normally-aspirated engine, but compression was raised for the introduction of the HC in October 1986 and we made some significant running changes at this point. For example, the pistons were by Mahle and ran in detachable aluminium liners. The compression was now 8:1 in place of the original 7.5:1, but we still only used fuel injection on American models and there was obvious potential in some kind of formal intercooling and the further spread of fuel injection. In the end, we combined European and American specifications to produce the SE as an answer for all markets and to make a significant power gain on unleaded fuels.

May 1989 and Lotus unveil their fastest Esprit, the 163mph (262kph) SE, at the Millbrook test facility in Bedfordshire.

Worldwide sales in common catalytic converter form, and incredible performance, were released from the Chargecooled version of the traditional Lotus 2.2 litres.

What colour would you like? The press line-up of Esprit SE variants awaiting test drives in May 1989.

First acquaintance with the Esprit SE underlined that a world-class car had emerged from Hethel. Quality had taken a big step forward with the softened outlines of 1987 and the SE built a new standard of performance to complement those constructional advantages.

The front-end spoiler accommodated extra lighting and hid a battery of cleverly sited water and oil radiators.

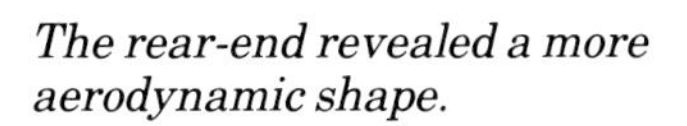

The rear-end revealed a more aerodynamic shape.

The best Esprit interior to date. The leather trim was part of the phenomenal performance package that Lotus created for the Esprit SE.

The steps which were taken toward SE specification and more effective emissions controls included:

1. A 2.2-litre open-loop catalytic convertor Esprit for the USA in May 1983.
2. The use of Bosch K-Jetronic in conjunction with a GM closed-loop catalytic convertor from October 1985 to September 1988.
3. The fabled GMP4 electronics.

In Hugh Kemp's words, the GMP4 offered:

Much better control of all engine functions via GM engine management systems that we adapted for Lotus needs. We particularly benefited from the lack of mechanical air-pressure sensing [as used by Bosch at this stage] and the accurate controls we could gain of pre-ignition and over-boost from the turbocharger.

TO THE FUTURE

As Simon Wood revealed at the formal presentation, the heart of both GMP4 and SE management was the Electronic Control Module (ECM). Lotus were working upon Delco software that was processed by a 32K on-board computer within the central 'black box', a plastic apparition that was sealed to prevent unauthorized tampering in search of yet more power. I am told that the box would continue to operate under water and that it previews the future by meeting Californian standards of diagnostics.

That simply means that the ECM prompts

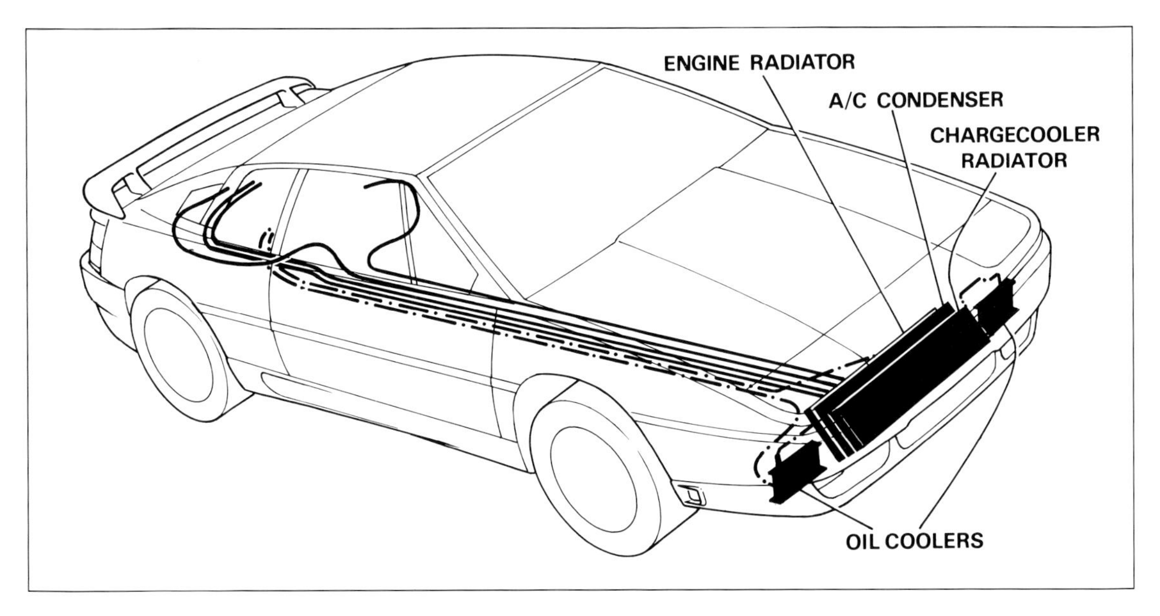

Plumbing for 160mph (260kph): the mid-motor Esprit SE needed the services of an automotive plumber to provide the services listed in this 1989 factory diagram.

a dashboard display whenever faulty engine operation is encountered. This is a particular concern in California, because all the emission parameters are monitored, so that there is no excuse for continuing to operate a noxiously faulty vehicle. One day, all cars will be this way, and Lotus engineers are already facing the challenge of building engines of warranted emission compliance over 100,000-mile periods.

A further electronic refinement was the adoption of direct ignition, a term popularized by Saab to perfectly describe the use of high-voltage coils and microprocessor-managed spark timing to replace the more conventional coil and distributor assembly. Saab, and some rivals, utilize a coil for each cylinder but the Lotus system features two coils reporting to the main ECM.

More Power

Mechanical changes over the existing 910S (HC) turbo 2.2-litre were comparatively confined, yet horsepower grew by 14 per cent and torque by 17 per cent. That extra pulling power was achieved at 1,000rpm less than the previous European turbo Esprit.

Most of that extra power – the engine is capable of holding a transient 280bhp for periods of up to 30 seconds, and an almost unmatched production 121.5bhp a litre is routinely achieved – can be attributed to the use of a compact Behr intercooler. This runs

Lotus Claimed Performance Figures

Max speed	163mph
Acceleration	
0–60mph	4.7sec
0–100mph	11.9sec
Fourth gear	
50–70mph	3.8sec
70–90mph	4.0sec
Fifth gear	
70–90mph	5.3sec
90–110mph	6.1sec

Lotus Esprit Turbo SE Technical Specification (as issued by Lotus, May 1989)

ENGINE

Cylinders	Four in line
Capacity	2,174cc (132.6cu in)
Bore/Stroke	95.3mm × 76.2mm (3.75in × 3.0in)
Max power	264bhp (197kW) at @ 6,500rpm
Max torque	261lb ft (354Nm) at @ 3,900rpm
Max engine speed	7,400rpm
Block	Aluminium alloy, Nikasil-coated wet liners
Head	Aluminium alloy
Pistons	Forged aluminium, chrome plated
Valve gear	Dohc, belt-drive four valves per cylinder. Sodium filled exhaust valves
Compression ratio	8.0:1
Turbocharger	Garrett TB03, water-cooled with integral wastegate
Boost pressure	0.85bar (12.4psi)
Chargecooler	Engine mounted intake chargecooler with independent mechanically-driven liquid cooling system. Front-mounted chargecooler radiator
Fuel system	Electronic multi-point fuel injection incorporating knock sensing and self-diagnosis capability to Californian Air Research Board requirements
Fuel	Unleaded, 95 RON minimum
Ignition	Electronic distributorless twin-coil

TRANSMISSION

Type	Five-speed, all-synchromesh manual transaxle
Clutch	Hydraulically operated, 9.25in (235mm), single plate diaphragm

Ratios

Gear	Ratio	mph/1,000rpm
5th	0.82:1	23.1
4th	1.03:1	18.4
3rd	1.38:1	13.7
2nd	2.05:1	9.3
1st	3.36:1	5.6
Final Drive	3.889	

BODY

Styled by the Lotus design studio, the bodyshell is manufactured by the Vacuum Assisted Resin Injection process and includes Kevlar reinforcement of the roof structure.
Removeable roof panel in composite Nomex honeycomb.
Front and rear bumpers manufactured from RRIM offering protection against minor impact damage.
Aerodynamic rear wing mounted on tailgate.
Engine air intake located behind the rear right-hand quarter light complemented by further ducting in the lower body sills for cooling. Warm air exits via cooling slats above engine bay.

CHASSIS

Galvanized steel backbone, guaranteed against corrosion for eight years.

SUSPENSION

Front	Upper and lower wishbones with anti-roll bar. Coil springs co-axial with telescopic gas pressurised shock absorbers.
Rear	Upper and lower transverse links with box section trailing radius arms. Coil springs co-axial with telescopic pressurised gas shock absorbers. Aluminium hub carriers.

STEERING

Type	Rack-and-pinion
Castor	1°
Ratio	15.4:1
Turns lock-to-lock	3.0
Turning circle (between kerbs)	36ft (10.97m)

BRAKES

Front	10.2in (259mm) dia ventilated discs
Rear	10.8in (274mm) dia outboard discs
Actuation	Dual hydraulic circuits split front/rear. Vacuum servo.

WHEELS AND TYRES

Wheels	Lotus-styled alloy wheels
Front	7J × 15in
Rear	8.5J × 16in
Front tyres	Goodyear Eagle 215/50 ZR 15
Rear tyres	Goodyear Eagle 245/50 ZR 16
Spare tyre	175/70 R 14

FUEL SYSTEM

Tanks	Centrally mounted twin tanks
Capacity	15.4gal (18.5 US gal/70l)

Twin, electrically-operated fuel filler caps mounted on rear flanks

EXHAUST

Stainless steel system incorporating two-part ceramic matrix catalyst, back pressure valve for rapid catalyst warm-up and acoustic exhaust muffler.

COOLING

Front-mounted cooling pack consisting of chargecooler radiator, air-conditioning condenser and main engine cooling radiator. Two side-mounted oil coolers.

ELECTRICAL

Polarity	Negative earth
Alternator	Valeo 90amp
Fuses	Front, 35. Rear, 5
Headlights	Four circular 6.0in (152mm), units. Electrically-operated headlamp pods
Foglamps	Two square halogen high intensity units
Battery	Low maintenance, 340amp cold crank DIN, 620amp cold crank SAE
Harness	'Ristex' thinwall cable

EQUIPMENT

Air-conditioning. Radio fitting kit. Single wiper with two speed plus intermittent. Screen wash by two single eyeball high flow jets. Central door-locking. Electric windows. Electrically-operated and heated door mirrors. Heated rear window. Warning lights include: oil pressure, cooling fans, coolant level, low fuel, screen wash level, emissions system malfunction. Three-phase ice warning lights. Fascia rheostat. Speedometer incorporating odometer and tripmeter, tachometer, boost pressure, oil pressure, oil temperature, coolant temperature, fuel gauges. Digital clock. Polished elm burr fascia. Full leather trim.

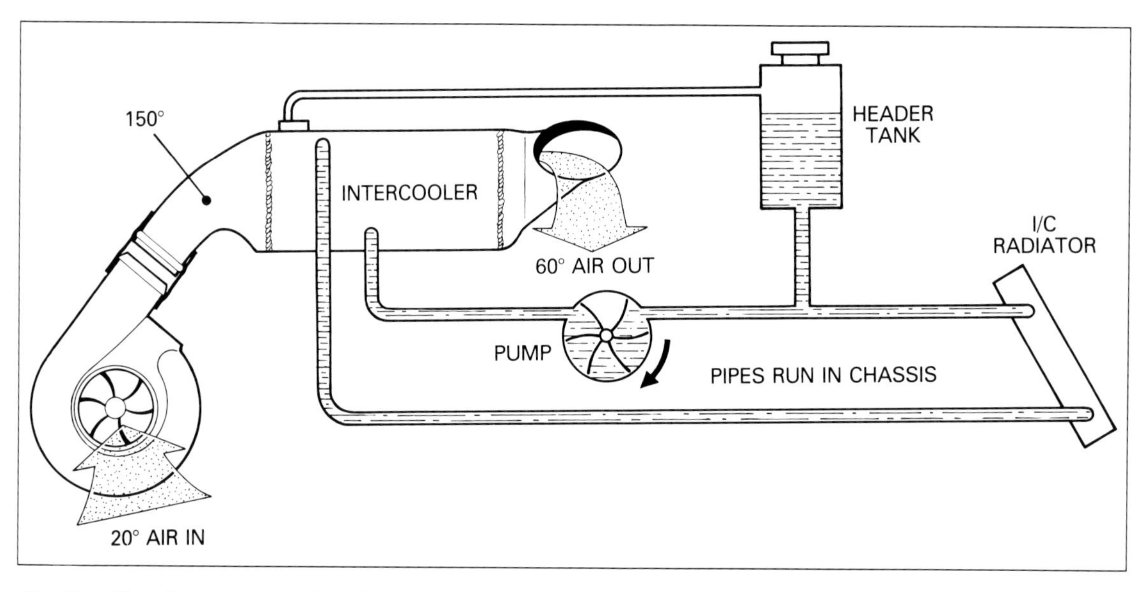

The first Esprit to run any kind of intercooling device, the SE featured such a compact yet effective system that its Behr heart was also featured on the subsequent twin turbo Lotus Vauxhall/Opel Carlton/Omega saloons.

an unspecified 'cooling liquid' mixture around a separate layout that features its own header tank and forward radiator; its plumbing runs forward and aft within the chassis, just like any number of sixties and seventies racing cars.

It is this small liquid-filled cooler that is dubbed the 'chargecooler'. Conventional intercoolers are air-to-air radiators that require a lot more space, and create unwanted extra aerodynamic drag. A Jabsco pump drives the chargecooling liquid system, taking power up from the old distributor slot. Reduced intake temperatures that Lotus claim for the system, operating in a warmish 4°F (20°C) ambient are: 238°F (150°C) into the chargecooler and 76°F (60°C) outward bound, ready for induction delivery.

The fuel injection system was based on components from the GM-Rochester division, but also featured two supplementary injectors to the primary four, all by Multec. The secondary injection pair operate within the plenum chamber to meet maximum power demand conditions. This is a sophisticated alternative to the common fifth (four-cylinder) or seventh (six-cylinder) injector found in many UK aftermarket turbo systems.

Hugh Kemp continued:

The engine changes included chrome-plated crowns to forged Mahle 8:1 compression ratio pistons and detail induction and exhaust work. We equalized the tract lengths to reach that of the shortest distance between exhaust valve and turbocharger entry, finding that turbo-charged engines are not so sensitive to exhaust manifold changes at this point.

We reduced exhaust manifold system weight significantly (up to 30 per cent) by analysis of the iron castings that we had been using and the substitution of more advanced material mixes. At the HC Esprit stage, we had introduced the integral wastegate as part of a new Garrett AiResearch TB03 fitment, which also allowed us the use of water-cooling in the central casing. In

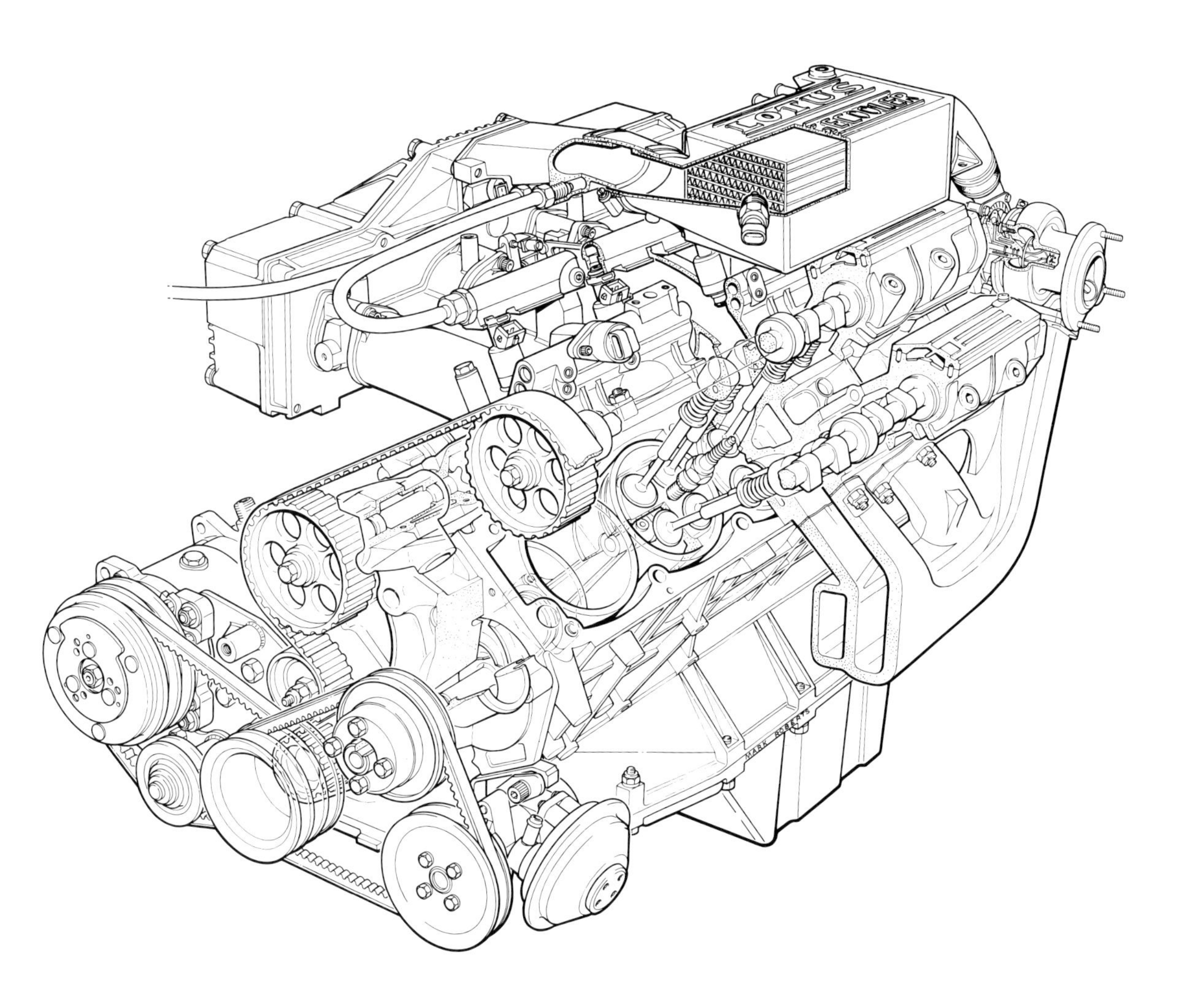

Contrast this Mark Roberts cut-away of the Lotus 910S Chargecooled turbo with the original dry-sump and non-intercooled unit and you will see that the basic engine principles remained, but that the ancillaries commanding turbocharger performance were radically altered.

itself, this prevents the kind of oil 'coking' deposits that had been a problem for Saab and ourselves in earlier turbo installations.

Under Pressure

On the sensitive question of maximum boost pressures, Lotus had their electronic management hold a cold-start figure of 0.65 bar/ 9.4psi and a warmed pressure of 0.85 bar/ 12.4psi for the SE. Rapid acceleration at less than 3,000rpm is allowed a degree of overboost upon this figure (how much more was not specified, but I was told by Lotus that 'the high boost condition is available only for short duration to provide initial vehicle acceleration').

For comparative purposes, the original turbo ran a maximum of 8psi, whilst the GMP4 American emission specification,

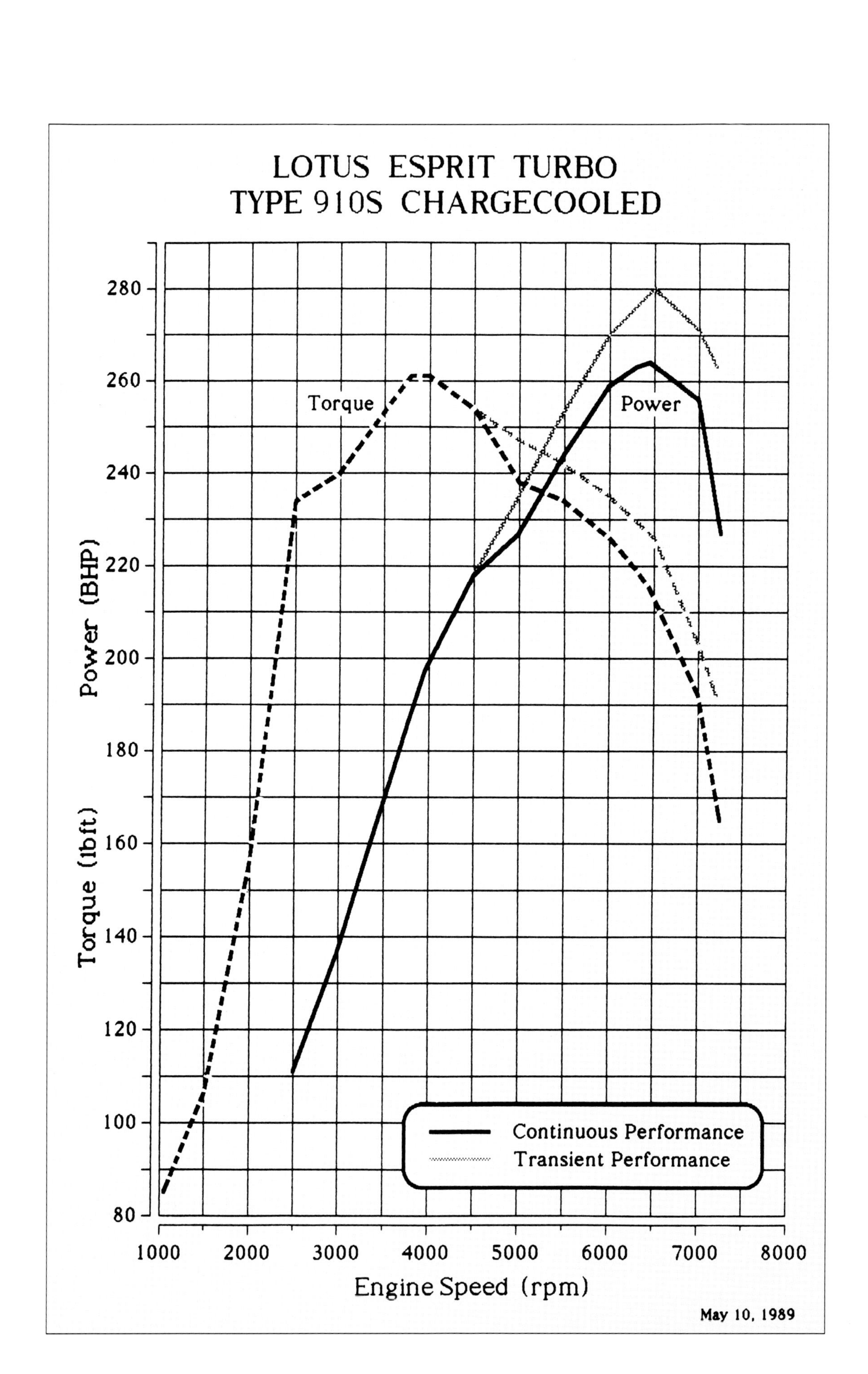
LOTUS ESPRIT TURBO
TYPE 910S CHARGECOOLED
Torque
Power
Power (BHP)
Torque (lbft)
280
260
240
220
200
180
160
140
120
100
80
1000
2000
3000
4000
5000
6000
7000
8000
Engine Speed (rpm)
Continuous Performance
Transient Performance
May 10, 1989

non-intercooled predecessor to the SE held 12psi to 3,000rpm and then dropped back to a constant commitment of 10psi.

Hugh Kemp commented:

There were some dimensional changes to the aluminium-block liners because the material strengths were altered, but there was also an extra boss to insert on one cylinder to install the knock control sensor. We drilled holes all over the place to get the optimum position for this sensor, but it has been worthwhile as the boost and ignition settings can be more precisely set without harming durability.

The exhaust system was new from the manifolds down and lowered back pressure was our design priority here, along with a lot of work from Southampton University and ourselves to lower noise and vibration levels in this area.

On the inlet side, longer tracts than previously used on the turbo showed an improvement in low-speed torque than we had seen on normally-aspirated engines. For the turbo, it also meant a better transition in power characteristics when boost was building up.

Hugh Kemp

A graduate in 1973, Hugh Kemp brought to Lotus extensive engines engineering expertise gained at Perkins and British Leyland.

Hugh joined Lotus in January 1979 and immediately started work on the 2.2 Lotus Sunbeam version of the 16-valve Lotus motor. From that successful project – later adapted to all Esprits of course – Hugh went on to develop the turbo-charged Esprit engine, working alongside Martin Cliff (working for Ferrari at the time of writing).

Once the turbo was completed, Hugh moved on to Lotus Engineering where, he finds, '10 per cent of the work is Lotus orientated and the rest is for external clients.'

I understand Hugh Kemp's engine development techniques have been applied to the Chevrolet ZR-1 V8 of 5.7 litres; the Chrysler 16-valve DOHC design, Lotus Omega/Carlton and others he 'cannot mention'.

We are indebted to Hugh Kemp and fellow engines engineer Simon Wood for such a thorough insight into the progress of Lotus engines engineering into the nineties.

HANDLING EXPERTISE

Despite the Lotus track tradition, about '95 per cent' of all handling research and development is carried out: 'On the road. Circuit work is to look at absolute on-the-limit handling and we often find that a car which is good on the track is not the best on the road. When we get it right, both ride and handling qualities come along together', reported former Goodyear engineer Tony Shute.

Mr Shute is the man who has been responsible for press quotes such as: 'The charge-cooled Esprit SE is just so blindingly quick from A to B, and yet comfortable with it. The ride is taut and the body control superb without any low speed choppiness and the grip . . . you can feel it tugging at the car through fast corners, rocking the body on its springs, but it never moves off line.' (*Fast Lane*, 1989 test of the Esprit.)

Under the sharp eye of Roger Becker, who knows exactly what he wants of a Lotus in terms of driving pleasure and safety, Tony Shute ensures that the Esprit continues to stay ahead in the handling and adhesion stakes.

(Left) Both continuous and transient horsepower are clarified in this diagram of the most potent Lotus power unit. Up to 280bhp is briefly available at 6,500rpm, but more important to most road users is the allowance of more than 230lb ft of torque between 2,500 and 5,750rpm.

Ride and Handling Changes, 1988 vs 1989 Esprit SE

	1988 Model Year	1989 Model Year
Wheels		
Front	7J × 15	7J × 15
Rear	7J × 15	8.5J × 16
Goodyear tyres		
Front	195/60 VR 15 NCT	215/50 ZR 15 Eagle
Rear	235/50 VR 15 NCT	245/50 ZR 16 Eagle
Shock absorbers	Twin tube, Monroe	Twin tube, gas, Armstrong
Castor	3deg	1.5deg
Camber	0deg 30′ to 0deg ± 30′	0deg, ± 30′
Front springs	23N/mm	29 N/mm
Ride Heights		
Front	170mm	190mm
Rear	170mm	170mm
Anti dive	17 per cent	22 per cent pro dive

It took even Tony Shute some time to come up with the definitive chassis and date start-point for the 'Eagle' Esprit SE chassis, but here is the result of his research.
From 3.4–89 for the Esprit SE, then a couple of months later for the different variants at the following chassis numbers:

SE (264bhp)	SCCFC20A 1KHF65000
GMP4 (225–228bhp)	SCC08291 0KHF62728
DOMESTIC (UK) TURBO (215bhp)	SCC08291 OKHD13587
DOMESTIC (UK) N/A (172bhp)	SCC08591 2KHD13582

The Eagle Chassis

Tony Shute explained further:

For the SE, we made some fundamental changes and these became collectively known as 'The Eagle Chassis', a reference to the Goodyear tyres that we worked with, and finally specified, to suit the SE. I found in engineering Powertrain employee Murray White a natural driver, one without too many of the preconceptions that come with experience. We did all but 5 per cent of our mileage on the road, but used facilities across Europe to back up our findings, including those in Belgium, France and Luxembourg, besides our obvious Norfolk outings.

Our panel shows the statistics behind the changes, which were most obvious in the larger, 50 per cent low-profile, Eagle Goodyears on OZ Ruote alloy wheels. The details summarize into stiffer and raised – 0.8in (20mm) – front springs and ride height; replacement Armstrong low-pressure gas shock absorbers; eradication of anti-dive suspension characteristics and lighter steering. The latter was obtained by a 1.5deg reduction in steering castor. Similar detail degree changes in bump steer, toe-in and hub-trail angles produced a chassis of enhanced stability *and* comfort, a rare achievement when starting from an already acclaimed chassis of the Esprit's calibre.

AIR MANAGEMENT

In proper Lotus tradition, aerodynamics were applied to make the Esprit a more efficient machine in more ways than just maintaining a reasonable (circa 0.35Cd) aerodynamic drag factor. Most obvious external additions were the elongated 'bib' front spoiler and a double-pylon rear wing. Neither were fashion accessories, however, and the technical briefing did mention alterations to the side sills and the management of some frontal air supply to be vented beneath the SE.

The front of the Esprit SE was now packed with coolers, and the front bib had to feed all of them, plus find a little air to feed to unchanged vented front-disc brakes. There were also oil coolers at either end; engine radiator *and* charge-cooling radiator. Both the liquid radiators were steeply raked back in the nose and ran entirely separate systems, although all the oil, water and charge-cooling liquids had to be fed back to the engine bay from the nose via the chassis. Also behind that bib, and equally vulnerable to a bump, was the air-conditioning condenser.

Lotus publicity reported of the aerodynamics:

Neutral balance is achieved throughout the car's speed range. Front and rear lift have been tuned to only a few points above zero, while particular attention has been paid to cross-wind stability . . . cooling capacity has been improved by 20 per cent.

Simon Wood mentioned that they had seen downforce figures at the rear of the Esprit, which would be a considerable achievement on a production car with such a squat outline.

SHOWROOM EQUIPMENT

At £42,500 on launch (£46,300 some eighteen months later), the Esprit SE did embrace a number of standard items of proven showroom appeal. These included a walnut burr fascia; leather trim; lift-out/tilt glass sun-roof, and air conditioning. Do not

Tony Shute

Chassis and suspension engineer Tony Shute is the kind of perennially youthful and cheerful individual that you would imagine putting the joy into Lotus handling.

The Esprit SE and its 'Eagle chassis' was just one of many projects to benefit from the former GM Institute graduate's attention. Tony has experience of GM (twice, for the Oldsmobile and the Buick) but is best known prior to his work for Lotus for his four-year tenure at the Goodyear ride and handling facility in Luxemburg. Shute recollected:

Under the Vehicle Manufacturing and Engineering liaison title, I came into contact with many UK and ex-Colonial countries, but Lotus was always something special to me.

When I came into contact with Roger Becker, I knew I would work for Lotus one day and I can honestly say I've thoroughly enjoyed the experience.

I started at Lotus four years ago [1986] and have worked on seven projects. These have offered the challenge of sorting front drive, mid-engine rear drive, simple rear drive (Lotus Omega) and even the inboard rocker suspension that we installed on a Toyota hatchback that we developed as part of the Elan programme. That car is still running round the factory and shows you that original thought continues at Lotus.

More specifically, I have concentrated on chassis work for the M100-new Elan; the Esprit S3 and was allowed a start-to-finish role on the Esprit SE.

Ask Tony to define the secret of Lotus handling and he smiles broadly before attempting to define the undefinable:

Lotus is about transient ride control. By which I mean that we still tend to use softer dampers than most; for example, the new Lotus Omega has softer units than the standard Opel 3000GSi.

Lotus also tolerate more roll than is often thought sporting; the secret then lies in damper control . . . and the fact that I drive the Esprit every day of the week, so we never lose touch with its current form.

ESPRIT

Lotus Cars Limited, Hethel, Norwich, Norfolk, NR14 8EZ. Telephone 0953 608000.

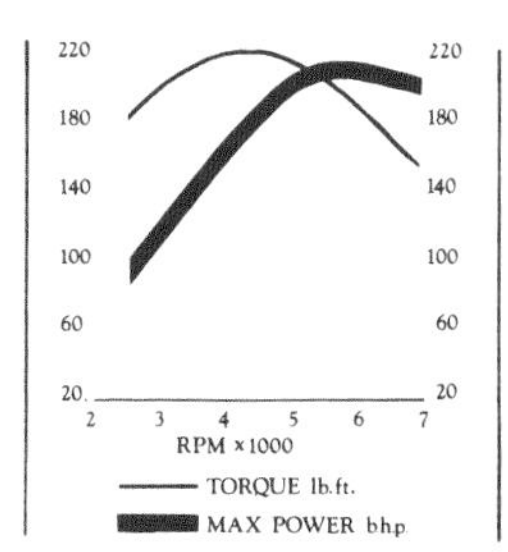

A 25% increase in engine power and the fitment of anti-lock power brakes as standard equipment are the major changes for the 1991 Esprit. Now featuring the 215 bhp version of the Lotus 2.2 litre turbocharged engine, the Esprit accelerates to 60 mph in only 5.3 seconds.

TECHNICAL SPECIFICATION:

ENGINE: Mid-mounted Lotus 2.2 litre (910S) aluminium alloy 16-valve DOHC.
Water cooled TB03 turbocharger with integral wastegate.
Maximum power: 215 bhp (160 kW) at 6000 rpm (DIN)
Maximum torque: 220 lb ft (298 Nm) at 4250 rpm (DIN)
Maximum speed: 150 mph
0 – 60 mph: 5.3 seconds
0 – 100 mph: 14.7 seconds

TRANSMISSION: 5-speed all synchromesh transaxle with hydraulically operated clutch driving rear wheels.

CHASSIS/BODY: Rigid steel zinc-coated backbone chassis, fitted aerodynamic impact resistant composite bodywork, providing seating for two. Guaranteed against corrosion for 8 years.

FRONT SUSPENSION: Independent by upper and lower wishbones, with anti roll bar, coil springs and telescopic shock absorbers.

REAR SUSPENSION: Independent by upper and lower transverse links, with radius arms, coil springs and telescopic shock absorbers. Aluminium hub carriers.

BRAKES: Dual circuit, full power actuated with three-channel electronic anti-lock brakes (ABS).
10.2" dia ventilated front discs
10.8" dia solid rear discs

WHEELS:
Front: 7J alloy fitted Goodyear Eagle 215/50 ZR15 Steel braced High Speed Tyres.
Rear: 8.5J alloy fitted Goodyear Eagle 245/50 ZR16 Steel braced High Speed Tyres.

GOVERNMENT FUEL CONSUMPTION TEST RESULTS:

	Imp mpg	Metric l/100 km
URBAN	16.5	17.2
56 mph	33.9	8.3
75 mph	26.6	10.6

Fuel tank capacity: 17.3 gallons (78 litres)
Fuel requirement: 97 RON 4 star or 95/98 RON unleaded

STANDARD EQUIPMENT:
The standard equipment for the Lotus Esprit includes tilt/removable sunroof, electric windows, central door locking, electrically adjustable heated door mirrors, plaid cloth trimmed seats and raven leather interior trim.

OPTIONAL EQUIPMENT:
The Esprit can be purchased with a range of options including air conditioning, glass sunroof, audio equipment and full leather upholstery in a range of colours. Ask your Lotus dealer for full details.

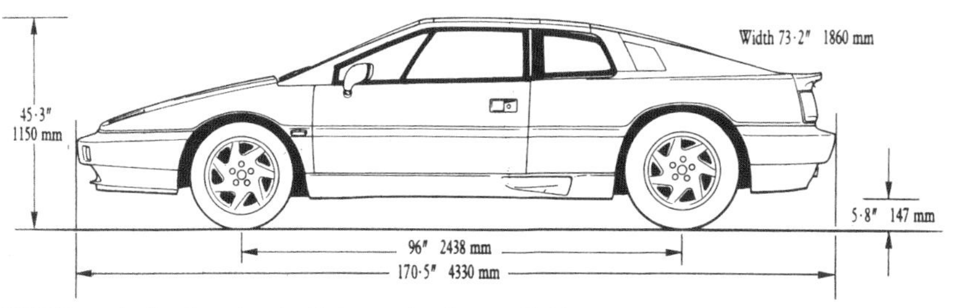

The Esprit SE marked a new high point in sales of the mid-engined Lotus, and this silver example displays how successfully the basic shape entered the nineties.

despair if a red dashboard light comes on in chilly conditions, an LED ice alert was included in the SE fascia from the start.

In-car entertainment was provided only in 'a radio fitting kit' initially and it is worth emphasizing that anti-lock brakes did not become available, optionally or otherwise, until the autumn of 1990.

(Left) Lotus continued to use self-explanatory showroom data throughout their three-Esprit model line of 1991; the reverse of this single page pamphlet was a simple single car picture.

THE 1991 ESPRITS

At the end of August 1990, under embargo until the British Motor Show (NEC, Birmingham) press day of 18 September, Lotus were ready to reveal extensive changes to the 1991 Esprit range, which now comprised entirely turbocharged models. All had Lotus-Delco sourced, three-channel, electronic anti-lock braking as standard. A feature any prospective second-hand buyer should value.

Three familiar Esprit specifications were now lined up for the UK market. At £34,900, the simple Lotus Esprit was actually the old

215bhp, carburated Turbo but equally capable of running on leaded or unleaded fuel. Standard equipment included the tilt-or-remove glass sun-roof; electric windows; central door locking; electrical assistance for heated door mirrors and an interior trim that comfortably combined plaid cloth and raven leather.

Options embraced items like air conditioning, audio equipment and full leather upholstery. Standard wheels and tyres were those of the Eagle chassis, right down to the 15in diameter fronts and 16in rears accommodating 215 and 245/50 section rubber. All three Esprits now shared their chassis as well as wheel and tyre specification.

Performances

Claimed performance for an Esprit using leaded (97 RON octane) or unleaded (95/98 RON) petrol were as strong as ever. The new 'starter Esprit' embraced a 150mph (240kph) maximum; 0–60mph (0–100kph) in 5.3 seconds and 0–100mph (0–160kph) in 14.7 seconds. Government fuel consumption results were: urban, 16.5mpg (600km/100l) 56mph, 33.9mpg (90kph, 1,020km/100l); 75mph, 26.5mpg (120kph, 900km/100l).

At £38,900 in autumn 1990, the Esprit S brought the GMP4 multi-point fuel injection specification to a wider European audience. Its 228bhp was accompanied by the visual clue of the 'glass-back' tailgate and the standard features of the 215bhp turbo (plus front fog lamps, adjustable seat backs and trim composed of leather with tweed).

Lotus performance claims on the catalytic convertor Esprit S, running 95 octane unleaded only were: a 155mph (250kph) maximum; 0–60mph (0–100kph) in 5.2 seconds; 0–100mph (0–160kph) in 12.7 seconds. Economy tests returned an improved 18mpg (600km/100l) Urban; 34.1mpg at a constant 56mph and 28.4mpg on 75mph (1,020km/100l at a constant 90kph and 1,000km/100l on 120kph).

The Esprit in the Fast Lane

The Esprit SE was such a sensational performer that there were few quarrels over Lotus performance claims. To show just what it could do when timed with electronic equipment, the best set of figures published for the 1989 Esprit SE have been selected. These come courtesy of racing driver/journalist Mark Hales and the monthly British magazine *Fast Lane*.

Mph (Kph)	Seconds
0–30 (0–50)	1.8
0–40 (0–65)	2.5
0–50 (0–80)	3.6
0–60 (0–100)	4.6
0–70 (0–110)	6.4
0–80 (0–130)	7.9
0–90 (0–145)	9.6
0–100 (0–160)	11.9
0–110 (0–180)	14.6
0–120 (0–190)	17.6
0–130 (0–210)	21.4
50–70 (80–110) in 4th gear	4.0
50–70 (80–110) in 5th gear	4.4

Maximum timed speed: 160mph (260kph)

Note *Autocar & Motor* showed these figures were no fluke. They recorded 159mph (256kph) around a banked track; 0–60mph (0–100kph) on the flat in 4.9 seconds, a standing quarter-mile in 13.5 seconds and an excellent overall fuel consumption of 23.5mpg (800km/100l).

The Esprit SE (from May 1989) was the performer we are all familiar with and it is worth reiterating that the company claims of 0–60mph (0–100kph) in 4.7 seconds and a 163mph (260kph) maximum were achieved by some independent testers using electronic measuring devices.

THE FIRST LOTUS ANTI-LOCK BRAKES

'The inclusion of anti-lock braking as standard equipment across the range is a further

The SE not only survived into 1991, but led the trio of Esprit turbocharged derivatives offered in Britain. All had electronic anti-lock braking systems as standard equipment for 1991.

step in the car's development', felt Michael Kimberley in August 1990. He went on to add, 'It is our policy to continuously evolve the Esprit. Following the successful launch of the charge-cooled version in 1989 we have now added a sophisticated anti-lock braking system.'

Adding anti-lock braking (usually dubbed ABS from the German original systems, which literally translates as 'Anti-Block System') to a mid-engined car can upset the dynamics and the driving pleasure that are the Esprit's *raison d'être*. Lotus therefore spent some time evaluating all the established systems. Working from the summer of 1989 onward with the GM division Delco Moraine, Lotus proudly claimed that their ABS 3A system could 'achieve braking capability (under controlled test-track conditions) up to 1.2g.'

The Lotus ABS 3A layout utilizes a high-pressure hydraulic brake circuit, where the hydraulics are powered by an electric pump/accumulator. The master cylinder receives fluid pressurized at 150 to 180 bar/2,135psi to 2,561psi. A pressure-control valve provides 'single modulated pressure output that operates the rear brakes directly and is fed to a boost chamber to assist pressure for the front brakes', in the very words used by Lotus at the launch.

A limiting valve is conventionally fitted in

Jim Clark, OBE (1936–1968) – An Appreciation

All the truly great racing drivers dominate an era. In a tragically curtailed life (4 March 1936–7 April 1968), Scotland's Jim Clark dominated the sixties, scoring twenty-five Grand Prix victories, two world titles (1963 and 1965) and deserving to win more than the one American Indianapolis 500 (1965).

What were the ingredients that brewed this extraordinary champion? The Scottish Border farming community was one strong influence. Clark was born in Kilmany, Fife, but his family moved to the Borders when Clark was only six.

A committed motorsport enthusiast, Clark graduated from motor club member and organizer to rally navigator and thence to driver. Ian Scott Watson, whom he met through the local young farmers' club, acted as his mentor and Clark was soon on his way to success.

His 'big break' came in 1958, when he campaigned one of the legendary Jaguar D-types for the Border Reivers racing team. Clark then went on to his first overseas race: 18 May 1958, at Spa Francorchamps.

On 26 December 1958, the traditional Brands Hatch meeting saw his first public appearance in a Lotus (an Elite). In that race, Clark competed against fellow Lotus drivers Colin Chapman (the 'Old Man' himself) and Mike Costin.

It was in single-seaters that Jim Clark's World Championship destiny lay. After a few false starts, the Lotus Formula 2 contract for 1960 proved a winner from the start; first with the Lotus 18 (the Esprit's natural great-grandfather if you like, for it was the first mid-motor Lotus), then the Lotus 21-Climax FPF in 1961 and in the first monocoque Lotus, the 25, in 1962. That 1962 season saw him achieve his first Grand Prix win, at Spa Francorchamps.

So, what happened at Hockenheim in 1968? As with many racing accidents, there are many theories advanced. In brief, Clark was driving the Lotus 48-FVA, a 220-plus bhp Formula 2 car. It was a wet weekend and just eighteen cars took the start of heat 1. The Number 1 Gold Leaf Team 48 sank from fifth to eighth in four laps. At 139mph (224kph) in a flat-out section, the Lotus started to oversteer violently and at 120mph (192kph), it struck some young trees, one of which slammed through the side of the Lotus cockpit, killing Jim Clark instantly.

Lotus investigation, under the supervision of Farnborough Air Crash investigator Peter Jowett, discovered the likely cause of the accident. A right rear tyre had a small cut and would not reinflate. It seems that this tyre was the cause, holding less and less pressure during the opening four laps. The punctured rubber finally defeated even Jim Clark's reflexes when it went down one of the fastest parts of the track.

In all the millions of words that have been written about Clark, both before and after his death, I think a tribute from Colin Chapman tells us most about a man whose driving majesty remains undimmed.

This tribute appeared originally in *Jim Clark, Portrait of a Grand Prix Driver.* Colin Chapman wrote in 1968:

I think his most profound influence was not his ability as a racing driver, but his success as a man. He was so thoroughly adjusted to life and its problems . . . He was fit, he was honest – integrity is the best single word to describe his qualities. He was a man who set an example to others.

the rear brake circuit to prevent excessive pressure generation and premature wheel-locking. The front brakes are effectively power-assisted whilst the rears are 'direct actuated' with power.

ABS CONTROL

The ABS control is of the microprocessor type. It is fed information from all four wheel hubs on rotation speeds and system pressures. It controls the anti-lock process through constant 10 millisecond updates (i.e.: 100 times per second). Front and rear wheels are paired off for control purposes, using solenoid valves that are fed three primary levels of instruction by the computer. These are: Step-Up; Step-Down or Hold selected pressure application in each brake circuit.

Naturally, there are a number of failsafe and self-check functions and a back-up of peripheral timers to maintain a safety back-up and avoid either wheel hop or undue vibration entering the system. There is also a neat anti-yaw provision that acts when the front wheels encounter differing adhesion levels under heavy braking (e.g., one wheel on grass, the other on tarmac). To avoid a potentially disastrous change in direction, the front-brake pressures are 'momentarily' balanced to provide 'feedback through the steering-wheel and enabling the driver to maintain full steering control.'

The rears are always controlled as a pair, but the tyre with the greatest lateral grip is contributing to stability across the axle in a further effort to avoid a directional change under emergency conditions. Lotus pointed out that they had spent a great deal of time and effort on obtaining a linear brake progression, to which the high pressure system was a key factor.

Proof Positive

One fine endorsement of Lotus's success is the Texan 1990 Esprit SE Racing Team. The majority of drivers agreed that the Lotus ABS was worth having in the wet, which argues enormous sensitivity in the way stopping power is apportioned on the lightly laden, wide tyres of the Esprit's front wheels. In dry conditions, development was described as 'progressing'.

From my own experience in Ford and BMW racing saloons, this may simply reflect that anti-lock, *any* anti-lock brake system, is presently at odds with the dry road racing driver's objective. That objective is to slow down from enormous speed in the shortest possible distances on a predetermined pattern that is (usually) free of the unexpected hazards that clutter road driving. The racing or rally driver is not so concerned with that other vital ABS benefit: the ability to steer whilst braking heavily, because the driver achieves that through a cadence braking routine whenever it is (rarely) necessary.

Lotus Grand Prix Records

World Champion Car Constructors	Lotus World Champion Drivers
1963	Jim Clark
1965	Jim Clark
1968	Graham Hill
1970	Jochen Rindt
1972	Emerson Fittipaldi
1973	—
1978	Mario Andretti

8 The Esprit SE on the Track

Considering the mid-engine racing heritage that is such an obvious part of Lotus's history, keener owners of the Esprit may well ask why it has not become a racing certainty? The brief answer is that the Esprit was conceived as a road car – without the parallel racing programme characterized by the Europa and Type 47 – and the Esprit did not easily fit into any racing category. In fact, it took until the advent of the Turbo SE and the interest of American Pure Sports racing team entrepreneur/driver Doc Bundy to bring the Esprit the kind of track success you would expect of a genuine Lotus.

Earlier Esprit sorties had been privately funded British affairs from Elan stalwart Richard Jenvey (2 litres, normally-aspirated) and Pete Hall/Andy Rouse Engineering, who campaigned the Esprit Turbo of 1982 in a production-based formula.

As a pure racing 2-litre, the Esprit was not reliable enough to capitalize on its reasonable qualifying abilities against factory-funded Porsches in the 1979 World Championship

A publicity shot of the Lotus Esprit Turbo SE, dated 1989.

Advertised as 'Lotus's 163mph Esprit Turbo SE', this road-going model certainly looks the part.

of Makes. As a 1982 production racer, it was handicapped by its roadgoing weight and the inboard rear disc brakes, which tended to overheat in British sprint events.

DREAM DEBUT

The answer proved to be the 1990 Sports Car Club of America (SCCA) Escort World Challenge. This series caters for modified production sports cars in events from 45 minutes to 24 hours. The Lotus Esprit SE was prepared by an Anglo-American effort in less than six weeks. It scored a dream debut win in California at the Sears Point Three Hours (drivers: Doc Bundy and Scott Lagasse). It always showed speed enough to lead the Corvettes thereafter, and had won four of eight events at the close of 1990; the racing statistics will be found in our separate panel.

In one of the events that eluded an Esprit victory, Bundy bundled into the undergrowth. That incident prompted the thought that more cars were needed in 1991, but on this occasion, a complete re-build ensured that only three Esprits were prepared and shipped from Hethel in 1990.

The racing Esprit was so well received that the American arm of Lotus marketed twenty 'World Challenge Race Car Replicas' at the end of the season. All were street legal, and safety and emissions equipment unchanged. Many features were shared with the racing version discussed in this section.

LOTUS ESPRIT TURBO SE

Draft Specification World Challenge Race Car Replica

How Oliver Winterbottom outlined the specification of the roadgoing race replica (twenty for sale) on 9 October 1990 is shown on page 174.

Inspiration for the programme came from Doc Bundy, who demonstrated the track potential of the Esprit SE to Lotus Cars USA president, Ron Foster. There was a thoughtful reception from the UK factory for the idea of racing an Esprit in the USA. On the one hand, it was a terrible commercial risk. The Lotus was twice as expensive as the dominant Corvette, with a racing heritage that would also be at risk if the Esprit was off the pace. What seems to have prompted a rather reluctant 'yes' from the lips of Michael Kimberley was the knowledge that the Esprit needed another dose of current reputation to overcome its American image of frailty. Another contributory factor was the sheer enthusiasm of test driver and development engineer Roger Becker, who had been actively plotting a lightweight Esprit along the lines of the Porsche 911 opposition.

Esprit Race Record 1990

This is a summary of how Ronald T Foster, president of Lotus Cars USA, saw the debut Esprit season:

- Four victories (50 per cent of the races)
- Six pole positions (75 per cent)
- Two finishes in 1-2 formation
- 2,900 race miles, no mechanical problems
- Led seven of eight races
- Set fastest race lap in six events
- Pure Sports Esprit was placed second in the Manufacturers' Championship; Chevrolet Corvette was first, Porsche third, Mazda fourth, Nissan fifth.
- Second in final points for Doc Bundy
- Lotus Cars USA awarded the annual Jim Cook Memorial Award for: 'Consistent display of good character and sportsmanship' and a 'significant contribution to the overall success of the series.'

The Turbo SE in action.

Lotus factory involvement was limited to Becker, John Miles (who also drove at one 24-hour round), pit administrator and ex-TWR technician Colin Marriott and transmission expert Alan Nobbs. Pure Sports were responsible for entries and USA preparation, but three complete Esprits were constructed at Hethel during the 1990 season.

Technical details (there were few of them) were published in two major UK magazine articles in 1990. However, Roger Becker, now Lotus associate director, chief engineer Vehicle Development and Proving, was extremely forthcoming. Talking vividly about a project which put Lotus Cars (as opposed to Team Lotus in Grand Prix) so

successfully back in the racing game, Roger revealed that initial preparation time had been 'about a week, but we had a lot of parts in place from our lightweight programme and our office does know an awful lot about the Esprit chassis.'

MODIFICATIONS

Externally, the biggest changes were the extension of the front spoiler below the production bib and relocation of the rear wing on two pylons that allowed a pronounced rearward rake. Small front-wheel air deflectors played a part, as did the use of composites to lighten the roof panel. I have been told unofficially that the Esprit used other lightweight panels to reach a natural racing weight of 2,500lb (1,130kg). Its success was greeted with a 2,600 to 2,650lb (1,180 to 1,200kg) ballasted racing weight during the season. However, Roger Becker emphasized: 'We did not have time to do anything about the central tub sections.'

The heart of production racing car technology is its roll cage, but not for the obvious safety requirement. Lotus ensured that their cage picked up the extraordinary loads of racing *very* efficiently and the UK team were somewhat surprised to find that it took the Corvette opposition by surprise. Lotus had ensured that their cage fulfilled this purpose, as well as proving extraordinarily

World Challenge Race Car Replica

Body
- Monaco white paintwork
- Deep-skirt front air dam
- Front-wheel air deflectors
- Optimized competition rear wing
- Reduced ride height
- Road type full-roll cage
- Matt black exterior mirrors
- Opening composite roof panel
- World Challenge decals
- Parts vendor identification kit

Chassis
- Fully adjustable competition suspension
- 225/45-ZR 16 Goodyear Eagle front tyres
- 225/50-ZR 16 Goodyear Eagle rear tyres
- Revolution 3-piece racing wheels
- AP racing 4-pot [piston] calliper brakes
- Competition brake discs with cooling ducts
- Revised steering geometry
- High-rate suspension springs
- Monroe shock absorbers with competition valves
- Brembo disc parking brake
- 'Get you home' tyre inflator replacing spare wheel

Powertrain
- Increased capacity engine chargecooler
- Hand-finished cylinder head
- Competition oil pan with anti-surge baffles
- Limited-slip final drive differential
- Competition transmission casing
- Special gear-selector forks

Interior
- Black doeskin upholstery
- Perforated hide-wearing surfaces
- Competition-type bucket seats
- Black anti-glare instrument panel
- 225mph electronic speedometer
- 4in tachometer
- Optimized foot pedal locations
- 'Trackgrip' brake-pedal location
- Competition-developed left foot rest
- Aluminium heel rest plate
- Door-mounted grab handles
- Lightweight grey carpet
- Reduced sound deadening package
- Cabin and windshield heater
- Optimized interior package deleting clock; ash trays; map pocket and air conditioning.

'The vehicle specification is full street legal and all occupant safety and emission control parts are unchanged.'

O C Winterbottom

robust in an incident-filled season. At the Mosport 24-hour event, the Esprit was put through what Doc Bundy graphically described as:

A torture test. We ran the car into a guard rail at least twice, ran it out of water twice, and ran the oil dry. I am sure there were not two wheels pointing the same direction at the end of the race. But the car just wouldn't quit, however desperately we tried to kill it. But if the engine will take that and have enough performance to run the fastest laps at the end, it's pretty durable.

The chassis changes – summarized at the close of the year – embraced: 16in Revolution three-piece racing alloys; Goodyear Eagle ZR tyres of 225/45 front section and 255/50 rears; AP Racing four-piston callipers clamping ex-Opel/Vauxhall Carlton 13in (335mm) diameter discs (themselves moulded on those of Group C World Championship racers); electronic Lotus-GM anti-lock braking was 'used in the wet and under development for dry tracks'; revised steering geometry; high rate suspension springs ('not so hard as you would think', said Becker) and competition-valved Monroe shock absorbers.

For 1991, Lotus looked certain to field more Esprits and were exploring the merits of 17in wheel diameters, possibly for use with even wider rear rubber.

ENGINE AND TRANSMISSION

Roger Becker recalled of the engine and transmission in 1990:

Lotus Esprit SE: Race by race, SCCA 1990

Date	Event	Practice	Result
5 May	Sears Point, 3 hours	5th	1st
2 June	Dallas, 1 hour	2nd	11th
1 July	Laguna Seca, 3 hours	1st	1st
14 July	Des Moines, 1 hour	1st	3rd
28 July	Road Atlanta, 3 hours	1st	1st
11/12 Aug	Mosport, 24 hours	1st	6th
25 Aug	Denver, 1 hour	1st	1st
3 Nov	St. Petersburg, 1 hour	1st	6th

Race-by-race record supplied courtesy of Hugo Tippet, Lotus UK.

We took out the air conditioning but took advantage of the condenser to plumb up extra direct-feed capacity for the standard chargecooling. This allowed us transient horsepower readings in the region of 300bhp and the motor proved absolutely reliable at 7,000rpm. The only engine trouble we ever had followed accident damage and loss of lubricant.

The Renault 25 transaxle was designed for front-drive use in a rather less powerful car, so it was not surprising that Lotus twisted the corporate arms of Renault and Alpine at Dieppe to get some new components fabricated – including the casing itself (it would flex under these racing loads) and individual gears. Incidentally, an SE gearbox in standard trim is no different to that of other Renault-sourced Esprits, but higher clamping loads upon the usual 9.25in (23cm) diameter clutch were introduced.

For racing, Lotus did have some alternative ratios, but the Corvette men spotted that and they were outlawed. A new Crown Wheel and Pinion (CWP) assembly was fabricated and was serviced by a conventional multi-plate differential.

As a general rule, the racers tried to avoid making vigorous use of second gear, or using that ratio at all. This was not too tall an order because, as John Miles reported of his 1.5-hour stint in the Mosport 24-hour race (*Autocar*, 12 September 1990), 'Our rev limit is 6,200rpm, but half the circuit is done in fourth gear because the engine pulls like a train from 3,800rpm.' The standard rpm limit was raised upon introduction of the Esprit SE in 1989 which, on road tyres at least, allows a convincing 60mph (100kph) in second and an honest 100mph (160kph) in third.

HARD GRAFT

Detail engine work that enhanced durability included fitment of a larger Garrett turbocharger, one that spun at lower rpm for enhanced race durability but reportedly hurt the amiable power delivery considerably. The fuel injectors were also enlarged.

The progress that the factory made with the Esprit SE in American racing trim can be judged from its lap times at the Hethel circuit. After its hasty original preparation, John Miles turned laps in the 1min 21sec bracket; by the end of the year the Esprit was returning laps of the 1min 16sec order.

I think it is the Audi slogan that translates 'Progress through Technology' (*Vorsprung durch Technik*). In the Lotus case they would be justified in merely adding the strap line: 'Progress through Ingenious Hard Graft.'

9 Buying an Esprit in the Nineties

'There are never any service body problems – and from 1980 onwards even the steel chassis had any rust problems cured.'
Brian Atthews, London Lotus Centre, 1990

To close our historical record of the Esprit's evolution, we will return to the realities of the nineties and assess the practicalities of purchase and ownership today. Since Esprit production spanned fifteen years at the time of writing, I thought this was the place to set out the production records of the variants and give some brief personal comments on each model. This will hopefully give some shade in degrees of desirability to suit your needs.

First, a few 'insider' conversations to allow an overall insight into Esprit ownership during the nineties. We spoke to a pair of the larger British Lotus dealers about their more recent and warranted stock, and followed this up with a private Esprit S2 owner's point of view.

THE DEALERS

Norfolk Motor Co Ltd says unequivocally that it is, 'the largest Lotus dealer in the World' and managing director John Hewitt has very firm opinions about the customers he meets in the sale of more than 300 Lotus cars a year:

Most Lotus buyers are enthusiasts and know more about the cars, and the Lotus company, than most salesmen! Often they have a very specific knowledge of the car they are looking to buy.

I feel the best way to buy is from a Lotus dealer, who will be fully knowledgeable about the car and has no excuse to sell a bad one. The difference in price from a reputable dealer, as opposed to an ordinary car, or private, sale outlet, could be £5,000 . . . But this should be looked at as a kind of insurance money.

I do not feel service history is that important, nor mileage. It all really depends on how sympathetically the car has been driven and cared for.

By contrast, Brian Atthews, joint managing director at the London Lotus Centre on Edgware Road, is very particular about service histories and frequently comes up with astonishingly young examples of obsolete models. Some of that acute purchasing is owed to his record with Lotus products over all but two years since 1975, but it is also owed to a genuine enthusiasm that shines through when he imparts a gem such as: 'I bought a Turbo that did not exist last week. Registered in 1988 it was, but the old shape model. Took me six weeks to get ownership, I just had to have it when I realized it was the ninth from last made and had covered 871 miles!'

More mundanely, Brian Atthews gave us an overall view of prices in the chaotic 1990/91 car market (when vehicles over £30,000 of any brand were struggling to find new owners) and had some interesting basic observations to make on purchasing an Esprit. Some of these observations were

Despite a sharp recession in used car values as Britain entered the nineties, the Esprit more than held its ground, an emphatic endorsement of the distinctive design and increased Lotus prestige.

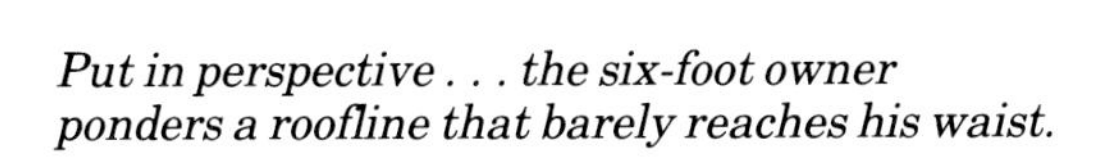

Put in perspective . . . the six-foot owner ponders a roofline that barely reaches his waist.

supported by the fact that an S1 was going through workshop restoration as we spoke and that he is interested to buy and sell the older models that most dealers shudder at and avoid:

Most important is to get a car with a full service history, carried out by an authorized Lotus dealer. As cars pass from one owner to another, they can become neglected, suffer cheap servicing [or none at all] and non-Lotus replacement parts. Second-hand values started rising twelve months ago on early Esprits, so it is worth keeping them properly. Remember that the Esprit is a design from the Chapman era and that the originals were styled by Giugiaro.

We never see any with a body problem in service (accident damage is a different matter, of course), and from 1980 onward we have never had to replace an Esprit chassis because of rust. To be honest, I am not sure that we have ever had to replace a chassis, certainly not on the S1 we are restoring at the moment. That will cost the owner about £6,000, but I expect he only paid £3,000 to £5,000 for it and, if he hangs on a bit, there will be a profit there for the taking with the 'stem to stern' restoration.

In general, I would say it is always wise to have a second-hand Lotus inspected by a recognized dealer because a Lotus is just as likely to suffer from a bad gearbox or poorly engine as a used Ford Escort.

This was Atthews' sage conclusion, and he should know, he sold 52 second-hand examples in 1990.

THE PRIVATE BUYER

Buckinghamshire-based Aiden Shutter is an engineer for his local council authority and an avid Lotus owner whose white S2 Esprit (EBO 307V) should be seen adorning our earlier pages. How had he come to choose the Esprit and was it all he had hoped? There was a characteristic snort of laughter before he admitted:

I used to go and ogle the S1 when it was new at my local dealership. At ten years old, there did not seem much chance of ever owning one, so when I did find that I had enough money to buy one, a sort of red mist descended and I probably bought *the* Esprit of all Esprits to avoid! It had been both raced and crashed, but I am actually extremely pleased with it.

The candid Shutter owned the certified last Europa Twin Cam before the price of a house demanded that they part. An Escort RS2000 Mark 1 and more mundane Ford products have kept him mobile, but let him tell us the tale of his 64,000-mile S2 purchase:

I knew I couldn't afford an S3 on the money I had, which was a budget of £5,000 to £7,000 in 1988. The car I finally bought cost £6,700 and I reckon I would probably get about the £7,500 originally asked today. Values seem to be appreciating, even in this recession.

I rang up after a few S2s, figuring that I would buy a good one of them, rather than a doggy S3. Most were gone, so one of the first I saw, I immediately bought. As I said, it had the *worst* history you could imagine. It had passed through *nine* owners, and the second one [Terry Kyte] raced and sprinted it, nearly winning the 1984 BARC Trophy, so it was a familiar sight on the pages of *Motoring News*.

The third owner possibly crashed it. I found that the front-end and one side wing had been changed. But none of it mattered; I just melted and bought the thing.'

It seems that Aiden was very fortunate, for previous owners had spent 'literally thousands on it. I have got most of the service history now, and there is no doubt you just have to keep throwing money at it.'

Aiden continued his improbable tale:

The engine has been fantastic, just 100 per cent, but some of that can be attributed to a £700 cylinder-head overhaul just prior to my purchase. I paid special attention to the chassis condition; it's obviously sensible to look out for the kind of accident damage I found, as people do smash them up. In fact, I have not had any of the more likely problems, such as wishbone mounting-points cracking up, nor any trouble in the engine-bay area. Frankly, it pumps out so much oil in the motor area that the chassis is lovely and silver-bright beneath the grime!

The main troubles I have with the car in a very small annual mileage [2,000 miles (3,200km) in two years] are those you would expect. That badly designed rear-end has cost me a wheel-bearing and universal joint replacements, but it is the electrics that drive you crazy. There *always* seems to be something wrong with the thing, especially after winter storage. Most typical is for only one headlamp to flip up, or the indicators to fail. Frankly, it needs just one huge earth . . . , because it is always suffering whenever there is damp about.

But these are minor problems compared to the pleasure of owning and driving it. I only operate it as a second car – I reckon you would have to be a brave man to operate an S1 or S2 as everyday transport. I did that with the Europa, and it just was not a very practical proposition.

I reckon the Esprit is a lot more civilized than the Europa ever was, and I enjoy even the lay-back driving position. It is just so refreshing after something like a Cortina or a Capri. A different world. Let's be honest, it is also the cheapest pose in terms of exotic mid-engine sports car motoring. It is nothing like as fast as Lotus said it was at the time, but the turbo Esprits take care of that aspect. Meanwhile, I reckon I will hang on to this one for the foreseeable future . . .

PRODUCTION PERSPECTIVE

Now, the thorny question of production figures. Aside from BMW records, I have yet to find a manufacturer capable of producing definitive figures and sticking to them over the years. Totals always seem subject to revision, even when heavily hyped at the close of production, as was the case at the close of Ford Capri production.

Such experience has taught me not to regard any such information as 'cast in stone'. Yet, potential and actual owners are always interested in production statistics and, I find, persistence does yield results. In the case of the Esprit, where some variants have been produced in astonishingly small quantities, the figures become important to collectors, but I always feel uneasy about these and worry that fakers might like to use this information to construct replicas of desirable low-volume types.

The following Lotus figures were supplied by Warranty and Customer Services at the factory. They were further ratified by product planning manager Peter Riddle after a meeting on the Lombard RAC Rally of November 1990. I believe they are as good as we can get. They contain a yearly analysis of production (rather than prototype and production) Esprits, so I have quoted and depended on these.

The key points that emerge from the 1990 figures are that the original Essex Turbo was far rarer than at first thought, and that the S2.2 was *not quite* so rare as we thought.

First, the Essex Turbo. Peter Riddle revealed:

It was originally intended to build 100 Essex Turbos. Lotus manufacturing records show 57 Essex Turbos completed. However, Essex blue continued to be offered on Esprit Turbos and a number of cars were upgraded to Essex specification in 'post production' under the control of the sales department.

It looks more cramped than it actually is, but the 2-litre Lotus twin-cam engine is not easily accessible for every service function with the lid (incorporating tool kit compartment on this S2) raised.

The ugly standard steering-wheel of the S1 and S2 was a common item, but the extensive instrumentation was switched over to black and white (rather than the original green Veglia dials) for the S2.

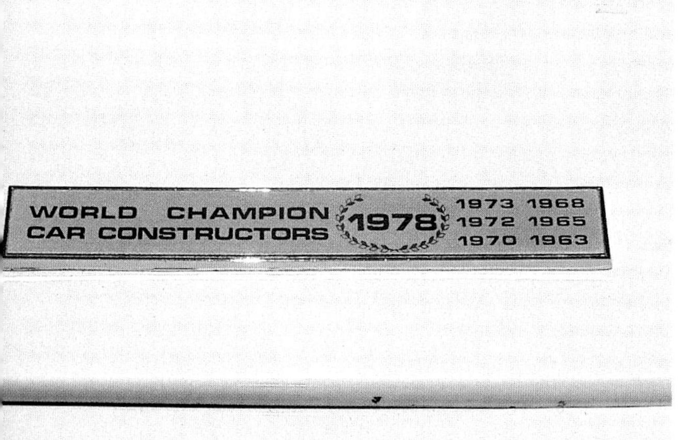

Lotus were never slow to tell buyers of their World Championship car racing record, one that unfortunately lacked any further titles during the eighties.

The second generation of Esprits dispensed with the original single-motor headlamp lift, but they are still quite capable of 'winking' one twin-lamp unit, particularly after winter storage.

The nose says it all . . .

. . . but Chapman and company had a major say in one of the boldest shapes ever marketed by a British car maker.

After an attempt to forget their heritage under new financial influences, Lotus recall that the founder's initials are still attached to every Esprit.

The price of affordable admission? Often criticized, the flap-action door handles from the Rover Cars parts bin are a persistent reminder that the Esprit was born not long after Lotus ceased kit-car manufacture . . .

1989 - NEW LOTUS CORPORATE IDENTITY

The definitive identifying feature of a genuine Essex Turbo is the Panasonic radio cassette player mounted in the windscreen header panel. Incidentally, no Essex Turbos were sold in the USA.

The S2.2 is still a statistically rare production Esprit; it did not reach 100 copies. However, I was first told by Lotus that only 46 were made. The 1990 analysis records nearly double that number: 88. Even that low number looks gross beside the 1987 output of the normally-aspirated 'soft shape' Esprit. For the latter, the closing months of a truncated launch Model Year provided an output of two examples! Here are the individual model totals:

Esprit S1

Comment The original will always have a unique value, but the first cars were flawed and far from as fast as Lotus claimed. Expect 1976–1978 examples to be either scruffy survivors (you may even find one, as I did, with a lopsided single extended headlamp grin resting in a city side-street), or full concours machines worth over £10,000.

Beware of the bodged half-restoration, particularly in areas such as chassis integrity (watch wishbone attachment points particularly closely). A visibly smoky engine will almost certainly cost thousands to return to its normal robust health and the gearbox should obtain all ratios cleanly, especially second.

The Esprit Turbo's new-style door mirror.

1990 prices From £3,000 upward, but below £5,000 you need a high degree of DIY ability and a knowledge of Lotus specialists to save the car.

Production: Esprit S1

Year	Output	Total
1976	134	
1977	580	**714**

Esprit S2

Comment Cosmetic changes to the cockpit and the exterior (Lotus wheel design), but no attempt made to address fundamental problems like excess wheel-bearing loads created by the rear suspension design, or material increase in performance.

Because of the larger numbers than in the first series, you – the long-term collector or enthusiast – may consider looking to the special editions (John Player Special: JPS) or visually similar S2.2 for rarity value.

When buying, the same comment as for the S1 applies: pay particular attention to the 'big thrcc' potential sources of large expense: chassis, engine and gearbox.

Production: Esprit S2

Year	Output	Total
1978	553	
1979	474	
1980	18	
1981	15	**1,060**

C61 XBF
esprit

German BBS alloy wheels of Turbo origin became optional fitments for the S3 and offered significant gains in road grip through more generous Goodyear tyres.

Aft of the rear wheel and proud of the prominent body crease (which marks the joining point of upper and lower Esprit body halves), the 1985 Esprit S3 wore this golden logo.

The cheap appearance of the apparently eternal door 'flap' handles from the old British Leyland justifies a regular criticism of the Esprit as a credible player in the higher-cost league.

(Left) The S3 Esprit was a vast improvement over its normally-aspirated predecessors but was always overshadowed by the presence of a turbo charged variant. Ridged tail-lights survived the S2/S2.2 production transition to S3.

JPS Totals

In regard to the JPS, the original intention was not just to manufacture 100 for the UK, but also 100 apiece in the 'rest of the world', or USA markets that provided up to a third of total volumes when the Lotus export effort was 'on track' (a rarity, especially in America). One Lotus employee did provide the JPS total and my information is that 147 were probably made: 94 for Britain; 10 for California; 16 for the other 49 US States and 27 for the 'rest of the world'.

Lotus tell me that the first commemorative JPS Esprit was completed by 13 December 1978 as unit number: 73120550G. The last was ready on 27 July 1979, unit number: 79070278J.

1990 Prices Good running examples with majority of service history will command around £7,000 (on a private basis), but you can buy from £5,000 upward in nastier fettle. The rarer JPS in pristine condition should attract bids beyond £12,000 and dealer stock in good, warranted condition can fetch up to £10,000.

Esprit S2.2

Comment The lowest production catalogue model, an S2.2 not only has a rarity value but also a historical one. It marks the introduction of the vastly improved 2.2-litre Lotus engine.

Compared to the S1/S2, the biggest apparent gains should be at the wheel, where the extra flexibility makes the car a lot friendlier in urban and suburban conditions. There is also a significant gain in fuel consumption, but not the 20 per cent that Lotus suggest would be the norm in the late seventies!

Performance was better. More realistic Lotus claims indicate 0–60mph (0–100kph) in around 7 seconds and an 80–100mph (130–160kph) time in fifth gear that was effectively halved.

Buying tips are very much as for the S1/S2, but note that this was the first Esprit use of a galvanized chassis. It is *not* the same design as the subsequent S3/Turbo galvanized steel, but it had a five-year warranty at the time and dealers speak well of chassis durability from 1980 onward.

Lotus also installed a larger clutch, new exhaust system and revised mountings. You should check that an apparent S2.2 is not a retro fit S3 motor into one of the more common S2s. Quote a chassis and engine number to Lotus Customer Services at Hethel.

1990 Prices I have not seen a genuine example for sale, but common sense argues that values could reach £10,000–£12,000 at current depressed values for a pristine example.

Production: Esprit S2.2

Year	Output	Total
1980	62	
1981	26	**88**

Esprit S3

Comment This was the normally-aspirated model that Lotus got right. Sharing the turbo chassis revisions (originally intended for a V8) enhanced strength and service durability considerably, whilst the driving pleasure was everything that you would expect of a mid-engine Lotus.

Cabin noise was considerably reduced at the point, because engine and transmission could be more flexibly and softly mounted (now freed from any excess suspension loads). There was also a lot more soundproofing, reflecting an approach that had first been tried in the rarer S2.2. A flexibly-joined exhaust system with ball joints and stainless steel sections offered better durability and comfort than the earlier Esprit.

At this point, the common S3/Turbo chassis design with enhanced strength and top-link rear suspension features galvanization and you can begin to trust company rust-proofing standards a little more. However, you still need to perform full under-body checks, as accident damage can always be a problem on such a high performer.

Any suggestion of poor handling should require a careful check as to the precise cause (is it possibly due to misalignment, a softening damper, or simply uneven tyre pressures?). The chassis is the literal foundation to a good Lotus and there are enough good examples of the S3 about to reject any duffers.

1990 Prices You should be able to buy on a private basis at under £10,000 for the earliest examples, but dealer stock tends to start around 1986 and commands £15,000 to £16,500. The earliest S3 we found at a main dealer was a 1982 example on a Y-plate. That model went to Japan (as so many do) for £13,000.

Such prices reflect not only that the S3 was a vastly improved product, but also that new Esprits are so much more expensive than before. Any example of the later shape is likely to command over £20,000.

Production: Esprit S3

Year	Output	Total
1981	144	
1982	160	
1983	84	
1984	104	
1985	127	
1986	72	
1987	76	**767**

Esprit Turbo

Note The Bosch fuel-injected version of the Turbo HC (HCPI in Lotus language) was sold with a catalyst in America and Canada, Austria and Sweden. A total of 407 such export injection turbo Esprits were made in the 1980–1987 body, so the *grand total* for the turbo in the older body ought to read: **2065**.

The Turbos start with the advantages of a better chassis foundation (six-year anti-corrosion warranty) and power to match the aggressive styling.

It is worth reading about the model's development carefully, because you will see that there was an early change-over from dry-sump engine lubrication. This is a significant point for collectors and for those who prefer the 'purist' approach to lubrication, but remember that those ahead of you may not have been so knowledgeable on cold-start procedures, or on checking oil level in the separate tank.

Generally, the later the turbo you can afford, the better proposition it will be to run, the water-cooled T3 casing and wastegate revisions enhancing durability.

1990 Prices A clever private buyer can find these at £15,000 but dealer stock tends to start at £17,000 for the best 1983 A-registration examples. The rarer and original Essex models would draw around £17,000 to £18,000, according to expert opinion at the time of writing, but it cannot be long before a genuine Essex rests firmly in the £20–30,000 region.

In fact, we were advised that £30,000 was around the top price paid for the latest of pre-1987 face-lifted Turbos, for which you could expect an HC specification. Special editions of this car look set to achieve over £30,000 in the depressed 1990/91 winter market, but (Essex and limited editions aside) you should expect prices to slip from those quoted here. Public preference for the softer shape has been established and demand is likely to slacken for anything other than the very special examples of the original breed.

The use of gold for side stripes and wheels is emphasized in this one-in-a-run, reported at Lotus in the 1990/91 winter to total 147 units. Just 94 of those were delivered in the UK.

Production: Esprit Turbo

Year	Output	Total
1980	57 (Essex)	
1981	116	
1982	205	
1983	343	
1984	418	
1985	262	
1986	136	
1987	121 (to shape change)	
*Plus . . .	407 (Emission Specials)	**2,065**

Post-1987 X-180 Esprit

Comment The 'NA' or normally-aspirated model is well respected by those who love driving (as was the S3) but the lower-powered car has always been over-shadowed by the Turbo and was finally dropped in 1990, for which Lotus supplied no production figure.

At the time of writing, the virtues of the new body ensured that high values were maintained and all would have been with manufacturer's warranty on the chassis anti-corrosion policy.

1990 prices It takes high annual mileage and private buying to depress these below £20,000. Dealer stock was achieving up to £23,000 regularly.

Production: normally-aspirated Esprit

Year	Output	Total
1987	2	
1988	176	
1989	90	**268**

Post-1987 Esprit Turbo

Note HCPI designation stands, as before, for High Compression, Petrol Injection. The MPFI stood for Multi Point Fuel Injection turbos that were fitted with a Lotus-GM injection system and three catalysts. These became available in the USA during the 1989 model year and found their way to Britain as middle-ranked Esprit S specification in September 1990. Esprit Turbo SE came in May 1989 to Britain and became simply the Esprit SE with ABS braking for 1991.

Production: Post-1987 Esprit Turbo

Year	Model	Output	Total
1987	Turbo	65	
1987	HCPI	99	
1988	Turbo	387	
1988	HCPI	375	
1988	MPFI	120	
1989	Turbo	103	
1989	MPFI	121	
1989	SE	563	
1990	All	754	**2,587**

Appendix

USEFUL ADDRESSES

Manufacturers

Lotus Cars Ltd.
Hethel
Norwich
Norfolk
NR14 8EZ
Tel: 01953 608000

Lotus Cars USA
1655 Lakes Parkway
Lawrenceville
Georgia 30243
Fax: 770 682 5222

Lotus Dealers

Norfolk Motor Company
242 Sprowston Road
Norwich
Norfolk
NR3 4HT
Tel: 01603 416613

Clubs

Club Lotus
PO Box 8
Dereham
Norfolk
NR19 1TF
Tel: 01362 694459

Lotus Drivers Club
Laurie Barton
15 Pleasant Way
Leamington Spa
Warwickshire
CV32 5XA

Lotus Specialists

Christopher Neil Ltd
Middlewich Road
Northwich
Cheshire
CW9 7BP
Tel: 01606 47914
Fax: 01606 41642

Fibreglass Services
(Miles Wilkins)
Progress Garage
Yapton Lane
Walberton
Arundel
West Sussex
BN18 0AS

Kelvedon Motors
Bourne Road
Spalding
Lincolnshire
PE11 3LW

Paul Matty Sports Cars
12 Old Birmingham Road
Bromsgrove
Worcestershire
B60 1DE
Tel: 01527 35656
Fax: 01527 575172

Lotus by Claudius
17411 Studebaker Road
Cerritos, CA 90703
Tel: 310 865 4439

Tingle's Lotus Centre
1615 Shawsheen St
Tewksbury
MA 01876
Tel: 508 851 8370

Index